ALARM IN THE FIREHOUSE

A Memoir of America's First Openly Gay Professional Firefighter

R. Kevin Mallinson

This honest account depicts real persons and actual events. The names of a few are omitted or changed to protect their privacy.

All photographs courtesy of the author unless otherwise credited. Cover design by author. Cover: Kevin Mallinson at the nozzle. [photo: State Archives of Florida]

Alarm in the Firehouse
A Memoir of America's First Openly Gay Professional Firefighter

2nd edition, November 2021

Copyright © 2021 by R. Kevin Mallinson

All rights reserved. Printed in the United States of America.

No part of this book may be used or reproduced in any form or by any means without expressed written permission from the author except for the use of brief quotations that may be used in book critiques or reviews.

Disclaimer: The author has made every effort to ensure the accuracy of the information within this book at the time of publication. The author does not assume and hereby disclaims any liability to any party for any loss, damage, or disruption caused by errors or omissions, whether such errors or omissions result from accident, negligence, or any other cause.

ISBN: 978-0-578-33437-0

DEDICATION

This book is dedicated to those courageous persons from disenfranchised groups who have endured the experience of being the 'first' person to integrate into a role not historically open to them. I hope that my story inspires other LGBTQ+ firefighters, especially those who continue to find it necessary to hide their true selves for fear of discrimination.

CONTENTS

	Foreword	1
	Preface	2
1	September 29, 1981	4
2	The Truth Will Set You Free	12
3	Man with a Plan	23
4	Settling into the Job	33
5	Gay Militants	39
6	Rear-End Man	43
7	Fire Station 1	48
8	Nonviolent Resistance	55
9	Butt Man	59
10	Assumptions & Accusations	68
11	Fire College	85
12	Two Different Worlds	111
13	GRID and AIDS	119
14	Dangerous Times	122
15	Captain Vidal	127
16	Life Saved, Lives Lost	133
17	The Man or Woman?	139
18	Mayoral Race	145
19	A Fundamental Shift	148

20	The Black Hats and the White Hats	154
21	White Boy Running…	160
22	City Safety Committee	174
23	Local 1424	180
24	Firemen have no Balls	190
25	Media Frenzy	196
26	Blaze of Glory	204
	Reflections	211
	After the Fire Department	215
	Odds & Ends	219

ACKNOWLEDGMENTS

I am grateful to the valuable feedback and editing expertise of both Jan Howell (*nee* Durland) and Robert C. Hansen. This story is more complete because several of my fellow firefighters (retired) in Key West agreed to be interviewed; their recollections and thoughtful perspectives were both illuminating and validating.

FOREWORD

Being First.

When we enter this world, we don't stop to think 'What would I be first in?' As we grow older, the importance of being first comes into play: in athletics, academics, birth order, etc.

As we continue in life, we come to learn of other first experiences: first car, first plane flight, first rocket, first in scientific discoveries…

Then, as we become more socially aware, we hear of minority members of our world becoming a historical First. The first African American…, the first woman…, the first Hispanic…and so on.

We begin to glimpse the struggle of what some of these pioneers went through by viewing photos and videos of, for example, young African American girls being attacked for being the First to enroll in a White school.

The true grit and determination of these treasured Firsts needs to be told in detail. To see the world though our Firsts helps us more clearly see the world in which we live.

I never thought I'd be a First, but I was in 1998. With nearly 15 years on the Fire Department of New York (FDNY), I came out as a gay man.

Kevin was America's first openly gay professional firefighter. The story that he tells here is gripping. It's raw and honest. This book details his life on the Key West Fire Department. It should be required reading for all First Responders.

Thank you, Kevin. Thank You to all those First's out there. Life is better because of you.

>Tommy Ryan
>Firefighter, retired FDNY Ladder 12
>Board Member, Key West Firehouse Museum

PREFACE

Since I was a young child, I have learned much about people, life, and the world by listening to stories. Everyone has a story, a narrative that reveals as much about them as it does about the events they describe. An unfolding story may be a personal fantasy, a creative refashioning, or an objective record. In telling this story, I chose the truth.

I am a gay man who has a story to tell. History, as told by those who didn't live it, may be distorted. If we don't tell our stories, someone else might write our history. My life and accomplishments could be overlooked or denied. Too often, historical accounts of the lives of LGBTQ+ persons are rife with mistruths and confabulation.

This is an American story. Writing this book, I sought to document my experiences as the first openly gay professional firefighter in the United States. It's an honest memoir, as much as my notes, documents, photos, and interviews can relay the truth. The events are written from my perspective. Much of what my fellow firefighters 'knew' about me may have come from malicious gossip, colored by stereotypes, inflammatory innuendo, and intentional mistruths. I need to set the record straight.

I decided to use real names for most individuals in this recounting, but not to disparage anyone unfairly. I hold some firemen accountable for their contemptible actions. Conversely, others are to be recognized for their support and professionalism. I hope that the reader gains some insight into what it might means for someone to be the 'first' in a situation. What was experience of the first Black student in an all-White school or the first woman to enter a corporate boardroom as the CEO? Each experience would have its unique nature, though elements of their struggles may be similar. I needed to tell this story before it was lost.

I acknowledge that my experience in the fire department occurred in a 'moment in time.' The social and political upheaval in Key West during the early 1980s was the background against which this story unfolded. Further, the events took place in a particular time in American history and early in the evolution of LGBTQ+ rights in our society. I joined the Key West Fire Department in 1981. Americans did not yet have personal computers, cell phones, the *world wide web*, or the Internet. People communicated with each other over landline telephones or via snail-mail letters that were typed or hand-written. Documents were stored in filing cabinets.

I offer a few notes about language. Most of the men in the Key West Fire Department (KWFD) identified as being a Conch [pronounced *konk*; a native-born Key Wester]. Every member of the department was male. When I refer to this cohort of men, I call them 'firemen.' However, when I discuss the larger population of persons in the profession, I refer to them as 'firefighters.' Similarly, I use the terms 'gay men' and 'lesbians' or 'gay rights' as this was common language in the early 1980s. When the language in this story is vulgar, it is meant to reflect the reality of the situation and not intended to be crude or tantalizing. Finally, there are no pornographic depictions of the 'gay fireman' in these pages. The reality of my experience doesn't lend itself to sexual fantasies.

I have the greatest respect for the firefighting profession. With time, I have come to a greater understanding of the events described herein; it has fostered in me a degree of forgiveness towards those who didn't know better at the time. Ultimately, I find that I need to tell this story as much for myself as for others.

R. Kevin Mallinson

CHAPTER 1: September 29, 1981

Oneri was so full of himself. "We heard you're a faggot," he said. "We heard you were a *goddamned* faggot!"

What could I say to that? This wasn't exactly how I thought this day would go.

It was 5:50 a.m., and as I was dressing, I was thinking that I should have a second cup of coffee before leaving for my first day on the new job. Honestly, the anticipation was killing me. Today I will finally realize my dream of being a firefighter.

The crisp new uniform looked as if it had been tailored for me. Despite its gray color, it inspired me with a sense of pride. I fumbled with pinning the Key West Fire Department badge on the left side of my shirt. A *badge*? I hadn't imagined firefighters wearing a badge. Was it meant to communicate a sense of authority? Did it signify that I would be held to a higher standard in the community? Finally, I clasped my silver name bar to the right side of the shirt. I felt a sense of pride in its simple statement:

K. Mallinson

I deferred my usual early morning 10-mile run. *I couldn't be late.* To account for any unforeseen delays, I planned to arrive in Key West early and find a place to park close to the Flagler fire station. Then, I could leisurely pull into the parking lot at 6:30 a.m. and make a timely entrance for the 7 a.m. shift change. I kissed my partner Joe goodbye and grabbed the keys to our classic 1952 Ford pick-up truck.

It was a warm morning, so I had opened the windows to catch the salt-tinged breeze and pulled out onto US 1 towards Key West. As one hops from island to island along this *Overseas Highway*, the scenery is some of the most beautiful in the world. This is the longest north-south road in the country, beginning at the '0' mile marker in Key West and ending in Fort Kent, Maine. As it winds down the Florida Keys, US 1 curves so much that I am now actually headed due west. We chose to build our house on a small waterfront lot in the Saddlebunch Keys, 15 miles from Key West, because land was more affordable this far away from the city. Bay Point is the first inhabited island west of Sugarloaf Key.

The sun wasn't up yet. Despite the early morning darkness, I knew I was driving past hundreds of mangrove 'islands' on both sides of the road. The Florida Keys are a coral cay archipelago situated between the Atlantic Ocean on one side and the Gulf of Mexico on the other. Our island, Bay Point, is about 150 miles south of Miami. It is relatively well protected from the Atlantic Ocean by an extensive barrier of red and black mangrove islands. The Saddlebunch Keys are situated in shallow waters, usually less than 2 feet deep. They are home to a wide diversity of wildlife that find protection in the red mangroves and plenty of food in the estuarine shallow waters. The deep green islands are usually dotted with white egrets, blue herons, and brown pelicans. Occasionally, the patient bird watcher is handsomely awarded with flocks of roseate spoonbills searching for a meal in the crystal-clear waters.

At 25 years old, today was the start of a new chapter in my life. Wearing this uniform, it would be my mission to protect the city that I have come to call home. Driving into Key West, I had high expectations – and only minor apprehensions – about this new position. I could never have guessed how the day would unfold.

To be honest, Fire Station 1 was unkempt and unappealing. Situated at the intersection of two main roads in the 'New Town' section of Key West, it was a concrete block structure of little architectural note. The building had been designed by a previous Mayor, "Sonny" McCoy. The main bay for the fire trucks faced Kennedy Drive on the west side of the building. The entrance to the parking lot for firefighters was on Flagler Avenue. My tires made a loud grinding noise when I pulled off the main road onto the gravel – coral rock – parking area. The lot had no definition, no lined parking spots. It had rained overnight, so I parked our pick-up truck away from the mud puddles that remained.

I donned my Key West Fire Department cap and walked towards the back door. I glanced up and noticed a group of firefighters peering out through the windows on the second floor as I approached. *OK. I am more nervous than I expected.* It occurred to me that these guys had just completed their 24-hour shift and were anxious for the next shift to arrive so they could go home. As it turned out, they were in no hurry to leave on this particular morning.

The heavy steel door led to a drab concrete stairwell that had no windows. At the top of the stairs was the second floor 'public' area of the living quarters. On the left was a wall of concrete that was only interrupted by an interior set of stairs leading to the third floor sleeping bunks and a large bathroom with showers. On the right was an open passage (no door) to the small kitchen. In a few more steps, you found yourself standing in the dining area. The kitchen had a standard U-shape design with an elevated counter that opened to the dining area, an easy pass-through for food. There were two men in the kitchen preparing Cuban coffee. The enticing aroma was comforting.

There were seven men in the dining area, but only one firefighter was sitting at the table. He was overweight and disheveled; I guessed him to be in his mid-40s. He was wearing a wrinkled white t-shirt which didn't quite cover his oversized waistline. I could see another fireman talking on the phone in the next room. The room seemed unusually crowded. I suddenly felt conspicuous, everyone seemed to be staring at me. *I guess they are curious about the new guy.* Though the shift wasn't due to start for another 30 minutes, it became apparent to me that everyone from the oncoming shift had already arrived. *Was I late?*

I hadn't met any of these men before, so I was relieved when an older, wiry firefighter stepped forward and introduced himself as Captain Stephenson. I knew that he was to be my commanding officer on this shift. The wrinkles around his mouth and eyes made me think he had been a smoker for many years. He was at least as tall as me and quite thin. His presence suggested a leader that was direct, but not intimidating. He didn't offer a handshake. Instead, he motioned for me to approach the standing counter that was open to the kitchen.

"Do you drink Cuban coffee?" he asked.

"Sure!" I said. The offer put me at ease. I thought sharing morning coffee was a good start. A couple of the firemen backed away as I approached the counter. I could see the can of *Bustelo* next to the stove. Clearly, these guys knew their coffee. I added some condensed milk to my cup, took a sip, and turned to scan the room.

Was it just me? Or was there a palpable tension in the room? The firemen were not engaged in animated chatter that would suggest collegiality. They were mumbling to each other, almost whispering. They glanced at me occasionally, but none of them met my gaze. Suddenly, amidst the low hum of chatter in the room, one of the guys suddenly snarled at the seated fireman.

"Shut the fuck up, Oneri! Don't start that shit with me!" he said.

The room went eerily silent. The captain looked around at the other men, as if for some direction, before turning back to me.

"What do we call you? Robert? Kevin?" he asked.

"Yeah, my first name is Robert, but I go by my middle name. I go by Kevin," I explained.

There was another awkward silence. Feeling quite uneasy, I took another sip of my coffee. *Why was I feeling so uncomfortable?* The guy in the chair, Oneri, looked directly at me. The smirk on his face should've given me warning. He leaned slightly forward.

"We heard you're a faggot!" he stated.

Whoa! OK, I was not expecting this turn of events. I tried to remain calm, despite feeling like I had been punched in the stomach. I focused for a second on not dropping my coffee cup. I turned to face him head-on.

"What?" I asked. I purposely emphasized my surprise, hoping to suggest that the assertion was incredulous. I hoped this ruse would give me a minute to think. The room was terribly silent, and all eyes were on me. Oneri was unfazed. He was so full of himself. He leaned back in his chair, appearing overly confident. Again, he spit it out.

"We heard you're a *goddamned* faggot!" he said.

Then, displaying as much disbelief as I could muster, I looked directly into his eyes.

"Who the *hell* would say such a thing? I am not a *faggot*!?" I said, stressing the antigay epithet. Deep down, I was quite terrified, but I would be damned if I was going to let any of them realize it. *I need to stand my ground.* I was squeezing the coffee cup so hard I could have broken it.

My calm demeanor and emphasis on the slur seemed to have worked; Oneri looked stunned. The other guys were looking at each other, baffled. Maybe, for just that second or two, I had Oneri and the other firefighters thinking that they had been woefully misinformed about me. Maybe someone had given them incorrect intel on the new guy joining the fire department. Now, wouldn't they all look foolish if this ambush had all been a big misunderstanding!

As if tripping over his own two feet, Oneri tried to support his accusation. Now, he was nearly stuttering.

"We heard you…you're building a house on Bay Point?" he asked.

"Yes," I said. "I am building a house on Bay Point."

"With another guy?" he asked.

"Yes, with another guy," I repeated his words, "my partner, Joe." From his expression, I could see that he was trying to juggle more mental balls than he was able. Still, he stuck to his initial conclusion.

"So, you're a *faggot*?" He seemed to enjoy the emphasis on the slur. Clearly, he intended to offend me.

At this point, I thought I should bring this uncomfortable exchange to a close.

"No," I said. "I am not a faggot. I am a *gay* man. But I would *never* consider myself a faggot. I don't think anyone I know would consider me a faggot." Again, silence across the room. They all seemed dumbfounded.

Good. They deserved to be stunned.

It was only at this point that I noticed that no one else in the room was jumping in on Oneri's attack. Maybe they were just stupefied? Maybe they were more curious than they were ill-intentioned? I didn't know why they stood as mere bystanders, but I was relieved to have to confront only one malcontent. As calmly as I could, I took my last sip of the Cuban coffee, placed the cup on the counter, and turned towards the captain.

"Thanks for the coffee," I said. "I'll go look at the fire truck, if you don't mind." It was more of a statement than asking permission. I turned around and walked downstairs. Once on the ground floor, I leaned up against the concrete wall of the truck bay. I was shaking all over. There was a sudden aching tightness in my belly. I was so angry at being set up for that ambush. I had to calm down. I'd be damned if I would allow Oneri – or any of them – to see how the incident had affected me. *Still, I can't kid myself; this was an outright assault.*

Faggot. I'd heard that term all my life. However, long ago I decided not to let such verbal attacks defeat me. I needed to take control of the situation by removing the power of the bully who uses such epithets. Those who call on the adage that *'sticks and stones will break my bones, but names will never hurt me'* have likely never been the target of such hateful attacks. Slurs always have the potential to hurt. Hate speech, whether motivated by homophobia, racial bigotry, or anti-Semitism often leaves the victim with feelings of fear, vulnerability, and self-doubt. Words like *'faggot'* are intended to intimidate, demean, and dehumanize. Public assaults can be worse if they set a hostile environment that encourages violence. If the bystanders who witness verbal assaults remain quiet, it may be assumed that they are agreeing with the aggressor. I understood that it would be difficult for any of these firemen to stand up and advocate for me in the macho firehouse environment. If one had objected to Oneri's crude attack, I am sure he would have faced an inquisition. *What? You defending this queer? You love faggots? Are you a faggot, too?* Many men would not risk such an attack on their 'manhood' in a public forum. I expected that Capt. Stephenson would approach me with an apology. He never did.

While this initial firehouse confrontation was unexpectedly hostile, I wasn't eviscerated by the attack. I had experienced plenty of homophobic assaults in my life. True, I was concerned about potential violence. I was relieved that my use of wry humor seemed to deflect Oneri's belligerent offensive. My aim had been to defuse the tension while holding my ground. I knew who I was. I wasn't going to let anyone tell me otherwise.

Yet, questions remained. *How did they know I was gay before my first day at work? How did they know where I lived?* Yes, Key West is a small island, but this level of personal detail surprised me. I wanted so badly to phone Joe for some support. Unfortunately, I didn't know where to find a phone to use. Joe would have given me some reassurance that I could get through the remaining 24 hours of my first shift. Of course, I knew Joe well enough; his response would likely be to storm over to the firehouse and give Oneri a piece of his mind! Joe would have had a much more forceful and aggressive response to such an attack. That kind of response I didn't need or desire. My approach was to use nonviolent resistance in an attempt to avert physical confrontation. I just needed to stick with my plan and find a way through the muck.

Once my heart rate returned to normal, I walked out to the edge of the truck bay and watched vehicles pass by the station. I was imagining that anyone driving on Eisenhower Drive might look over and think: *There is a guy in a uniform. He's a city firefighter.* After all, didn't wearing this uniform make me a professional firefighter? That gave me some hope. Still, it had just become all too clear that wearing a uniform provided me no real level of protection from being beaten up by a couple angry men.

The remainder of that first day was extraordinarily tense. I learned how long a 24-hour shift can be when one feels apprehensive and unsafe. When the firemen from the previous shift finally left for home, the firehouse quieted down. The men on my watch only spoke to me when necessary. At the direction of the captain, we collected our turnout gear, boarded the truck, and proceeded to drive around the neighborhoods in our part of town. We stopped, occasionally, to retrieve the hydrant wrench and test if water would pour out when a hydrant was opened. An article in the Key West Citizen newspaper had recently revealed that several hydrants across the island were found to be non-operational. When opened, some either supplied no water or had water pressure so low as to be useless during a fire. So, it was now standard practice to conduct random testing.

We responded to only one small car fire that day. As the rookie with no training, I was not allowed to handle the hose at the scene. Rather, I was relegated to sweeping the street clear of debris and rolling up the hose when the fire was out. In this incident, I learned that there were different hoses for different needs, various ways to deliver water, and even ways to draft water from a swimming pool in the absence of an available fire hydrant. I decided that I needed to learn something new each day to be a successful firefighter.

I left the firehouse at the end of my first shift grateful that I would not be back for another two days (48 hours). I needed time to recover and strategize before returning to the firehouse. When I told Joe my tale of woe, he was furious. His natural reaction was to strike back. "Fuck that," he would say, "I'd beat the shit out of them and teach them some respect!" This was not my style. I thought long and hard before walking back into Fire Station 1 two days later. I held my head high.

CHAPTER 2: The Truth Will Set You Free

I grew up in an immigrant household. My parents were raised in a small town near Leeds in Yorkshire, England. During World War II, my father had served in the Royal Navy, stationed in North Africa. My mother was a nurse's aide in the Royal Air Force, caring for wounded pilots outside of London. After the war, they returned home and fell in love. Their families were not pleased by their plans to get married; my father was of English, Protestant stock and my mother's family was Irish Catholic. Still, they insisted on becoming husband and wife. Consequently, their wedding gifts included two one-way tickets to the United States. The unspoken message from their families was clear: "If you want to marry, leave."

When my parents arrived in this country in 1948, they had no jobs and little support. Fair to say that both my mother and father were intelligent, though neither had advanced education. My father was skilled at mathematics and my mother was a voracious reader. Over the years, they had four children. In addition to juggling unstable employment, they struggled with finances, depression, and alcoholism. I was the third in the line of three boys; my one sister – three years my junior – came last.

At the age of 13, my attraction to other males crept into my consciousness. It had been there for a while but was nothing that caught my attention. Suddenly, I couldn't stop staring at the handsome handyman at the apartment complex. I found his big mustache strangely intriguing, tantalizing. In high school, I stared at the senior students performing gymnastic feats in phys-ed class. The older guys had developing muscles and small tufts of chest hair that captivated my imagination. The idea of sex wasn't even on my radar. The allure of the males was sensual, not sexual. I had the desire for physical closeness with a guy, but it was a couple of years before I was aware of the need for sexual intimacy. I was particularly attracted to the confidence shown by the older boys and young men. Teenagers my own age held no fascination for me.

At 16 years old, my junior year in high school was unremarkable. Though my grades were outstanding, my classmates hardly ever heard me speak up in class. I was a loner both in and out of school. My passions were reading, walking on the beach, and taking long bicycle rides. There were no opportunities for me to gather carnal knowledge. Somehow, I knew I was different from my peers and had something to fear from sharing my inner thoughts about men with friends. When the adolescent banter centered around 'getting some' from girls, I couldn't relate. The allure of dating escaped me. My self-imposed isolation from the other adolescent boys in school probably contributed to my naiveté about sexual matters. My world was about to change in a brief 60-minute period.

I was standing in the hallway with a group of boys before Geometry class. Mathematics was one of my favorite subjects and our teacher was excellent at explaining the material. Several boys next to me were abuzz, overly excited with a rumor.

"He must be a *faggot*," said one of the boys.

That word seemed to intensify their interest and their voices dropped to whispers.

"I'm sure of it," another boy said, nodding his head confidently. "He must be a faggot."

"What are you talking about?" I asked. I knew enough to keep to a whisper.

"Mr. Lonergan. We think he's a faggot," one of them responded.

It wasn't clear to me what they were saying about our teacher. Of course, I had heard the slur 'faggot' many times but was not exactly sure what it meant. All I gathered was that it was a terrible insult. It was as bad as being labeled a *fem, queer, sissy, pansy,* or *fairy*. This made no sense in the context of our teacher. Mr. Lonergan is a faggot?

"Why do you say that?" I asked, innocently.

Then, laying out the evidence, one of the kids explained. "He isn't married. He doesn't have a girlfriend. He's probably a faggot. He likes to *do it* with guys. You know, a homosexual."

As I was scrambling to put together the clues – and his emphasis on the phrase 'do it' with guys – the door opened, and we dutifully filed in to take our seats. I sat in class, dumbfounded. My mind was ablaze with new possibilities. What were these boys suggesting? I wasn't focused on Mr. Lonergan, per se, but how they tied their points together to arrive at their scandalous accusation. "Not married?" "Doesn't have a girlfriend?" "Likes to *do it* with guys?" Even the word *homosexual* was a mystery to me. I admit it; I was naïve about sex. I couldn't focus on geometry. I left school immediately after class. There was no way I could pay attention for the rest of the day. I jumped on a bus into New Haven. One of my favorite pastimes was sitting on a bench in the Yale University quadrangle and watching the guys as they played Frisbee or soccer in the greenspace between the dormitories. I was having an epiphany. I was finally becoming aware of *why* I liked staring at the college men.

I had only a fleeting experience with internalized homophobia in that first year of accepting my sexual orientation; it brought me to the edge of suicide, though. However, since that crisis, I have not experienced the years of handwringing or the burden of self-doubt that interferes with so many gay men's ability to have a happy and fulfilling life. I accepted who I was with no apologies.

In the Spring of 1973, my high school graduation was approaching. The more I excelled in my schoolwork, the more unhappy my parents seemed to be. Being from the working class in northern England, my parents struggled to embrace the American concept of children trying to 'do better' than their parents through higher education. They undermined my attempts to attend college; I had won a scholarship to study architecture at Bucknell, but they would not sign the papers. My father was disappointed that I wouldn't quit high school to work with him and my brothers repairing cars.

By this time, my family had already surmised that I was gay. One brother, just a couple of years older than me, frequently taunted me with insults, the usual *sissy, fairy, pansy*. My family often told me that I would amount to nothing. Neither of my parents attended my high school graduation. I walked across the stage to obtain my degree on a warm Wednesday afternoon. At 6 a.m. the next morning, I stepped onto a Greyhound bus and left home. I was 17 years old and had an accumulated savings of $88 in my pocket. My message was clear: "I am going to be who I am, so I will leave."

I traveled to Rome, a small town in Upstate New York. Over the months prior to finishing high school, I had been corresponding with a gay man I met through neighbors. I had written to him describing my intolerable homelife. My intention was to escape for a better life and, hopefully, to attend college. Ron allowed me to move into his house with explicit conditions: I would have to get a job, pay rent, and open a savings account to save for tuition. He mentored me like an older brother.

Ron was in his early 30's and a successful businessman. Through his social network, I met a wide variety of gay men. They included lawyers, Air Force officers, building contractors, hair stylists, and restaurant owners, among others. *Wow, any type of man can be gay!* Still, most of the men were not open about their sexual orientation. They lived closeted lives to protect their reputations and their careers. I had very little idea of the dire consequences that could befall a man who was found to be homosexual. There were no laws protecting a gay man or lesbian from being fired from their job or denied housing because of who they loved. At that age, I had little to lose by being true to myself, as long as I didn't put Ron at risk. I would not be forced into a life of hiding that was inauthentic and caused me to be dishonest.

Only a month or so after I settled in, Ron took me to a gay bar in Utica. Though it only took us 30 minutes to get there, it might as well have been a world away! The bar was filled with so many kinds of gay men out for some Saturday night fun. They were tall, short, Black, White, older, and younger (me!). As with most gay bars in those days, it was the proverbial 'hole in the wall.' Situated on a dark street in a semi-industrial area, it saw little pedestrian traffic after dusk. The one room bar/dance floor was small with dark walls that were sparsely decorated. It astounded me to see a public space in which men could hold hands, kiss, and dance! At not quite 18 years old, it had not occurred to me that two men could dance together. Ron kept me close as the bar became more crowded.

We had been there only an hour or so when I was approached by a stranger asking me to dance. He was a tall, good-looking bearded guy in his late 20s wearing a white outfit with fringe (so much the fashion at the time). I had always been attracted to the cowboy motif. *Hell yeah!* I was going to dance with this man! He had an alluring musky cologne that I later learned was patchouli oil. As we swayed to the Moody Blues song *Nights in White Satin,* I was transported to another reality. Dancing with a man was intoxicating. This was my first opportunity to see men being romantic with each other. I had rarely danced before, but my partner didn't seem to mind. The freedom of expression among the gay men was unlike anything I had ever imagined. Sadly, the evening fun ended all too soon. Ron jerked me closer so I could hear him over the loud music.

"Kevin," he said, "walk out the front door right now! I am right behind you." He was in a near panic. When I didn't respond immediately, he began to push me towards the door. I still didn't understand the urgency to leave. He was aggressively pushing me through the groups of men who were drinking beer and laughing. We flew by a uniformed police officer.

"Strange?" I thought. I couldn't imagine what a cop would be doing in a gay bar. Then, I noticed another officer to my right. He didn't see me as we rushed past. Ron gave one last push.

"Get outside," he said. "Go!" I got out the door and walked quickly towards the curb. As I looked back, I could see 3, 4, or 5 more policemen entering the bar. Ron, however, didn't make it out. I crossed the street to keep an eye out for Ron without being caught in the fray. Over the next 15 minutes or so, I witnessed terrified patrons scrambling out of the bar, running in all directions. Clearly, they were trying to avoid getting caught by the officers. The cops seemed unduly rough, pushing the men out the door and lining them up on the sidewalk. I could hear the police shouting derogatory comments at the men, intending to shame them for being homosexual.

Finally, I saw Ron. He was being escorted to the police van. My heart sank. A few of the guys successfully wrangled themselves free and made a break for it into the night. None of the cops pursued. Unfortunately, Ron didn't have the opportunity to escape. I walked a half block away so the police wouldn't notice me.

I was alone. I was in a city where I knew no one. It was the middle of the night. I had no idea how I would get back to Rome. I was so angry that I wanted to rip open the paddy wagon doors and release the "criminals" the cops had captured. I couldn't understand why this was happening. As quickly as they had arrived, the police were gone. Miraculously, there were still men leaving the bar. One of Ron's friends saw me and came over to check on me. Tommy explained that this type of police raid on gay bars occasionally happened. Traditionally, the police extorted money from the owners of gay bars to "look the other way" and not bother the customers. At times, though, the officers wanted to emphasize that they were in control. It was 1973, a time when homosexuals were vilified by clergy, politicians, and the press. Sex between men was illegal in all states. It was even against the law to sell alcohol to "a known homosexual" in those days! The police had the legal authority to arrest patrons in a gay bar on suspicion of intent to engage in immoral behavior. Just that year, the American Psychiatric Association (APA) had removed homosexuality from its list of mental disorders, acknowledging same-sex attraction as only one in a spectrum of possible sexual orientations among humans. However, it was years before the lives of average gay people were impacted by that action.

Thankfully, Tommy drove me back to Rome. He assured me that Ron would return soon. Ron was released from jail the next morning, retrieved his car, and arrived home safely. On Monday morning, however, his name – along with the names of 20 or so other patrons – was published in the Utica newspaper. The gist of the article was that these "perverts were arrested in a homosexual bar." Over the next week, I could see the pain in Ron's eyes as he had to face his family, friends, and customers who were quick to judge. I found the police raid to be unfair, unnecessary, and outrageous.

Ron tried to make light of his arrest by telling me about how Oscar Wilde had been arrested several times for "cavorting" with men thought to be homosexual. I swore that I would not tolerate being debased and humiliated without a fight. I made a commitment to myself that I would stand up if my rights – or the rights of other gay men and lesbians – were being abridged. From that point on, I never considered hiding the fact that I was gay. A closeted life not only breeds internalized homophobia, but requires one to continually lie to family, friends, and coworkers. I was unwilling to sacrifice that much to satisfy a self-righteous heterosexual's need to oppress gay people. Forcing gay men and lesbians to hide "in the closet" only perpetrates stereotypes. My choice was to live my life openly and honestly.

I had always heard that 'the truth will set you free.' Well, it seems that it might slap you across the face, first. Then, it will set you free!

There are times, of course, when homophobia leads to violence. After leaving home, my primary goal was to get a college education. Two years after graduating from high school, I began my studies at the State University of New York (SUNY) at Geneseo. Located in the Finger Lakes region, the college of approximately 6,000 students was in set in the middle of a town of approximately 4,000 residents. I had been learning sign language and selected this college for its Special Education program. However, my college experience taught me more about how to stand up for myself than anything else.

The second week of my first semester, September 1975, the cover of *TIME* magazine featured Sergeant Leonard Matlovich. He was a Vietnam War veteran and recipient of both the Purple Heart and the Bronze Star. He was pictured in his Air Force uniform. In big, black letters, the title of the lead article across the cover boldly stated: *"I am a homosexual": The gay drive for acceptance.* Wow! Sgt. Matlovich was a handsome, well-decorated American hero challenging the military's policy of discharging active-duty personnel simply because they identified as gay or lesbian! I had so much respect for someone who could stand up and resist in such a public manner.

I trimmed the front cover off the magazine and taped it to the side of my study desk. My two roommates saw me do this, but never asked me why I displayed it. About an hour later, a student from across the hall walked into our room. He spoke with my roommates before turning towards me. Seeing the TIME cover, he stopped and read the caption out loud.

"I am a homosexual," he said. He sounded genuinely puzzled.

I stood and reached out to shake his hand. I looked him straight in the eye. "I am, too," I said. "Nice to meet you."

The room was stone cold silent as the three of them tried to find their footing. I was as nonchalant as I could be. I sat back down, opened my book, and continued studying. Amazingly, they didn't respond to my outright declaration. Eventually, they resumed their discussion. *OK. I did it. I have come out. They will just have to accept that I refuse to hide my sexual orientation.* I wasn't ashamed of it. Why should heterosexuals feel free to be themselves while expecting me to 'sell my soul' by hiding in the closet? They were no better than me. Over the semester, neither of my roommates ever discussed the issue with me.

The year was 1975, only six years since the riots at the Stonewall Inn in Greenwich Village, a pivotal event that ignited the modern gay rights movement. To its credit, the college already had an established Gay and Lesbian organization on campus, and I became its President. The position was easy to slip into as there were only two other students willing to place their names on the organization's roster; others were fearful of being 'found out' and harassed. Sadly, this position allowed me access to the details of the numerous instances of harassment and gay-bashing reported by lesbian and gay students across campus. It became clear to me that many incidents of assaults and intimidation were swept under the rug and minimized by college administrators as innocent "normal male adolescent behavior." Soon enough, I became a target for one of those bullies.

Schoony, as he was known, was particularly disturbed by my presence. He was a senior who lived down the hall in my dorm. I hadn't had any meaningful interactions with him, but we frequently passed each other on the small campus. He never failed to target me, hurling the usual homophobic insults: *faggot, queer, homo, sissy, fem.* Of course, this was nothing I hadn't heard before. Sometimes, in the middle of the night, he would awaken me and my roommates by banging on our door and screaming obscenities as he walked down the hall to his room. One day, though, he went too far. It hadn't occurred to me that he would try to physically harm me.

After finishing my last class of the day, I was walking back to the dormitory. As I approached the entrance, I felt a 'swoosh!' next to my left shoulder and a loud crack of something smashing on the concrete. I quickly jumped aside to see what had nearly struck me. On the ground was a large ceramic flowerpot, shattered into a thousand pieces. When I looked up, I saw Schoony peering from his third-floor window directly overhead. His projectile had missed my head by mere inches. It was obvious that he meant to hit my head with the plant container.

My first instinct was to dart into the building lobby for protection. I was shaken. Quickly, my shock turned to outrage. Enough was enough! I picked up the lobby phone and reported the assault to the campus Security Office. Within minutes, a campus officer pulled up on a Cushman golf cart. After I had described the incident, the security officer suggested that it could have been an unfortunate coincidence and nothing intentional. I pressed the issue, assuring the officer that it was an act of malice. Reluctantly, he agreed to go upstairs and talk with Schoony. I was following him.

"Stay here," the officer directed, "I will talk with him."

"Oh, no," I said, "I have every right to be there." Motioning to the stairwell, I directed the officer, "Third floor, to the right at the top of the stairs. Room 311." Ascending the stairs, I imagined that Schoony would be enraged upon seeing the security officer. Would he start yelling about me being a homosexual? I was prepared for a tense confrontation with the guy who had just tried to cause me grave harm. It couldn't have unfolded more differently.

Schoony answered the door. Rather than being puffed up like a cock with ruffled feathers, he appeared surprisingly meek and overly respectful to the officer. "Yes, sir," He replied repeatedly. He seemed stunned – if not a little intimidated – to see me standing just a few feet away in the hallway. I guess he never expected me to face him directly. Other students began gathering in the hallway, curious about what had happened. Schoony muttered softly that he was guilty of pulling a stupid stunt on the gay guy. Several times he apologized for taking up the officer's time. I had never imagined he could be so submissive and acquiescent. I assumed that the officer's authoritarian manner was more threatening to Schoony than I thought. The security officer attempted to settle the situation by asking us to 'leave this behind us' and agree to no further hostilities.

Once downstairs, the officer summarized for me that this was just a case of 'boys being boys' and that he didn't think that it rose to the level that needed to be reported to the municipal police.

"Except that I could've been seriously hurt by that fucking stunt!" I snapped back. The officer ignored my objection. I was astounded that the incident would be minimized by someone sworn to provide 'security' for students. Apparently, security didn't apply equally to homosexuals. He gave me a copy of his report and headed out the door. I decided not to pursue the issue further. I was somewhat satisfied seeing Schoony backed into a corner. He seemed humiliated by both the presence of authority and my willingness to publicly call him out for his behavior. He appeared uncharacteristically subdued for a few weeks. I wondered if this wasn't his first encounter with law enforcement. Perhaps, my act of submitting a formal complaint to the university security department undermined his confidence. Eventually, however, he resumed bombarding me with slurs when we encountered each other.

It was a cold, snowy day in mid-December 1976 and most of the students in the dorm had left for home to enjoy the winter break. I had no home to return to, so I remained on campus. I gathered my dirty clothes and descended to the basement laundry. Walking into the small room, I could see that Schoony was the only other person present. After placing my basket at an open washing machine, I retraced my steps and closed the door to the hallway. Schoony and I were now alone in an enclosed space. As calmly as I could, I started placing my clothes in the washer.

"Why the hell did you close the door?" Schoony barked. He adopted a rigid posture.

I turned to face him head-on. "I think it's time you and I had a talk," I said. With my arms slightly raised and open, I spoke in an honestly curious tone of voice. "Schoony," I said, "just what is it about me that bothers you so much?"

"I don't like you talking about being a homo and getting others to act like you!" he said. If he hadn't sounded so anxious, I might have believed the pretense of anger. Clearly, I had rattled his cage.

"What do you mean, others?" I asked. I was a bit surprised. What could he be thinking?

"You have that organization to make others gay. It's disgusting," he said. Now, his tone sounded more explanatory than angry.

"You think that they aren't already gay when they join?" I asked. "They come to the group because they ARE gay." His assertation seemed preposterous. I tried to reveal the flaws in his thinking.

"Do you think," I asked, "if you hung around me for a couple of weeks that you would become gay?"

"I don't know," he said. His voice was low and meek. He was staring down at his feet. His aggressive stance had wilted to the point that I thought he might collapse. I could sense his defeat.

"Well, Schoony," I said, now concluding, "*there* is your problem. You *don't* know."

I turned, placed my coins in the washer to begin its cycle, picked up my empty basket, and exited the room. I left the door open. Schoony never bothered me again. In this case, perhaps, *his truth* set me free; I hope it did the same for him.

CHAPTER 3: A Man with a Plan

The firemen seemed surprised that I returned for my second day on duty. There were no mean words...there were no words at all. After settling in that morning, I started checking the equipment on the fire truck. I verified that the ax, bolt cutters, K-12 saw, and others were in their assigned storage bin and ready for use. This was a daily ritual for which the rookie was responsible. Then, I would have to wash the truck.

We didn't have enough staffing at Fire Station 1 on this day, so one of the men from another firehouse, Carlos, was being transferred to us for the shift. Since I was new, he would work alongside me. I glanced up as he approached the station and tried to be congenial.

"Good morning, Carlos," I said.

"Oh, fuck you!" he growled. His tone implied he wanted nothing to do with me. I calmly looked at my watch before replying.

"Oh, geez. Not now, I'm busy. But catch me after noon, OK?"

Then, I turned back to begin washing the truck.

It took him a moment to rebound from my unexpected response and then he climbed the stairs to the second floor living quarters. Carlos returned in about 10 minutes or so, alone. He came directly up to me with his hand outstretched.

"Hey, I appreciate a guy with a sense of humor!" he said. He shook my hand. I was so pleased that he made the effort to come back to say it.

Whew! Maybe my approach will work, after all?

So, an openly gay young man becomes a professional firefighter. At this point, anyone might be wondering *What was he expecting? Did he have a plan?* Well, aside from my long-held desire to be a firefighter, no. Truth be told, I could not have imagined the challenges I was going to face by taking a position in the Key West Fire Department (KWFD).

Most often, my approach to coming out was nonchalant. I began working regular jobs at 17 years old. Of course, I wouldn't introduce myself as a gay man, but I never hid my sexual orientation from my workmates. In most instances, there was the opportunity to get hired, develop basic relationships with coworkers, and earn their respect as a hardworking and engaged colleague. Eventually, my coworkers would ask about my private life. I would be nonchalant when saying 'my partner' or 'my boyfriend.' I wasn't trying to make a big deal about being gay. It made no difference to any job I held. Still, when part of the workplace environment is sharing personal stories, I surely wasn't going to lie about who I was or diminish the importance of those I loved. I was not going to apologize for being myself.

To be sure, not everyone I met at work had been accepting. There were occasional snide comments or snickers intended to make fun of me as a 'gay boy.' I realized early on that referring to a gay man as a gay 'boy' was not unlike calling a Black man a 'boy' or a woman a 'girl.' The goal of these diminutive terms is to deny respect for the individual's adult personhood; it implies that the person is 'less than' or less capable. However, there had never been a time when a co-worker or boss was so intolerant as to suggest that I didn't *belong* in the workplace. So, casually revealing myself as a gay man had worked well for me in the past. Apparently, having an openly gay man in the firehouse wasn't going to go as smoothly as I might have expected. *Why was I such a threat to these guys? What will I have to do to win their confidence and acceptance?*

Before I applied for a position in the KWFD, my friend Jan Durland and I had been working our small business maintaining lawns, hauling junk, and cleaning houses. Our income was neither stable nor enough to live on. Jan was raising two kids and I was building a house. I supplemented my income with washing dishes at the Sugarloaf Lodge motel. After a couple of years working together, Jan and I both decided it was time for each of us to pursue a job that would be more rewarding and profitable. Jan found her way into teaching and established a successful, creative alternative school. I had heard from a neighbor on Bay Point that the fire department was hiring. Suddenly, my imagination was ablaze with excitement! The next day, I walked into City Hall at the corner of Angela and Simonton Streets in Old Town to register for the upcoming Civil Service examination. I had no idea what to expect.

"I haven't been a fireman before," I admitted to the clerk. "How do you think I should prepare for the exam?"

"Oh no, you don't need to have experience," she explained. "If you completed high school, you can take the exam."

After registering, I decided to walk to the Monroe County library and see what resources they had on taking a 'civil service' test. I exited out onto Simonton Street. *Isn't that funny? It had never occurred to me that one of the fire stations was in the City Hall building.* As I passed the open bay door, I could see the bright red fire truck sitting silent, but apparently ready to race off at a moment's notice. Exciting!

I was a regular patron of the library on Fleming Street. Usually, I used the card catalogue to find my own materials. However, I was eager to avoid a tedious search, so I asked the librarian for her advice. "Oh, you don't really have to study for a civil service exam. It tests your fundamental abilities in reading English and doing basic math," she said. This seemed to align with what I had heard from the clerk in City Hall.

"Well, do you have books on firefighting?" I inquired. With the few resources in hand, I sat down to familiarize myself with the basics of fighting fires. The first book was fictional schmaltz, a story about imaginary firemen who battled grand conflagrations. The second book, however, was more sobering; it was a training manual for firefighters who were seeking to advance from basic firefighter to the role of *'engineer.'* The engineer controls the water pumps on the truck to assure that adequate streams of water are available to the firefighters on the frontlines at a fire scene. I was intimidated by the terminology, the geometry of water stream arcs, and the complex math involved in managing hydraulic pressures during a fire! My initial thought was that I had bitten off more than I could chew. Maybe firefighting would be too much of a challenge? I concluded that this book was written for experienced firefighters who were looking to be promoted. The library visit wasn't a total loss, though. I was even more convinced that this was a career I was meant to pursue.

The Civil Service exam took place in City Hall. There were 20 or so guys who showed up to take the exam, each hoping to get the firefighter position. Most of them were Conchs who knew each other. I had to laugh. They greeted each other with 'manly' handshakes, feigning support and wishing each other good luck. In fact, these guys were all applying for the same job opening; they were likely sizing up the competition. Half of the conversations were in Spanish. There were no women sitting for the exam and only one young Black man present.

The exam met my expectations. It covered basic reading skills, math (algebra and geometry), and general knowledge. I finished the exam relatively quickly. After taking a few moments to check that I had answered every question, I returned my materials to the proctor.

"Done so quick?" he asked, as if surprised. "Well, if you want to wait, I can score them right away." I thanked him and took a seat in the back of the room. Slowly, but surely, the other guys finished and turned in their forms. The proctor would lay his answer key over the response sheets to mark any incorrect answers. A few men left after handing in their forms, but the majority stayed on to receive their scores. I waited about 45 minutes.

"Mallinson!?" the proctor yelled.

"Mallinson, that's me," I said.

"Well, congratulations. You got the highest score on the exam."

"Thanks," I said.

"Oh, it's to your benefit," he volunteered, "I hear they will be hiring three firefighters this year. You will be sure to be called by the Chief for an interview." *Not to worry, Kevin, there were three positions to be filled.* I didn't realize how important my score would be until weeks later. According to the policies, the Chief could overlook my job application once…even twice; he could not jump over it three times, though, without interviewing me because of my score on the exam. Leaving City Hall, I drove over to a bodega for lunch. I felt like celebrating, so a chocolate dessert was in order. Practical questions began to pop into my head. *When might the Chief call? What do I wear to an interview for this job?* I should have asked for more questions.

The call came the next day. I was given instructions to show up for an interview with Chief Gilbert (Gibby) Gates at Fire Station 1 on Flagler Avenue. My physical abilities would be tested, so I was to wear comfortable clothes and sneakers. I was comfortable with my physical condition by the time I became a firefighter. My partner, Joe Dietrich, and I had been living together for three and a half years and, for the past year, we had been building a house from the ground up. We had been digging holes, laying concrete, lifting truckloads of lumber, and grading the landscape at our property. To be sure, I was no bodybuilder. However, at 5' 9" and a mere 130 pounds, my body was lean and agile. Optimizing my 'body mechanics', I was able to lift or move heavy objects despite my relative lack of muscle and bulk. I was to learn that the firefighter's turnout gear (jacket and pants), gloves, boots, helmet, and air tank can add an extra 40 pounds or more.

Firefighting entails lifting, dragging, and stabilizing hoses full of water at high pressure. I was surprised to learn that firefighting often requires physical endurance rather than brute strength. Firefighters need to withstand hot, difficult conditions for extended periods of time. One needs stamina to carry hoses up and down ladders. Finally, one must be mentally disciplined enough to perform under pressure in a dangerous and unpredictable fire scene. The public should revere firefighters for their grit, tenacity, and fortitude as much as for their bravery or brute strength. Endurance was one of my best qualities. I enjoyed distance running. In 1981, I was usually hitting the pavement for 10 miles or more a day in the heat and humidity of the Florida Keys. One of my personal goals was to complete a marathon someday. Long distance running required dedication to training, a disciplined mind to pace oneself, and an ability to tolerate physical discomfort. I had these qualities before entering the fire service and they would prove to serve me well.

I showed up on Monday morning, as instructed. The interview with Chief Gates was brief. He didn't seem like the kind of guy who laughed very much. He was about my height and thin…no, *gaunt* might be a better descriptor. His facial wrinkles suggested a lifetime of cigarette smoking. His questions for me were non-specific and, frankly, not memorable. Then, he reached over for a crutch and lifted himself out of his chair carefully, trying to avoid pain or losing his balance (I wasn't sure which).

"OK. The other candidates are out by the field," he said. We walked out together and made our way onto the football field next to the firehouse.

"Kevin, this is Captain Castro," he said. "Eddie, this is our third guy."

The captain reached out to shake my hand, smiling widely.

"And this is John and Johnny," the captain said, motioning towards two other recruits.

John was taller than me. He had a full-sized body and was quite strong from the looks of it. The other candidate, Johnny, on the other hand, was considerably shorter than me. He also appeared quite muscular. I laughed to myself. In the gay community, we might refer to a man with Johnny's stature and body shape as a 'fireplug'. Ha! *I think it best not to mention that at this moment.*

Over the next 30 minutes or so, we had to demonstrate our physical speed, agility, and strength. We began with my daily pastime; we were timed for how fast we could run 5 laps around the football field. This was a cinch for a guy who already averages 10 miles a day for recreation. Within two laps, I was already passing John and Johnny who were just completing their first. There was no shame in their struggle to run; they were clearly going to beat me in the strength categories. Completing my fifth lap, I was thinking *I'm just getting warmed up.*

"Great Kevin. I guess you like to run?" Capt. Castro laughed.

When John and Johnny were done with their laps, they looked winded. The next task was to pick up two rolls of fire hose and carry them up three floors to the top of the wooden platform overlooking the sports field. Each of the rolls weighed about 45 lbs. or so. I was beginning to doubt myself. How would I do this when I weighed only 130 pounds? Then, I quickly strategized how I could balance these hoses without dropping them. Grabbing each with one of my hands, I made sure that my arms were pointing straight down to allow my legs to bear the weight, and I bounded up the steps. Whew! It was not easy. I thought I would pass out from the exertion in such heat and humidity.

John and Johnny had a tougher time than I expected. I think they were still recovering from their laps when they were asked to endure another aerobic activity. It occurred to me that few folks had a well-rounded exercise workout. For example, I focused on aerobic exercises that improved my agility and endurance but tended to ignore strength-building activities such as lifting weights. Others focused on building muscle strength but lacked overall flexibility and stamina.

The last test took place in the firehouse. Capt. Castro brought us back into the truck bay. At the rear of the building, two firefighters were holding three facemasks that firefighters normally used with air tanks when entering burning buildings. But right now, the end of each air hose was not connected to an air tank. The test was to put the mask on your face, tighten it securely by pulling on the side straps, and keep the mask on for at least 30 seconds while someone cuts off the air supply by placing their thumb over the open end of the hose. Once our masks were secured, Captain Castro and the two firemen each took responsibility for an air tube.

Oh my god! Can I do this? I could hold my breath when snorkeling on the coral reef. But, to have your air supply cut off by someone else is another story. I focused my thoughts, attempting to achieve a state of tranquility. I tried to assure myself that the test was no big deal. *I can do this.* It was surprisingly difficult.

"30 seconds!" the captain said. He took his thumb off John's tube. The guy holding Johnny's also immediately let go. The fireman holding my tube did not immediately release his thumb. I couldn't pull in any air. Almost immediately, Capt. Castro noticed that I was still holding my breath.

"I said let go!" he snapped at the fireman.

Once the fireman removed his thumb, I was able to draw in air. It was obvious that Capt. Castro was particularly pissed off at this guy for blocking my air intake for the extra few moments. At the time, I didn't think that he had done anything malicious. All was forgotten. Then, Chief Gates rejoined us.

"You all did good," he started. "You all will report to duty next week. Capt. Castro will give you specific details. Bringle, report to Station 3.

Rodriguez, Station 2. Mallinson, you will be here at Station 1."

I was hired! We received instructions on how to obtain the necessary uniforms, badge, and name tag for our first day on duty. Within minutes, I was back on my motorcycle, heading for the cable TV offices to share my good news with Joe before he started his workday! At the time though, I couldn't have imagined the challenges I would face in the Key West Fire Department (KWFD).

Key West in the early 1980s had a unique sociopolitical environment that complicated my position in the KWFD. The island is approximately 4 square miles of coral rock positioned at the confluence of the Atlantic Ocean and the Gulf of Mexico, about 150 miles south of Miami. Until I lived on an island, it was difficult to understand how insular your world becomes. There are no neighboring communities. In this small space, the permanent residents numbered about 30,000 people. The population more than doubled during the winter months as tourists and 'snowbirds' flocked down from the north. The circumscribed living space leads to 'everyone' knowing your personal business, your comings and goings. Some locals were short-sighted and intolerant; there were Conchs who had rarely – if ever – set foot on the mainland of Florida or elsewhere in the country.

Up until the late 1970s, Key West had been a 'sleepy' town. The lifestyle was relaxed, and no one was in a hurry; things could always be left until 'mañana.' The city government was rife with corruption and there were few checks and balances. If a local wanted to obtain a city position or secure a municipal contract, nepotism was the best option. For some of the men I was working with, entry into the fire department was secured through favoritism by family or friends (as opposed to eligibility for the job). Becoming a firefighter for the city was coveted because it assured the man a secure base income, health benefits, and exceptional flexibility. The shift schedule (24 hours on/48 hours off) allowed a fireman to hold down a second job. Once a month, each fireman received a 'Kelly Day' off to avoid being paid overtime for the extra hours that mounted up due to the unusual work schedule. The Kelly Day provided a run of five days off away from the firehouse. It wasn't surprising that the Conchs wanted my position in the KWFD to go to one of their own. Once 'outsiders' were hired into positions traditionally given to family and friends, the Conchs might lose their long-held chokehold on municipal functions. My entrance into the KWFD coincided with a call by the City Commission to end nepotism and enact fair and equitable hiring practices.

Any casual visitor to the island cannot deny that the Key West social scene is unique. Cayo Hueso (Spanish name for the island) has a core of longstanding Conch families, most of whom originated in Cuba or the Bahamas. In addition to the local Conchs, there are many transplants (*newcomers*) who have settled into the relaxed and, often, quirky island lifestyle. Dozens of famous writers, artists, and celebrities had been drawn to the sleepy little island since the early 20th century. Following my arrival in late 1977, I encountered such luminaries as Tennessee Williams, Jimmy Buffett, Leonard Bernstein, Shel Silverstein, and Roy Scheider. There was also a sizable population of 'hippies' who had migrated to the island. Their creativity and quirky, offbeat lifestyle brought an anti-establishment irreverence to Key West. The islanders were wildly diverse.

By the late 1970s, local Conchs were beginning to experience a rapidly increasing transition of their island culture. Gay men and women were moving to Key West and establishing businesses. By 1978, dozens of businesses with gay or lesbian owners (and others that were gay-friendly) collaborated to launch the Key West Business Guild. This new association served as an alternative 'chamber of commerce' that pooled advertising funds to reach out to a new demographic: the gay tourist. No longer were gay and lesbian businesspeople hiding their affinity with the broader homosexual community. This new venture was extraordinarily profitable as there were few options for the gay traveler to indulge in a tropical vacation in the United States. Tourism to Key West was exploding!

It was no secret that many Conchs were not happy that well-financed newcomers – gay or straight – were relocating to 'their' island and buying up homes and businesses. This new wave of gentrification was leading to dramatic increases in property values. Conversely, local Conchs who were tradesmen central to building renovations – plumbers, electricians, and carpenters – were in high demand. So, there were financial benefits to the restoration of old Conch-style homes and the influx of tourist dollars.

Amid these radical social changes for the local Key Westers, I was hired by the fire department. Perhaps, the initial confrontation with the firemen was simply because my presence symbolized the adaptations they so feared. Once they got to know me, perhaps I would be accepted as a fellow firefighter.

CHAPTER 4: Settling into the Job

The first two weeks in the Fire Department were particularly stressful. The firemen would converse throughout the day, but purposely avoid including me in their discussions. Admittedly, most of their chats were inane. It seemed that their conversations were simply opportunities to boast – unconvincingly – about their exploits while hunting, fishing, or pursuing women. Many of them had worked with each other for years on these 24-hour shifts. My guess was that they had long ago been 'talked-out' and had little new to share with each other.

Occasionally, if the conversation was related to firefighting, I would jump in with a comment. More often than not, I observed quietly and tried to figure out their personalities. This had its dangers, though. If I was in the dining room, kitchen, or living area, it gave them the opportunity to denigrate me or the gay community as *faggots, fairies, cocksuckers,* or any other offensive term they could hurl in my direction. It surprised me that they continued with such adolescent bullying behaviors. I remained convinced that they would, eventually, realize that my personal life had nothing to do with being a firefighter.

The department had about 45 or 50 men, including Chief Gibby Gates. The city had three fire stations. I was assigned to Fire Station No.1 at the corner of Kennedy Drive and Flagler Avenue. Fire Station No. 2 was situated in the City Hall building at the corner of Angela and Simonton Streets in Old Town. The oldest firehouse (circa 1907) was Station No. 3 at the intersection of Grinnell and Virginia Streets. Each of the stations had assigned firefighters who served on a 'watch' under the direction of a Fire Captain. Each watch rotated, working 24 hours on-duty, followed by 48 hours off-duty. Although I wasn't sure if I would remain on Capt. Stephenson's watch for any length of time, I knew that I was settling into my position. I fell into a routine of washing the fire engine and checking the equipment each morning. There were no other scheduled activities on most days; occasionally, we would monitor the fire hydrants or conduct practice drills.

When I left the firehouse one morning at the end of my shift, I took my yellow fire helmet home with me. With some heat-resistant paint I had purchased at the hardware store, I carefully wrote my last name onto the 'beavertail' – the helmet's elongated back flap that protects the back of the firefighter's neck from hot embers.

Mallinson

Damn! It looked good. Like the effect of seeing my name badge, the helmet validated my position as a Key West firefighter. Having your name on your helmet is common practice among firefighters. It allowed others to readily recognize you, particularly in dark, smoky, and hectic fire scenes. Further, if I became injured – or worse – in a fire, they could identify me by my helmet. When I got back to the firehouse two days later, one of the men sneered at me upon seeing the helmet.

"What?" he asked in a contemptuous tone, "you think you are staying around that long?"

"That's the plan," I responded.

"You'll never pass Fire College anyway. They won't even let a fag through the front door," he said as I was walking away.

Fire College? I had heard only bits and pieces, but it was a recent requirement that a new hire had to be certified by the State Fire College before securing a permanent position in a professional department. The certification was optional for volunteer firefighters. All I knew was that some of the Key West firefighters had been 'grandfathered' in and were exempt from the training. Others had attended Fire College with mixed success; some were certified while others failed and were released from their positions. *I need to find out more about this Fire College program.* It struck me that I was making a serious commitment to stay in the KWFD, despite the attempts by these guys to force me to quit.

One morning, we had a scheduled visit by a group of second grade schoolchildren. Capt. Stephenson seemed to be struggling with which fireman to send down to greet them and provide a tour. I wanted to help, so I volunteered. With his permission, I turned to descend the stairs. Behind me, I could hear some of the guys grumbling and whispering loud enough for me to hear them.

"Kiss-ass little bitch," one of them sneered.

Once downstairs, I started up the engine on our bright red American LaFrance fire truck and slowly pulled it out onto the driveway. It was a beautiful day in the Keys and my spirits were up. I was looking forward to accepting this new challenge. Exiting the truck cab, I could already see the school bus pulling off Kennedy Drive. As I watched the kids disembark, I couldn't help but remember the excitement I felt when on elementary school trips.

It was a blast! There were about 18 kids, their teacher, and a teacher's aide. The teacher was so excited to be able to bring the children. She was engaging and attentive to the kids. I tried to assess what they already knew about firefighting and then asked them what they wanted to know. Some of them had good questions and others had funny, off-the-wall inquiries. I did my best to answer them all with a sense of humor. The real fun, though, began when bringing some of the less-dangerous equipment off the truck and letting them touch it to their heart's content. *Second-graders are easy to please.*

It seemed only right to give the kids a thrill. "Do you want to hear the sirens?" I asked. There was a roar of agreement, as expected. I jumped up and opened the fire truck door. The kids were all crowding in as if they needed to be closer to hear. I reached over and flipped the switch.

"Waaaaaahhhhhh! Waaaaaahhhhhh!" That was enough. Though I knew that the guys upstairs would have expected I might run the siren for the kids, I didn't want to overdo it. The kids had their hands covering their ears, enjoying the loud whining.

"OK, kids," I yelled "one more sound."

"Nhhhnnnnnn!" The truck's air horn boomed impressively as the truck bay was acting like an echo chamber. The children were jumping around, feigning deafness for a few moments. At this point, I thought I might be running out of ideas for my dog-and-pony show. What was I forgetting?

Of course, the kids wanted to slide down the fire pole. I explained in a kind way that it was much too dangerous unless you were in high school. They responded with awe, mixed with disappointment, as they tried to think of how many years it would be before they were old enough to slide down the pole. However, it occurred to me that this was something some of the other firefighters could do to contribute to this school visit. In hindsight, maybe that was a mistake.

I climbed up into the cab of our fire truck and turned on the radio. The kids could all see me as I called into the dispatcher. They didn't know that Jackie, our dispatcher, was located on the second floor of our firehouse, about 100 feet away from the truck. They were mesmerized as I spoke into the hand-held microphone and (amazing!) someone answered back! Ha! I was having fun. I asked if one or two of my fellow firefighters wouldn't slide down the pole so that the kids could see how it functioned. My stomach tensed as I imagined that the guys would refuse to cooperate. Surprisingly, their response was affirmative.

The teacher and aide helped me to position the kids around the base of the fire pole at a safe distance. They were impressed when I explained that there had to be a foam rubber landing mat surrounding the base of the pole to protect the feet and legs of the firemen as they slid quickly towards the concrete floor. Suddenly, I remembered how loud the floor plates at the top can be when activated to open.

"Hey kids! It's going to be loud!" I blurted out while putting my palms over my ears. The warning was just in time. "Bam!" The metal doors flew open, and a fireman came sliding down the pole, followed by the second firemen. Seeing the excited reactions from the children, I realized that we could have avoided the tour and simply had firefighters slide down the pole. Ha! *Second-graders are so easy to please.*

After a few minutes, the captain made an appearance. He made a beeline for the teacher and introduced himself. Then, the other two guys began engaging the teacher and her aide. I sensed the guys had an ulterior motive in talking to these two young women, so I moved closer. Yeah, it was clear that the guys were leering and making the female visitors just a little uncomfortable. Maybe it wasn't such a good idea to have them come down from upstairs.

"Oh, it's getting late. We should be going," the teacher said. It seemed like a good time to bring the visit to a close. I turned around and yelled for the kids to come in close.

"Did everybody have a good time?" I asked.

"Yes!" they responded.

"Then, everyone say 'thank you' to the firemen," the teacher added in a tone of finality. The roar from the children seemed to bring a smile to the captain's face. The teacher motioned the kids towards the bus and they were on their way.

"That was fun," I said.

"Good job, Kevin," Capt. Stephenson said. He seemed pleased. The other two firemen were not amused. As he walked back upstairs, I began checking that the equipment I had used for the demonstrations was sufficiently secured and back in their rightful places on the truck. Suddenly, the two guys appeared just behind me. They were much too close for comfort.

"*Good job,*" one of them sneered. "Good job, *faggot*!" He had moved so close to me that *my* back was pressed up against the truck. His face was contorted by his anger and, I surmised, his utter distain for me. "Just who the fuck do you think you are?" the other guy asked. He had shifted forward so quickly that I feared he would strike me on the spot. "You think you belong in this department? You don't. You never will."

I was speechless, too scared to utter a retort. Somehow, I managed to keep eye contact with each one for a few moments. My mind was racing with possible tactics should they decide to hit me. *Would they dare attack me out on the tarmac where the public might witness it?*

"Excuse me," I said. I pushed myself away from the truck and both guys. "I have to get this truck back into the bay." I walked around to the driver's side and climbed up into the cab. I glanced over at the sideview mirror and could see the two of them returning upstairs. I leaned back on the seat and closed my eyes. Though I was really close to crying, no tears came. Every muscle in my body was taut; I thought they were going to physically harm me. I thought that I might vomit. I took slow deep breaths, trying to relax. It took about 15 minutes to get myself together. I started up the engine and returned the fire truck to its place in the bay.

For the next hour or so, I sat on the bench outside the firehouse, watching cars go by on Flagler Avenue. It seemed like such a contradiction that we present ourselves to the community as brave firefighters, worthy of their praise. Yet, the environment in this firehouse was toxic; the men were ill-tempered and unprofessional. I was trying to fathom how adult men could devolve into behaving like hostile adolescents.

CHAPTER 5: Gay Militants

Joe and I were called 'militants' because we acted to bring about change. We were part of the 'resistance' movement. It is said that the 'gay liberation' movement began 1969 with the Stonewall Riots in New York. Throughout the 1970s, gay men and lesbians were increasingly standing up for their rights, at times with radical actions. One goal of the liberation movement was to eliminate stereotypes of male and female homosexuals that contributed to social stigma, legal discrimination, and unfettered violence against the community. However, gay liberation also aimed at emancipating the individual from their internalized homophobia, allowing each person to enjoy a fulfilling life in which they could freely choose their partners and their professions. Joe and I resisted the status quo, acting as change agents in the gay liberation movement.

In the late 1970s, and into the beginning of the next decade, there was a rash of gay-bashing incidents in Key West. A self-righteous minister had been spewing anti-gay rhetoric, suggesting that the 'gay problem' "could be solved by 100 good men with baseball bats." There were outrageous claims that gays would take over the city and force Conchs off the island. This crusade against 'immorality' followed in the wake of the 1977 anti-gay campaign by Anita Bryant in Dade County. So, it wasn't surprising that adolescents and young men began attacking gay men on the streets of Key West. Joe and I were the victims of an assault by 6 or so high school boys who wanted to beat up faggots. Our complaints to the police were not taken seriously. The response smacked of victim-blaming: "Well, what did you expect?" In the case of gay-bashing, the police often looked the other way, failing to hold assailants accountable, and rarely documenting the incidents.

One evening in Key West, Tennessee Williams was assaulted. The publicity surrounding an attack on one of the island's most famous artists was extensive. It was not just any gay person complaining of being harassed or beaten, it was a well-known celebrity. This type of violence was putting gay tourism at risk and the Key West Business Guild began calling for a halt to the attacks. They hosted a visit by Rep. Elaine Noble (D-MA), the first openly gay [lesbian] person elected to a statewide office in the United States. She spoke of the critical need to address the underlying hateful attitudes that spur gay-bashing. Joe and I believed that hosting open and honest discussions would change attitudes.

We wanted to do more than simply call for calm. In 1979, we formed a speaker's panel by loosely affiliating with a few others as the Oscar Wilde Liberation Society (OWLS). We were officially listed in the Key West Business Guild's *Discover Key West* brochure, along with 52 businesses. Joining Joe and me were Phoebe Bangle, Greg Strickland, and Carmen Baños. We were invited by sociology and psychology professors at the Florida Keys Community College to host panel discussions with their students. We addressed the many questions students had about sexuality, coming out, and homosexual relationships. Ultimately, we aimed to humanize the homosexual and reduce homophobia through shared understanding. We also conducted sessions for police cadets at the Florida Keys Institute of Criminal Justice. The director, Clinton Leslie, felt that police officers needed to be better informed and face the prejudices they held towards gay and lesbian citizens. He believed that police officers with positive attitudes could affect the health and safety of the community. He appreciated our candor, relaxed and informal presentation style, and ability to laugh at the most ridiculous questions. We answered all kinds of questions as best we could:

"What do you guys do in bed anyway?"

"What does your family think of you being gay?"

"How can police officers be more supportive to gays and lesbians?"

One evening, we were talking about gay-bashing and the urgency to take the situation seriously. A female cadet agreed with us; she stated that her boyfriend had recently been beaten in an anti-gay attack and they were both traumatized by the incident. I was surprised at her candor and asked, "Your boyfriend is gay?" She laughed and said, "Oh no. He is very good-looking, and they thought he was gay!"

According to some KW Business Guild members, Joe and I were 'militants' that would hurt gay businesses by speaking to these audiences. The misguided members thought we would disturb the 'peace' that existed between the Conchs and gay business owners; they fooled themselves into thinking that the simmering, unpredictable mutual discomfort was a state of peace. The Conchs, of course, wanted gays to be invisible and quiet.

Admittedly, Joe and I did think quite differently than others in the gay community. Both of us had participated in 'consciousness-raising' (CR) groups when we lived in upstate New York. The groups were based on the feminist tenet that "all politics are personal" and each of us is responsible for initiating the change we wish to see in the world. We were also influenced by the work of Paulo Friere, a Brazilian educator who asserted that people needed to examine the institutionalized oppression affecting their lives if they ever wished to dismantle it. We recognized the similarity in the civil rights, women's rights, and gay rights movements as a struggle for human dignity and respect.

Joe and I resisted the status quo. We believed that institutions must fundamentally change if we wish to eradicate prejudice, social injustice, and discrimination. However, our 'activism' was not meant to offend; we felt that one-on-one encounters could only initiate change through mutual respect and understanding. We hoped that hosting the discussions would, eventually, raise awareness in the general population and, ultimately, lead to societal change. I was keenly aware that I would also be changed by listening to people who thought differently than me.

The firemen had much 'down time' between calls, so I was able to reflect on the experience of being harassed. The opportunities for introspection helped me maintain my sanity. I had the luxury of taking time to deconstruct the stressful encounters and glean some wisdom about how to respond in the future. I contemplated how to mitigate the potential for violence. I decided I wouldn't mock the firefighters or suggest that their concerns were not of value; still, I couldn't dismiss their despicable behaviors. Sometimes, I tried to address their erroneous assumptions with rational explanations. However, mocking or disrespecting the firemen would only have promoted a vicious cycle of conflict that would fail to establish mutual understanding.

I found inspiration in other openly gay and lesbian folks. One night, Joe and I attended a 'concert' at the Monster Restaurant & Bar on the corner of Front and Duval Streets in Old Town. As an interesting aside, the bouncer at the door of this gay venue was a Conch, an uncle to one of our firefighters. This was the hottest disco/dance bar at the time. On this weekend, however, the visiting musician was Steven Grossman, a gay folk singer from California. He was on tour, promoting his album *Caravan Tonight*. He would sing a song or two and then hold discussions with the audience on the nature of gay male relationships. His lyrics were heart-warming, insightful, and humorous. He also sang about the struggles of being a gay man. I was awestruck by the simplicity of his message and the gentle manner in which he relayed his 'militant' thoughts. He encouraged gay men to be proud and live an authentic life unencumbered by society's stereotypes. *Now, this is the kind of music we need.* Rather than the superficial, tongue-in-cheek, satirical style we saw with the *Village People*, this folk singer was reminding me of our fundamental need for love, tenderness, and self-respect.

CHAPTER 6: Rear-End Man

The more I came to appreciate the unique aspects of life in the firehouse, the better I understood why my presence was such a disruption for some of the firemen. First, the fire service is based on a paramilitary structure, replete with ranks (Chief, Captains, Lieutenants, etc.) and a chain of command that adheres to relatively strict guidelines for behavior. This is intended to keep firefighters from arbitrarily deciding what they want to do at a fire scene; they must rely on orders from the officers who appreciated tactics, available resources, and personnel constraints. Above all, the command structure is designed to assure the safety of everyone at the fire scene. Each time I donned my KWFD uniform, I realized that I may have to follow orders without knowing their purpose. In other words, there is a surrendering of some individuality when joining a fire team. This was unlike any other job I had ever held. Nonetheless, I was the rookie with a lot to learn.

Each morning, the commanding officer at each of the three firehouses reported on their manpower status. If a fireman called in sick, for example, personnel would be readjusted by transferring an extra man from one station to another. Of course, temporary reassignments were also due to vacations and other foreseeable circumstances. So, a firehouse may need to 'borrow' a captain, lieutenant, or firefighter for a day or more. As a rookie firefighter, I was more likely to be temporarily transferred to fill in for a frontline firefighter at another station. One morning, I overheard Capt. Stephenson talking to his counterpart at another station.

"No," he said, "he called in sick. The only rear-end man I have is Kevin and he is only a rookie."

"Rear-end man?" *What!? Did I hear that correctly? He called me a 'rear-end man'?* Once he got off the phone, I got up the nerve to ask the captain what he meant by that comment. He laughed out loud. Then, he explained that the firefighters who ride on the back of the truck are referred to as 'rear-end' men. The captain supervises the fire response, and the driver/engineer manages the delivery of water by adjusting the pump controls on the fire truck. It is the rear-end men who pull the hose and advance to fight the fire. The irony of the label being applied to the gay guy was quite funny. I laughed out loud; I didn't want him to think I was offended by the term.

A few minutes later, Capt. Stephenson approached me to request that I work an extra shift on Christmas Day so that one of the firemen on the next watch could have the day off. I asked him if he meant 'swap' a shift or if he was asking me to work a run of 48 hours. He was requesting the latter; the fireman also wanted to have off on Christmas Eve because, as the captain stated, "Kevin doesn't have family." I assured him that I did, very well, have family and that we also enjoyed the holidays. I agreed to swap days so that the other guy worked my Christmas Eve shift, and I took his regular duty so that he could enjoy Christmas Day off.

It was generally quite stressful for me to work on a different shift. The firemen who regularly relieved us at the end of our shift only saw me for a matter of minutes. They didn't engage me in conversation. *What would others think of a fireman that wanted to get to know the gay guy?* Consequently, the men on the adjacent shifts knew little about me. In fact, I imagined that my coworkers confabulated stories about me that distorted the true picture of my time in the firehouse. So, I found myself on edge and vigilant whenever joining an unfamiliar group of firemen for a 24-hour shift.

In line with most professional departments across the country in 1981, the KWFD was entirely male. Society's stereotype of a fireman brings up images of a muscular, blue-collar male who exudes 'masculinity' and virility. This caricature is bloated by the 'hero' label that individual firefighters are happy to accept, even when they do little to earn the title.

One needs only to see the popularity of calendars with half-naked firefighters in various degrees of undress to see how sexual fantasies of firemen are promoted. This has contributed, some writers say, to a homoerotic undercurrent in the firehouse environment. This is not to be confused with overt homosexuality, however. In our firehouses, I found incessant bragging about sexual escapades (or fantasies), the sharing of pornographic magazines, and a relentless attempt to cast doubt upon each other's manhood. There was 'innocent' physicality between the men that included pretend boxing, wrestling, and even 'ass-grabbing.' Along with the other horseplay, practical jokes, and pranks, the physicality has a role in building camaraderie among the men. It may also have been their only way to release pent-up frustration and bitter feelings they harbored. In an all-male living environment in which firefighters eat and sleep, there are likely to be 'bromances,' alliances, and 'family' squabbles. Surely, there was friction between differing factions in the KWFD; some firemen were engaged in unethical or illegal behavior and others were honest and sincerely committed to being the best firefighters possible.

Like many firefighters, these men also took great pride in their heritage. Several came from a long line of firefighters who had protected their city from burning to the ground. Not only did they have a family tradition of firefighting, but some were currently serving in the KWFD alongside their brothers, uncles, and fathers. This added to the familial feel in the firehouse. Conchs were particularly fond of nicknames for each other, and the firemen were no exception. I heard stories told about retired firemen like *Bolo* and *Squeaky*; I worked with *Viti, Pic, Buddha,* and *The Kid,* among others. These monikers served as indicators of familiarity, acceptance, brotherhood, and respect.

I had a good laugh thinking of the nickname that my coworkers might have created for me, but I was sure that I would never be honored in such a way. I was expecting to endure practical jokes during my first weeks. Rookie firefighters often find their bunks short-sheeted or sprinkled with itching powder. Such playful, though adolescent, shenanigans are not uncommon in all-male environments. Alas, I was not the target of such pranks. It made sense that these men didn't want me to feel that I was being initiated into their 'club.' They had no intention of making me feel welcome. They seemed bent on reminding me that my presence in the KWFD wasn't acceptable to them.

There had been a lot of turmoil in the KWFD the year before I joined. The equipment was aging and dangerously ineffective. The department was in desperate need of at least two new fire engines. The older fire trucks would be out of commission for weeks on end due to mechanical problems. The air tanks were old and outdated. Both Fire Stations 2 and 3 were dilapidated and in serious need of renovation or replacement. There were as many as 14 firefighter positions that had remained unfilled due to budgetary constraints. Due to insufficient manpower, City officials had proposed closing Station 2, a suggestion that raised vigorous opposition, particularly from the Black community that would have suffered the most from the lack of timely fire service. Several fire hydrants in the city were found to be non-functional (dry) and the city's aging system of water lines could not consistently provide the volume or pressure needed for effective firefighting. These were serious risks to our ability to combat structure fires, let alone a conflagration.

The poor state of the fire hydrant network wasn't the only challenge facing Key West firemen. The Old Town neighborhoods are charming, but the gingerbread-decorated homes are old wooden structures that catch fire relatively easily. The historic structures were built in close proximity and a fire could spread rapidly from one structure to another. The city also contains many narrow alleys and lanes that cannot accommodate a fire truck. There was a sense that the KWFD were woefully unprepared for a worst-case scenario: *What would happen if a conflagration started in Old Town? Would we be able to contain such a fire?*

The KWFD was under-resourced in both equipment and personnel. These challenges weighed heavily on the minds of the men whose primary interest was professional firefighting. However, it was also fodder for the firemen who were less dedicated; they attempted to leverage the unsafe conditions to justify their lack of motivation to do their job. Their firehouse banter inevitably led to political arguments and repeated denigration of the Mayor, the City Manager, and the City Council members. The firemen on my shift frequently vilified our openly gay City Commissioner, Richard Heyman, as if he was a political opponent. Richard was one of the first openly gay elected officials in the United States and that was enough for the men to invalidate his opinions. They ignored how Richard was practically a lone voice calling for new fire engines, updated equipment, and higher salaries for the department.

Not surprisingly, the overall morale among the men was low and there were newspaper reports of interpersonal conflicts between city officials and representatives of the firefighter's union. The department had suffered a considerable amount of bad press, as well. Several firefighters were on suspension due to drug-related charges. Others who had acted inappropriately and disrespected their superior officers were suspended for insubordination. Salaries in the department were well below standards set by the city. The KWFD had numerous problems.

CHAPTER 7: Fire Station 1

Fire Station 1 was only a couple of years old, though its unfinished state made it look older. Structural engineers were unconvinced that the concrete walls could support a set of large truck bay doors. Therefore, the truck bay was open, exposing the fire engines to the elements, vandalism, or theft. There had been no attempt to decorate the interior living spaces with the usual photos of memorable fires or firefighters in action. So, the building (inside and outside) had an industrial, impersonal feel with its concrete walls and smooth, terrazzo floors. The paint was already peeling off the walls. The two oversized couches in the TV room were worn and looked as if they had never been cleaned. The design was 1970s frat house.

There was a very small room off the living area with a single chair for the radio dispatcher. The dispatcher for our watch, Jackie, was older and obese. He no longer responded to fire calls with the others; he remained at his post to assure that communications between the fire companies and various agencies were maintained. He answered incoming phone calls and dispatched resources as needed. He also transferred personal calls to the phone on the wall in the TV room; this non-emergency line was reserved for the firemen's own use.

The interior stairs leading to the bathroom and sleeping area were also made of concrete. The handrail was cast aluminum to match the industrial motif. One passed through a glass door at the top of the stairs. Off to the right was a large open hall that held eight sleeping bunks. The beds weren't particularly comfortable, but they were practical. Each man had his preferred bunk. I learned quickly that snoring – and other noises that go 'bump in the night' – were easy to hear because of the concrete surroundings. We kept personal items next to our bunks. Each night, we would lower our turnout pants to the ankles and step out of our boots carefully. If a call came in the middle of the night, we could simply step into the boots and lift our pants up with one smooth motion. I quickly learned the value of having suspenders to keep my pants up when dressing quickly.

Turning left, away from the bunks, you would immediately find the fireman's pole. It had a loud, spring-activated mechanism that dropped the floor out and allowed us to grip the pole and slide down to the truck bay on the ground level. Admittedly, I enjoyed sliding down the fire pole. Your hands provided some braking, but most of the control and speed came from wrapping your legs around the pole. I have never had an irrational fear of heights. I did learn, though, that jumping out of the shower and grabbing the pole with wet hands could lead to a much faster descent and, potentially, injury!

The rookie was responsible for washing the fire truck each day to remove dust and inspect for damage. We counted the tools, made sure that supplies were stocked, and the equipment ready for use. I learned that sometime in the previous year when the firefighters were at odds with the municipal administrators over limited resources, one of the gas generators disappeared from our fire truck during the night. This is a crucial piece of equipment when the electrical power is shut off at a fire scene, leaving us in the dark. It was rumored that the theft of the generator was an 'inside' job. I had my suspicions as to the likely suspects.

Over the first couple of weeks, I was learning the rhythm of my shift. The men incessantly told stories – sometimes in half Spanish/half English – that were usually intended to make themselves look like expert fishermen, good mechanics, or great lovers. Their conversations didn't include me, of course. They didn't want to give the impression that I should feel welcome. I could clearly sense the tension each time I came within a few feet of any of the men; the kitchen was particularly close quarters. It was their discomfort, not mine, I decided. Slowly, I became comfortable with not moving for another fireman if I was already making coffee or preparing food. They would simply have to wait their turn.

There were many days when the firemen would gather around the open truck bay entrance and shoot the breeze. Frequently, their friends would drive up on their lunch breaks. The conversation frequently focused on municipal politics and, in particular, our openly gay council member. If they noticed I was within earshot, I usually got one of two responses. At times, some guy in the group would loudly complain about Richard, noting his sexual orientation as the fundamental reason he was unqualified for the job. At other times, the group would revert to speaking Spanish, thinking I couldn't follow their conversation. I understood more than I was willing to let them know.

One morning, there was quite a bit of yelling on the tarmac. As I got closer, I could hear the men complaining about the Chief's decision to keep an older fire truck and try to find parts for its repair. The firefighter's union had been demanding that the City purchase a new fire engine. Uncharacteristically, I joined in on this heated discussion about the use of limited departmental resources. I added my opinion to the conversation. We complained that officials made decisions that might jeopardize our safety without asking our opinions.

The next day, Chief Gates walked up from his office into our living quarters. This was unusual. I learned that the chief had recently returned to duty after nearly a year and a half due to a terrible accident that took the life of his son and left him with mobility challenges. So, it was an effort for him to climb those stairs. I was sitting at the dining table, reading the newspaper. He walked over to me.

"Come down to my office for a minute?" he asked. His voice was calm and quiet.

"Sure," I replied. *Who am I to refuse a request from the Chief?* I closed the paper and followed him back to his office. The chief closed the door and motioned for me to sit down. He sat down behind his desk and took a breath. I couldn't imagine what he had to say. Then it came....

"Kevin," he asked, "did you call me an asshole?"

I was stunned and a little more than baffled at the question.

"What? I'm sorry, Chief. What do you mean?"

"Two of the guys came in here this morning telling me that you called me an asshole yesterday," he said.

I thought for a minute. Then, I realized that one of my comments had been twisted to place me in a difficult position with the chief.

"Chief, we were discussing the negotiations for a new fire truck versus fixing the old one. I think I was wondering out loud 'what kind of asshole would make decisions that might make us unsafe at a fire scene," I explained. "So, in a roundabout way, I guess I did."

"So, you admit it?" he asked. He seemed genuinely surprised at my candor.

"Chief," I said, "I have no reason to lie to you. I make mistakes."

I was thinking how incredibly petty these guys were to report such an innocuous, sideways comment to the chief. It was not as if I intended to personally disparage the chief's character or disrespect his position.

"I'm sorry," I continued, "it wasn't personal." He leaned forward and spoke to me as if a mentor.

"Look, Kevin, these guys will look for anything to cause you trouble. Be careful what you say. In the future, I would appreciate it if you didn't call me an asshole."

He cracked a smile! I was grateful for the lighthearted way in which he handled this awkward incident. For just a minute, I imagined he might have been supportive of my presence in the department. I stood up with a great sense of relief.

"Thanks Chief. You can be sure I won't make that mistake again. My apology."

He motioned for me to leave. I walked back upstairs and got a cup of coffee and sat back down to finish reading the paper. I started thinking that I had to be much more careful in front of these sniveling cowards. My face still felt hot and flushed following my dressing down by the chief. On the other hand, I was encouraged by his treating me like a professional...like someone who was deserving of respect. *Wow!*

Over those first few months, it seemed that forming any camaraderie with these men might be impossible. It was bad enough that I was openly gay. My status wasn't helped by being an 'outsider' who was not born in the Keys. Even worse, I was a vegetarian. *Should I even mention that I am an atheist?* There wasn't much I could do to win their acceptance.

Frequently, the men would organize for one or two guys to walk across the street and get sandwiches from the corner Cuban coffee shop in Habana Plaza. In another effort to ostracize me, they would not ask me if I wanted anything from the shop. So, if I hadn't brought my own food for the day, I would get permission from the captain to walk over to the Cuban shop. Luckily, they sold sandwiches that didn't contain meat. If Joe were in town in the evening, he would occasionally drop by with a dinner from a restaurant.

The firemen on my shift purposely excluded me from conversations and firehouse socializing. Worse, though, was the incessant taunting. Though several of the men directed *faggot* comments to me, it was Oneri or Oscar who attempted to get me riled up. While the other men stopped and intently listened to see how these confrontations would go, they didn't seem to want to 'gang-up' on me by joining in on the harassment. Yet, they stood back and witnessed. They were complicit in their silence.

Some of the firemen would quickly scan the immediate area to be sure that no one would hear before verbally harassing me. Two brothers – Billy and Dickie – would only deliver derogatory, anti-gay comments when others were present. It seemed that they were only comfortable being bullies when someone could witness it. Neither of the brothers confronted me when we were alone. One day, Dickie was smoking out in front of the station. He and Louis were chatting about which firefighters might consider taking the examination for promotion to Engineer. Often referred to as the 'driver' or Lieutenant position, it was the engineer who was responsible for controlling the water pumps on the engine, supplying adequate water pressure to the hoses being wielded by the rear-end men.

"How long is it before a firefighter is eligible to sit for the exam?" I asked.

"Don't think you will be here that long, you little fairy!" Dickie snapped back. He smiled at Louis as if seeking affirmation for shutting me down. Then, he quickly took a long, final drag from his cigarette and threw it to the ground before walking away.

As they often talked about Key West being invaded by gays, it was not uncommon to hear comments like "Take them all out and shoot them." I was sure that the men were trying to offend me to the point of anger, but that rarely happened. My philosophy was to remind myself that they were frightened of what they didn't understand; they felt their way of life was being threatened. I knew that responding in a hostile or nasty manner would only lead to a worse outcome.

As a consequence of the social ostracizing, the firemen on my shift knew very little about me. There were some who feared that I might report them when I witnessed their illicit behavior. Sometimes, I would find a couple of the fireman behind the station drinking beer or smoking pot. At first, I was shocked. These men were on duty!? As we were working long shifts, it wasn't uncommon to have friends or family come by for short visits. However, a couple of guys on my shift were visited regularly by various suspicious, disreputable acquaintances. The firemen would often walk out to their vehicle and converse in whispers. If I were to wander anywhere near them, their visitors would quickly depart. It wasn't hard to imagine that drug exchanges were occurring.

I was beginning to grasp why the KWFD had a poor reputation; a few bad apples were misbehaving. I was sure that these men were afraid that I would report them to the captain, but I never did. It seemed obvious to me that the captain knew darned well what was happening with his men. I guessed that he had no desire to interfere.

After joining the KWFD, my personal life felt so much better than my time in the firehouse. Joe and I were busy erecting the exterior walls of our house on Bay Point. Most of the materials had come from Woodson's lumber yard on Stock Island. Owned by the Woodson family, it was a welcoming business that had a long history. Tom, one of the employees, was particularly engaging. He was as tall as Joe and sported an attractive beard. He had a wide smile and beautiful eyes. He had surmised that Joe and I were a couple at our first meeting. He seemed intrigued that we were building our own house.

"You're building a house on Bay Point?" he asked, "with your own hands?"

"No," I laughed, with a hint of sarcasm, "we're using our feet!"

On trips to Woodson's, Tom would often interact with us. He often would make jokes about gay guys. Don't get me wrong; Tom was funny and not trying to harass us. It was my guess that he had never met regular, 'down home' gay guys. He often dealt with wealthy gay guys who paid contractors to complete their renovations on Key West houses. Joe and I didn't have the funds to rehab a Conch house in Key West. We also wanted a more natural environment that came with a waterfront lot in the Lower Keys. City living often included the sounds of traffic, late night revelers, and early morning rooster crowing. Joe and I liked to lie in bed and listen to the soft whistling of the wind blowing through the Australian pine trees on our property.

"Lie in bed?" Tom queried. "I thought the house was under construction?"

"Oh, yeah, it is," I explained. "We renovated an antique Airstream trailer that we moved onto the lot. We live in it while we build."

"And it has enough room for the two of you to lie in bed?" he asked. I was guessing that Tom was titillated by thought of two men in bed together.

"Ha!" I laughed. "One of us has to sleep on top of the other in the small bed. We take turns!" We all burst into guffaws over the sexual inuendo that implied a variety of possibilities. Tom was surprised that Joe was a construction manager for the local cable television company, and I was a city firefighter. With that new knowledge, he ramped up his humor and innocent teasing. It was a pleasure for me to see a straight guy who was unafraid to be friendly with a gay couple. Tom wasn't stereotyping us as much as trying to get his head around how we could be a couple that seemed *so normal*. We were treated like any other customers. Tom gave me faith that not all straight men were intent on assaulting and demeaning gay men.

CHAPTER 8: Nonviolent Resistance

My unwavering commitment to being open and honest with others about my sexual orientation had a cost, of course. Overt homophobia was rampant in our country and, unfortunately, acceptable to the masses. Many straight Americans were disinterested bystanders while gay men and lesbians were publicly ridiculed, harassed, or assaulted. Rarely would others feel self-confident enough to stand up and decry the way we were disenfranchised, teased, beaten, and sometimes, murdered. For good reason, most gay men and lesbians distrusted the police. In 1981, very few cities in the United States provided homosexuals any legal protection against discrimination in employment, housing, and public accommodations.

I stood firm in my convictions. I never believed that one should 'fight fire with fire.' When the firemen taunted me, I didn't throw it back in their faces. I resisted the urge to respond with anger or counter threats. I resisted the temptation to ridicule their Conch culture or their relative lack of formal education. I felt that disrespecting others would only make me less respectable. I adopted an approach that sought mutual understanding and cooperation.

As a teenager in the early 1970s, I was influenced by the non-violence principles of Dr. Martin Luther King, Jr. and his followers. I understood that violence only begets violence. As the saying goes, if we adopted the 'eye for an eye' approach, we would eventually all be blind. The Black civil rights movement had inspired me. I was willing to acknowledge that my own preconceptions were based on racist stereotypes, and I worked to change my thinking. Similarly, when my thoughts were shaded by misogyny or internalized homophobia, I considered alternative explanations. I perceived that racist bigotry was similar to the debasement of women, the vilification of gay men and lesbians, or the rejection of persons with disabilities. Each of these groups had a common desire for inclusion, fairness, and acceptance. *How could I promote social justice?* If I wasn't going to make the change I longed for, who would? I had internalized the words of MLK, Jr. that *"injustice anywhere is a threat to justice everywhere."*

I did choose to respect the firemen, but I was also committed to non-violent resistance. I agreed, fundamentally, with Thoreau's support of civil disobedience. As luck would have it, fate brought me together with two older lesbians living on Upper Sugarloaf Key. Joe and I became friends with Barbara Deming and Jane Verlaine. Their property was extensive, including their cottage and several small houses. Barbara and Jane had established a 'women's community' that provided a safe place for lesbians (and other women bound by feminist philosophies) to meet and learn from each other. We knew Barbara and Jane as older women with voracious reading habits and kind hearts. Little did I know the extraordinary impact that Barbara would have on my life.

Barbara and I would walk through her garden, pulling weeds while discussing feminist and critical philosophies. Much to my surprise, she was nationally known as an advocate for non-violent social change. She had an extensive career in journalism and had published several books. Barbara had been jailed numerous times for demonstrating in support of voting rights for Black Americans. She helped me understand the insidious nature of institutionalized racism. She spared no details when describing the barbaric actions of White men who beat Black youth during school integration, raped Black women, and lynched Black men. The actions, she suggested, were to assure that Blacks who were 'uppity' were 'put in their place' and that a message was sent to others who might consider 'stepping out of line.' I described what I had heard about the unfair treatment of Black men in the KWFD and how my situation was similar. Barbara understood that my position in the firehouse might be threatening to some of the men and warned that it could put my life in danger.

With her stories of oppression, Barbara tied together the history of slavery, the subjugation of women, and vilification of gays and lesbians; all three were connected to the same need of White, Christian, straight men to maintain their power in society. It was during my conversations with Barbara that I began to see some of the firemen as scared little boys. *Did my presence cause them to look at their own lives, forcing them to reevaluate what it meant to be brave? Or masculine?* Were these men harassing me because they were unfulfilled in their lives? Were they lacking self-confidence? Why were they bullies?

I began to share Barbara's worldview that all humans are the same; we are imperfect individuals with specific strengths and weaknesses. Even the best of us is fallible, at times. I began to see that our lives are intertwined and that our relationships are forever in flux, always in a state of change. Strangely, this appreciation for our humanity allowed me to have some empathy for those who opposed my presence in the firehouse. I came to appreciate how much I might have been turning their world upside down. Barbara inspired me. I knew that I had to navigate my journey as a firefighter who just happened to be gay. Barbara encouraged my commitment to nonviolent resistance. Nonviolence does not mean being meek; it means you have the strength to hold your ground and not do what the opponent wants you to do (fight back).

One of the most helpful philosophical discussions I had with Barbara surrounded society's erroneous entwining of masculinity and bravery. There is no evidence for characterizing most actions as either masculine or feminine. Similarly, bravery is greatly misunderstood. Bravery is not being fearless; it is standing your ground and acting, in the presence of fear! It is the measure of a person and not the measure of a man! Surely, Barbara's stories revealed the incredible strength and bravery of a woman deeply committed to social change. A couple of years later, Barbara was diagnosed with ovarian cancer. Over the following months, women visited their Sugarloaf Key compound from all over the country. Barbara had impacted the lives of thousands of Americans. In August 1984, I received a phone call from Jane telling me that Barbara was dying. At her bedside, I was able to assure Barbara that my interactions with the firefighters continued to be guided by her sage advice about respect, forgiveness, and cooperation.

Back at the firehouse, I continued to receive nasty comments from my fellow firefighters. At first, it seemed ironic to me that I got no support from Oscar. He had the distinction of being the first Black firefighter in the KWFD (and, notably, only the second Black professional firefighter ever in South Florida). If there was anyone who might have an inkling of what it was like for me to be forging a new path, it should have been Oscar. Unfortunately, he had nothing but disdain for me.

Oscar probably hadn't had an easy time integrating into the firehouse. Before I joined the department, I read an article in the Miami Herald about the serious demoralization among the firemen. The KWFD was seriously understaffed due to sickness, suspensions, retirements, and economic constraints. Some of the equipment was woefully out-of-date. The department had also been scandalized by drug charges. One of the articles focused on Oscar being suspended for four days for 'unprofessional' behavior at the scene of a house fire. He was criticizing City officials for the poor state of the fire equipment and the lack of manpower, shouting to any neighbor who would listen. While not alone in this unprofessional behavior at the scene, he was described as 'preaching' to the bystanders when he was supposed to be focused on the fire scene.

I found Oscar to be distant and angry. The only time he would engage with me was to make homophobic remarks. I didn't know much about his own experiences, but he seemed to enjoy taunting others. Was he always irritable and ill-tempered? Was he always foul-mouthed and brutish? Or did he morph into this despicable personality to ward off racist attacks and try to become one of the guys? I couldn't tell if it was his nature or a defense mechanism he developed after being the target of insults, barbs, and jokes. I tried to imagine what Oscar's life in the KWFD had been like over those years. One of the firemen told me that Oscar was hired "...to meet a quota." It was clear to me that he still wasn't welcome in the ranks. He had his position in the KWFD, but not the respect and acceptance of a true 'brother' in the fire service.

CHAPTER 9: Butt Man

Some of the most stressful times those first weeks were during shift change. Many of the guys in the incoming or outgoing shifts knew little about me (and I knew little about them). Sometimes, they would stare – from a distance, of course – to see what I might be like; they only knew what stories they heard from the men on my shift. I would try to engage them in conversation at times, but it became painfully obvious that they would be held 'suspect' if appearing to be friendly with me. The hypermasculine environment in the firehouse doesn't make it easy for a fireman to associate with the gay guy.

Just as bad as shift changes, I found it quite difficult to be working with someone new who transferred from another firehouse for the day. One day, only Capt. Stephenson, Oscar, and I showed up for work. Oscar would be driving the fire truck. We needed a second rear-end firefighter to safely staff the truck for the shift. This is how I met Al Rahming.

Al was a Black man not of Cuban descent. He descended from one of the many Black families that immigrated to Key West from the Bahamas in the 1800s. He was only a couple of years older than me and had more than a decade of firefighting experience. There were only three Black men in the department at the time. I watched with interest as Al sat at the table interacting with Oscar. Their banter was full of jeers and disparaging remarks. Though the teasing appeared superficial – even jovial – at first, I began to sense the dubious nature of the 'camaraderie.' I concluded that there was 'no love lost' between them.

I finished my coffee and went down to sit on the outside bench. Al joined me on the bench about 10 minutes later.

"Don't you pay no attention to their shit," he said. I was surprised that Al would even sit and talk to me!

"So, you don't seem to get along with them very well?" I asked.

"Oh," he offered with a laugh, "they are nothing but lazy-ass know-nothings. They are a miserable lot."

"I don't think they ever have anything good to say about anyone," I added.

"Don't you listen to their shit!" he snapped. "You belong here as much as any of them. More than some of them." I was speechless. That was the first time that any of the firemen had given me that kind of respect. I found the way Al spoke to be entertaining. He had a deep baritone voice and the cadence of a preacher delivering a sermon.

"You know, when I first walked into this firehouse years ago, you could hear them whispering *'Oh, there's a Black man in the firehouse! There's a Black man in the firehouse!'* Oh yeah," he said. The rhythm of his story captured my attention; the seriousness of the storyline revealed his underlying anger and sense of rejection. "No, they didn't want me here. Not these goddamned Cubans! They didn't want no Black man. But you know what Kevin? After all these years in this department, when I walked in today," he continued with particular emphasis, "I can *still* hear them moaning *'Oh, there's a Black man in the firehouse!'* Ha!"

Al paused for a moment, and got a wide, wry smile on his face. He pursed his lips.

"You know what Kevin?" he said. "They gonna know there's a *faggot* in this firehouse for a very, very long time! Ha!"

I laughed along with him. At that instant, I knew Al was going to be a friend! As we talked, I was reminded that the island of Key West was really small. Al already knew a bit about me. He knew some of my friends. On his days off from the firehouse, he managed his own independent cab service: *Big Al's Taxi*. Driving around the island for business, Al noticed whose car was parked in whose driveway. He knew the comings-and-goings of his coworkers. He was privy to a lot of gossip. He met a wide diversity of locals, newcomers, and tourists. This second job also allowed him to meet plenty of gay and lesbian people. Al had an insatiable curiosity and engaging personality that allowed him to interact easily with many kinds of people. He also had a penchant for being provocative.

"You know, Kevin," he said, "you are not the first gay guy in this department?" I know I had a surprised look on my face. Clearly, I wanted to hear more. "No," he explained, "you are the first to be open and honest about it! You don't have a woman on your arm, hiding who you are. But, no, you aren't the only one." He didn't name names and I didn't ask.

I decided that Al would have been a good person to answer the one burning question that remained: *How did they know I was gay before I even set foot on firehouse property?* He laughed at that question. Then, he explained the convoluted process. When the short list of guys deemed eligible for an interview with Chief Gates was available, none of the firemen recognized my name. I wasn't a Conch. One of the firemen living on Bay Point claimed not to know me (though his home was across the canal from the house Joe and I were building). So, someone called the chief's ex-wife, Elsie, who lived on Bay Point; she, reportedly, revealed that I was a 'faggot' building a house down the road from her property. So, the entire department knew I was gay before I even came for the interview. I surmised that my being gay was the reason that the fireman did not immediately take his thumb off my air hose during the candidate testing. Al agreed that he was likely showing his displeasure with my being considered for hire. He ended his story with a laugh, saying "They got themselves so twisted up Kevin. They didn't expect YOU!" I took that comment as his expression of respect for my tenacity.

This was turning out to be the best time I'd had at work since joining the KWFD. Before we could talk much more, Oscar came down to tell us that the captain wanted to go out for a drive and to practice fire skills. We gathered our gear and jumped onto the back of the truck. As the captain came by, he looked at Al and told him that we would be teaching the rookie (me) some skills. Al broke into a wicked smile; I surmised that he knew how much the regular firemen on my shift hated practice exercises. After a short drive, we pulled into an open area on the edge of a sports field. In a few minutes, we were joined by a truck from Fire Station 3, with Captain Charlow in command. So, there were two rookies here now, me and Johnny. Clearly, Johnny was strong, but I doubted his flexibility and endurance after seeing his performance on the day we were interviewed. However, we practiced our skills separately, each with an experienced mentor to show us 'the ropes.'

Oscar stayed with our truck and didn't seem much interested in our practice. The engineer driving the other fire truck was Alan Vidal, the nephew of another captain at Firehouse 1. He and Al Rahming seemed to get along well; they laughed a lot and suggested various exercises for Johnny and me to learn effective firefighting skills. Both Al and Alan were truly engaged instructors and willing to share their experience.

"Don't breathe in fumes from a dumpster fire," Al offered. "They are full of harmful chemicals from all the plastics and shit." Really?! *Who knew that a dumpster could catch on fire?* Alan added that there were car fires that presented similar dangers from the artificial materials used in the dashboard and seat fabrics.

"Use this type of fan spray to provide a shield of water. It will protect your face from being burned by the intense heat," Alan said. *Who knew that there were so many ways to spray water?* Like Al, Alan seemed truly interested in helping us to learn. They were dedicated to firefighting. Their interactions with the captains were noticeably more respectful than what I usually witnessed on my shift. This practice session gave me great hope. I had grown accustomed to having the men on my shift undermine my position in the department. But, here with Al and Alan, I had no sense that either of them was treating me any differently than the other rookie, Johnny.

The two captains stood talking to each other through most of our practice. Occasionally, one or the other would shout suggestions. Finally, Capt. Charlow told us to break out the ladders. Al and I headed to our fire engine. I began to unhook the ladder stays. Al glanced around, assessing where we would be taking the ladders. I could never have guessed what he would say next.

"Hey Kevin. You're doing good. You be my butt man. OK?"

"Butt man?" What? I must have heard that one wrong? I am sure I had the strangest look on my face!

"What?" I asked, "now, you want me to be your butt man?" My tone was more of affable curiosity than indignation. Al stopped and thought for a nanosecond before bursting into laughter.

"Oh, man," he said. He was truly entertained. "No, no, no! You got that all wrong!? Ha! Butt man!"

Luckily, no one else was close enough to hear our exchange. Then, Al explained that the end of the ladder that stays on the ground – the end that has feet for stabilization – is called the 'butt.' Hence, the butt man is the one who stands on the feet of the ladder while the other man raises the tip of the ladder into the air. After the exercises, we were riding the back of the truck towards a Cuban sandwich shop to get lunch. I turned to Al and broke into a wry smile. I knew he could take a joke.

"First," I said, "I get the position of 'rear-end' man. Now, I am promoted to 'butt' man! This was more than I could have hoped for! Ha!" Both of us had a great laugh over the sexual innuendos.

Later that afternoon, Al and I continued our conversation on the bench outside the firehouse. He assured me that there were other good firefighters in the department like Alan Vidal. He seemed to enjoy having me in the KWFD. Perhaps, he reveled in the fact that some of the firemen were frustrated in their inability to scare me away.

"You are still here," Al said. "They thought you be gone after day one. They thought you be gone in a week. And here you are. You sure got a set of *cojones*, brother!"

Al divulged that some of the firemen thought I was a 'spy' when I was hired. They thought that Richard Heyman had pulled political strings to place me in the department so that I could uncover, and report on, illegal activities by the firemen. *Me, a spy? Now, wasn't that preposterous?*

"Al, think about it," I said, "seriously. If they wanted to plant a spy, why would they choose an openly gay vegetarian atheist?" We both had a good laugh. I was overjoyed that I had made a friend that day.

I did have rare moments during that first year when I was reminded how exciting it was to be a firefighter. My experiences with Al Rahming and Alan Vidal raised my hopes for finding support in the department; in other words, there might be fellow firemen who would see me as more than just a 'gay guy' and help me to become an effective firefighter.

On one beautiful day with moderate temperatures, a fire truck from Station 3 pulled up to our firehouse. Their captain spoke with us and announced that the three rookies (Johnny, John, and me) would be practicing how to lay hoses. I enjoyed these opportunities to hone our skills. We got into our boots and turnout gear and jumped on our respective pumpers. We drove to an open area to practice undisturbed. One of the men from the other station, Alex Vega, was assigned to instruct me in the exercises. I was told to jump off the truck when it (briefly) stopped; I was to hold my position, with nozzle in hand, while the fire engine pulled away. If I stood my ground, the hose should unravel and fall from the truck without tangling. Unfortunately, I hadn't set my footing fast enough before the truck took off. The hose yanked so hard, it knocked me down to the ground. I was still holding the end of the hose, though. Alex was laughing. Then, in a hushed tone, he moved in to give me advice.

"Get up quick! Get up before the chief sees you!" he said.

I jumped up and hugged the hose with renewed confidence. I realized that Alex didn't want me to look foolish in front of the chief and others. He laughed. I was sure he had seen this happen before with other rookies.

"Don't worry," Alex said, "you'll get it. I just didn't want the chief to see you on the ground!"

All it took for me to feel accepted in this job – to feel like part of the team – was someone treating me like everyone else. Just like Al and Alan, Alex was treating me with respect. Yes, he was teaching me what I needed to be safe at a fire scene; but he was also protecting me from being mocked for rookie mistakes. Like the other two supportive colleagues, Alex was willing to provide positive feedback with his advice.

"It's OK," he would say. "No one gets it the first time. Keep practicing. That's it, put your foot here, and lean forward with all your weight." Alex seemed to enjoy giving the rationale for each of the maneuvers we were learning. I couldn't help but think that he was putting his own reputation at risk by giving me such support. I was grateful that Al, Alan, and Alex took the time to help me learn and, by their actions, make me feel welcome as a member of the KWFD. *What allows them to risk their reputation by engaging with me so freely?*

After an hour or so of practicing, Capt. Stephenson directed Oscar to drive to a Cuban coffee shop for lunch. This was common when driving around town; it was also a chance for the firemen to see their friends. The neighborhood coffee shop served as a center of Cuban social activity. There were many options in Key West, but each captain had their favorite. It was always a treat for me to order a *café con leche* and a side of toasted Cuban bread.

Still, being in this (nearly) all-male social environment was often stressful for me. Depending upon which firemen were present, and which Conch friends they encountered, I might become their topic of derision. Most of the time, the guys would talk in Spanish, thinking they were having a private conversation. However, they didn't realize that I understood much more Spanish than I could speak. Surely, I understood when they spoke derogatory terms like 'maricón' [*faggot*]. So, as much as I liked Cuban coffee, a visit to the coffee shop could be distressing.

On this day, we stopped at the *Five Brothers* coffee shop and grocery on the corner of Southard and Grinnell Streets. This was a popular meeting place for police officers, as well as firefighters, construction workers, and retired Conchs with nothing better to do than gossip about Key West politics. There were about five police officers in the shop when we entered. The firemen got their coffee and walked over to talk to the officers. I noticed that Oscar stayed outside with the truck. I got my coffee and bread and turned to leave when I was hailed to join the firemen talking with the police. One of the cops was beckoning me to join them.

"Hernando says he knows you?" someone said as I approached.

The police officer was smiling, but I didn't recognize him. I suddenly felt uncomfortable. *Was this a set-up to embarrass the gay guy?* Seeing my blank expression, the cop reached out to shake my hand.

"Kevin came to speak to us recruits when we were in training," he said. "He and his partner talked about the gay community and the problems they face with gay-bashing. They were really funny, too!"

Wow, could this really be happening? I managed to get my footing once I realized that our OWLS panel had presented to his class when he was a cadet.

"Oh, yeah. I did talk to your class!" I said. "How has it been going on the police beat?"

"Great. I don't remember," he asked, "were you a firefighter?"

"Not when we came to your class. I joined a couple of months ago," I said. After a chit-chat, I wasn't sure where the conversation could go, but I wanted to savor the moment. Their conversation quickly switched back to details of their own lives. I said goodbye to Hernando and shook his hand again to wish him good luck. I hoped that the firemen's estimation of me was raised a few notches by the nonchalant manner with which their friend – a police officer - accepted me as both a gay man and as a firefighter. It seemed ironic that I could open a dialogue with police cadets to impart information about being gay, but there was no such opportunity to do the same with my fellow firefighters.

There were aspects of being a professional firefighter that I didn't expect. The uniform was the first surprise. It gave me a sense that firefighters were a part of something larger. We had a purpose, a mission. We were to hold ourselves to a higher standard – in morals and behavior – because we were there to serve our community. However, it didn't seem to have that effect on all the firemen. Still, my uniform centered me. When I donned it in the morning, I felt as if I were transforming from an ordinary citizen to someone who could be called upon that day to be brave. My short-sleeve shirt and pants fit me well. I had never been in such good physical condition as when I joined the department. The uniform implied that I was ready to serve in a manner that could make the City proud. Unexpectedly, the uniform raised in me an instinct to direct others when we got to a fire scene. Unlike the police uniform that imposed authority, the firefighter uniform communicated that we were there to protect the community from danger, not enforce laws. Despite my experiences with the men on my watch, I felt the KWFD uniform made me feel that I belonged to a team. I had an expectation that the uniform would somehow provide me a level of protection from being hurt by my fellow firefighters. I would eventually learn that the uniform wouldn't offer me much protection at all.

There were incidents around the firehouse that detracted from us having a professional image. One firefighting tradition was raising and lowering the American flag each day. Our flagpole was out front where the community could witness the twice-daily ritual. Admittedly, I wasn't a fan of reciting the Pledge of Allegiance in public ceremonies. As a gay man, I lived the hypocrisy in the words "with liberty and justice for all." It had become all too clear to me that not all Americans had guaranteed freedoms and that our system was rife with inequities. The system was not equally just for all. Still, I considered it an honor to ritualistically raise the flag of a country that, at least, *aspired* to be a land of freedom.

Some of the firemen were less than respectful with their handling of the flag, especially after taking it down in the evening. I cringed when one of them rolled it into a ball instead of taking the time to carefully fold it. On my shift, it seemed a daily chore that they would rather relegate to the rookie. These were the same guys, though, that came to work with wrinkled uniforms, smoked cigarettes in front of the firehouse, and didn't curb their cursing when engaging with the public. It had not escaped my attention that Alan and Alex both carefully handled the flag, refolding it with respect and care. To me, the daily flag ritual seemed much like the uniform; it sent a message to the community that "we respect you and we are here to serve you."

CHAPTER 10: Assumptions & Accusations

It took several weeks before I felt comfortable bringing any of my personal items into the firehouse. The only area for storage (next to our sleeping bunks) had no security; I suspected the firemen would not respect my belongings. I was right to be apprehensive; it turned out that my personal items were not safe.

Joe and I needed two vehicles to get back and forth to Bay Point; he would drive the old Ford pick-up most days and I used my motorcycle. The Honda CB450 wasn't a 'hog' by any means. It was sleek with a handsome blue body. When on shift at the firehouse, I parked my motorcycle inside the truck bay behind the fire trucks. If I parked in the lot behind the building, it could easily be stolen. I kept a thick locking cable around the tires when it was parked in the truck bay.

One morning, at the end of my 24-hour shift, I came downstairs to find that the back tire was flat. One of the oncoming firefighters was standing a few yards away.

"Oh, ain't that a bitch!" he said. By the tone of his voice, and the smirk on his face, I surmised that either he damaged the tire or knew who did. This wasn't a fireman I knew well, so I let it go. I returned upstairs to call Joe. I could feel the eyes of the men on me as I approached. I had not yet worked with this crew, so they were as much a mystery to me as I was to them. Joe said he was coming into town with the truck, so he could stop by and help me load the bike onto the bed. When he arrived, he parked on the tarmac at the entrance of the truck bay. He came over to assess the damage.

"I didn't find any cuts or nails," I said. I wanted to assure him that I'd done due diligence on the tire inspection.

"One of these assholes probably did it!" Joe said. He was clearly pissed off. At that moment, two of the firefighters from my shift were walking out to head home.

"Hey, you can't park your truck there!" One of them yelled. I knew he was just trying to irritate Joe. He had parked far from the exit lane that the fire truck would need to leave for a call. This was exactly where the firemen's friends stopped when they visited.

"Aw, shit," the other one said with a whiny tone of false concern, "looks like you got a problem."

Joe was getting riled. He quickly stood up and assumed a cock stance. He was ready to fight. Joe was tall and quick enough to present a threat. The guys took a step backwards, thinking they were about to be rushed.

"Fuckin' assholes," Joe snarled in a low voice. I quickly stretched my arm in front of his chest to hold him back.

"It isn't worth it, Joe," I said. "Come on, let's just get this fixed."

He dropped me off at our usual garage to have the tire fixed. It turned out that the air had simply been let out of the tire. *Whew!* An irritation, to be sure, but no damage to the tire. It took about a day or two before that incident really began to bother me. Yes, it was a silly adolescent act that could be dismissed. Still, some of these guys felt emboldened enough to fool with my bike, my property. *That* pissed me off. Then, about a month later, the seat of the motorcycle was slashed with a blade while I was working at the firehouse. That was a much more expensive fix. Still, I didn't think of reporting the damage because I thought the harassment would end once the guys realized that I wasn't going to be frightened into quitting. Denying the seriousness of these incidents was a mistake.

Slowly, but surely, I was getting experience fighting fires. The State Fire Marshall's office planned a 'controlled burn' of a dormitory barge on Stock Island to simulate an arson investigation and provide firefighting practice for our department. I was excited for the opportunity to wield the fire hose. There was so much to learn, though. The fire turned out to be bigger and hotter than expected and it quickly became a threat to us and our equipment. One fireman suffered significant burns. The fire engines had to be repositioned after their tires began smoking! Even a controlled burn fire is nothing to taken lightly.

Dumpster fires occurred more frequently than I could have imagined. We also had numerous calls for car fires. The most common reasons for auto fires were owners who ignored short-circuits in the electrical system or people simply being careless with their smoking materials. I learned it was a myth that cars always burst into flames and explode the way you see in the movies. This is not to say that they cannot be deadly. Car fires were particularly dangerous after collisions because gas may leak onto the pavement and ignite. Sometimes, the driver or other occupants are trapped in the vehicle when the doors are mangled and unable to open. As a rear-end man, I had to learn how to use the proper tools to force open vehicles to help rescue a person while a colleague was using water to fight the fire itself.

We were called for fires in outdoor sheds, deck-side grills, and scrub brush. For most of these smaller fires, we used a 'booster' hose. This smaller gauge hard rubber hose rolled off a reel. It was much like a garden hose 'on steroids' and considerably easier to manage than the larger diameter fire hoses. Even better, the booster line didn't have to be dried out (to avoid dry rot) like the hoses surrounded in layers of cotton ply. Despite their size, though, each of these 'insignificant' fires required time, effort, and some level of expertise. I found myself hoping that I could attend the Fire College training before we were called to any major house fire or other scenarios for which I was not yet prepared.

In fact, there was much to learn about my role as the rear-end man. When we approached a fire scene, the driver would have to position the truck far enough away from the incident to prevent it from being damaged by heat or flying debris. I would jump off and pull off a 1½ inch 'attack' line. The engineer would hook the other end of the hose to the pump. Then, with the nozzle in hand, I would advance the hose towards the fire. Each hose could be up to 50 feet long and weigh about 45 lbs. when dry and empty. However, it will suddenly increase to hundreds of pounds when filled with water. A hose under such pressure is no longer flexible and it loses much of its maneuverability. Often, a single firefighter doesn't have the capacity to wield the hose in a safe and effective manner. Then, I had to decide how much water to deliver and where it needed to go. Usually, the captain or one of the other men would give me the direction I needed. After the fire was out, it was usually my responsibility to drain the hose and roll it up. It was placed back on the truck and laid out to dry when we returned to the station. Even with the smallest fires, this could be exhausting in Florida's heat and humidity.

One day, we received a phone call from someone reporting a bomb threat. We were dispatched to a fast-food restaurant that had recently been constructed at a nearby shopping center. This wasn't something I had expected. Hanging onto the back of the truck as it sped down the road with the siren blaring, I thought *"Why is a fire truck needed for a bomb threat?"* When we arrived, we parked a reasonable distance from the restaurant. Capt. Stevenson directed me to follow him into the building. My rational brain was ablaze with questions. *Why are we entering a restaurant that someone has threatened to blow up?*

Once inside, the captain quickly spoke to the manager to assess the situation. He then turned to me and said "Kevin, you check the restrooms and meet me back at the kitchen."

"Captain," I asked, "what exactly are we looking for?" He seemed to draw a blank as well. "Well," I added, "I guess we will know it when we see it. I'll report anything unusual." Thank goodness, there was nothing to find. It had been a prank call. This was the first time, however, that I realized how much danger my job could entail. What if a device had detonated and I was injured, or killed? Who would phone my partner, Joe, and tell him? A more distressing thought was *how* would they tell him? These guys would probably fight over the chance to deliver the news to the lover of the faggot fireman. I felt, though, that the captain was starting to respect me as a rear-end man he could depend upon in times like these.

Aside from the continual *faggot* jokes, most days at the firehouse were relatively boring. Grand fires in the department's history were memorable and led to endless storytelling. I became quite disinterested in repeatedly listening to inane conversations and needed something to help pass the time between fire calls. Eventually, I began bringing my drafting board to the firehouse. I had designed the stilt house that Joe and I were building on Bay Point. Now, a friend of ours wanted me to draw up blueprints that they could provide to a builder. He and his wife had purchased a lot on the next island down from ours and were ready to move out of their mobile home. In the early 1980s, there was no requirement that the plans be created by an architect. If the blueprints were accurate, the Monroe County building inspector provided a permit to build. Because I didn't trust the men not to damage my belongings, I had to bring the board back home at the end of each shift.

I had also begun to teach sign language classes at the Florida Keys Community College. It was satisfying to spend time with adults who were interested in learning a new skill. My experiences as an interpreter in college had provided me with cultural insights into the Deaf and hard-of-hearing communities. As a group, they face misunderstanding, stigma, and discrimination on a regular basis; again, some human beings are not given respect or equitable opportunities in life because of the misperceptions of ignorant others with more power and social status. While teaching sign language, I would intersperse real-life stories to help bring the Deaf culture alive for the students. The small amount of additional income was helpful because my firefighter salary was quite modest.

One day at the firehouse, I received a phone call from a stranger. She verified that I was the fireman teaching sign language. *How did she connect those two disparate aspects of my life?* She asked permission to come by the station and talk with me that morning. After quickly checking with the captain that there were no planned activities, I welcomed her to come by and talk with me. My days were about to get more fascinating.

About an hour after the call, a cab – *Big Al's Taxi* – pulled up at the curbside and the passenger's window rolled down. I could see that it was Al Rahming driving his personal cab. Laughing, he yelled over to me "Hey! This woman is looking for a firefighter who knows sign language!" *So, Al told her about me.* I could see a beautiful woman getting out of the cab and closing the back door. I smiled and yelled back "Thanks Al!" Before rolling the window back up, he added "If you need some help, you just let me, you know! Ha!" Al was always one to keep an eye out for a pretty woman. *Who was this woman and what did she want?* She bounced over the piece of grass that separated us. With an outstretched hand, she introduced herself. "My name is Karen and I need to learn sign language." She was buoyant, animated! The lively introduction made any of my initial concerns melt away. I was intrigued.

Karen was from New York City where she worked as a writer for the *Saturday Night Live!* television show. She was visiting Key West for a two-week vacation. She explained that she had become pregnant out of wedlock when she was young (quite the scandal in the early 1960s) and gave the newborn baby up for adoption. Her son, now a young man of 21, had uncovered his birth mother's identity. Just before she left on her planned vacation, he contacted her and asked to meet in New York after her return. Her son, it turned out, was deaf and primarily used sign language to communicate. Karen pleaded with me, saying "I need to learn how to sign in the next two weeks!" I think she realized how ridiculous the appeal sounded. We both laughed at the absurd idea of learning a language in such a short period. Then, she adjusted her expectations. "Can I learn at least enough to introduce myself?" she asked.

We sat on the bench and, after we had talked for an hour or more, I noticed one or two of the firemen casually walking by. Clearly, they were curious why this lovely woman would seem to be having such a good time with Kevin. Finally, Capt. Stephenson stopped by to be introduced. I kept it cool and simply introduced her as 'Karen.' The captain was respectful enough to leave us to talk. When we were done, I went upstairs and called Al's taxi to come back and retrieve his passenger. When I got back downstairs, Oscar had already engaged Karen in a brief conversation. He immediately backed off, as if he was inappropriately intruding. He was. Approaching, I said "OK. Al is coming back to get you now. I'll meet you at the restaurant at 7:30 tomorrow morning?" She confirmed the plan and gave me a big hug. Feeling out of place, Oscar walked back upstairs. I stayed with Karen until Al swept her away in his taxi. Oh, I knew this encounter would stir rumors. The firemen will want details.

"Who was that blond?" Oscar asked. It was clear to me that he was the mouthpiece for the others who wanted to know more.

"Oh, that was just Karen." I responded, nonchalantly. I went into the kitchen and poured myself a cup of coffee.

"Yeah, but what is she to you? Does Joe know about her?" Oh, I was beginning to grasp the reason for their insatiable curiosity. They weren't simply interested in her because she was an attractive woman. They suspected Karen and I were having an intimate relationship. It struck me that most of these guys probably didn't experience platonic friendships with women. Maybe their encounters with women were primarily to satisfy their own sexual needs? They seemed to think that men and women were very different from each other and that gender-based limitations were intended to keep things in balance. Women were for getting some 'poontang,' not forming a relationship that is based upon mutual respect. *Heaven help the first female firefighter to join this department!*

"Joe?" I teased, "well, he knows what he needs to know."

"You wouldn't know what to do with a pussy if you had it," Oscar retorted. Yes, all he can think of is sex.

"You think gay men don't have sex with women?" I asked. "You really don't understand sexuality, do you?" I was sure it would blow their minds. But, why would they think I hadn't been with a woman? It was not anything I would ever discuss with this group of men. *Let them stew in their curiosity.* In my usual manner, I walked out of the room. Making my exit at the right time seemed effective in truncating conversations that I didn't wish to continue.

Karen and I became fast friends in a whirlwind of teaching sessions. We laughed a lot over the next two weeks. Almost immediately, though, we were a known item. It was hard not to be seen around the small island. When I returned to the firehouse for the next shift, there were more questions. "Tell us about this pretty woman you had dinner with at the Pier House." I think only Al Rahming knew what Karen and I were doing together, but I don't think he cared to share it with the other firefighters. Knowing Al, he was having fun seeing the firemen perplexed.

It was impressive how much sign language Karen managed to learn over her brief time in Key West. Her ability to create meaningful syntax and recall complex sign combinations was impressive. She was, by far, one of the most creative and funny individuals I had ever met. It was easy to see how she contributed to *Saturday Night Live!* Perhaps, it was her right-brain creativity that helped her absorb the conceptual nature of sign language. I never heard again from Karen after she left Key West. I only wished that her reunion with her son was all she had hoped it would be.

I appreciate the adage that "idle hands are the devil's workshop." It seemed when the firemen on my shift were idle, they would harass one another – or me – to break the boredom. One day Oscar was sitting at the dining table, scanning through a magazine. I had just made some coffee and was glancing out the sliding glass doors. Two other firefighters were just chatting at the table.

"*Coño!*" [damn!] Oscar said. He seemed surprised by the centerfold of his magazine. It was hard to tell from his expression if he was truly startled, or simply over-acting.

"Hey, Mallinson, look at this…" Oscar ordered. He laid the magazine open on the table in front of him. I walked over and saw a naked centerfold of porno star 'Long John' Holmes lying with a naked woman. Holmes was sporting a full erection. No doubt, anyone would be impressed, if not intimidated, by the length and girth of his penis. *No wonder Holmes makes money in the porn business.*

"Well, now that is impressive!" I said, playing his game.

"So, you think you could *take that*?" He said, with every intention of embarrassing me. I took a moment to answer as if seriously considering his question. I was suddenly aware that all eyes were on me.

"In the mouth? Or in the ass?" I asked, as if needing clarification.

"Oh, fuck you!" he screamed. Oscar flung his erotic 'reading' across the table and left the room so fast that his chair toppled over onto the floor. He continued to curse at me from the living area. I went back to the window, sipping my coffee. My heart was racing, but I maintained a cool exterior. Behind me, I could hear the two guys snickering about Oscar's failed attempt at humiliating me.

When we are attentive to our surroundings, we have the opportunity to experience personal growth from everyday encounters. One February morning, as I was driving home after a shift. I opened the windows of the truck to enjoy the lovely, cool weather that was characteristic of 'winter' in the Keys. As I made my way over the Cow Key Bridge onto Stock Island, I noted a young man with a backpack standing on the shoulder of the road. He had his thumb out, trying to catch a ride up the Keys.

It wasn't unusual to see young people hitchhiking up and down the highway, especially during the tourist season. In the early 1980s, there was less fear of being robbed or assaulted by hitchhikers. I found encounters with new people provided opportunities to gain intriguing insights into someone else's life. I wasn't in the habit of picking up couples on the road, but often gave a ride to an individual that I quickly assessed to be lower risk. Admittedly, such a superficial evaluation is hardly valid. I down shifted and motioned to the guy that I was pulling over to offer him a ride.

After tossing his backpack into the bed of the truck, he opened the door and climbed into the passenger seat. He appeared a few years younger than me, clean-shaven, and wearing a relatively nice shirt and shorts. He had jet-black, wavy hair that complemented his dark olive complexion. I quickly determined that his skin tone was due to genetics and not simply from basking in the Florida sun. Though he was not the 'type' of man I generally found attractive, he was quite handsome.

"Good morning. I'm Kevin," I said. I offered to shake hands. He smiled broadly and shook my hand firmly.

"Ali," he responded. "Thanks for stopping." Despite this friendly exchange, I could sense that Ali was slightly uncomfortable. "You are police?" he asked.

"*Police?*" I echoed, a bit surprised at the suggestion. Then I realized I was still wearing my uniform. He had noticed the KWFD badge and nametag on my shirt. "Oh, no. I am a fireman for the city. I just finished work." I explained. That seemed to put him at ease. However, I did wonder for a moment why he would be disquieted at the thought of me being a police officer. I shifted the truck back into gear and pulled out onto the highway. Ali was scanning the inside of the truck, seemingly fascinated with riding in such an antique vehicle.

"It's a truck from 1952," I said. "I am only going 15 miles up to the Saddlebunch Keys. How far are you going?"

"To Miami, now," he answered, "I've been in Key West for a week."

Ali had an accent that I couldn't easily place, and I was intrigued. Up to this point in my life, I had never traveled outside of the United States. It was always interesting for me to talk to people from other countries.

"I can hear that you have a nice accent. Where are you from?" I asked.

"I'm Persian," he responded. The answer was so soft that I think he didn't want me to hear it. It took me a minute to process what he had said. Thinking about geography, I quickly placed him as being from Iran.

"Persian?" I echoed. I was smiling. "Yeah, I guess being from Iran isn't so easy when traveling through this country, is it?" It had only been a year since the release of the American hostages who had been held for 444 days following the siege of the U.S. embassy in Tehran, Iran. I could surely understand why this young man wouldn't want to identify himself as Iranian. I was trying to let him know that I was sympathetic to his need to disguise his heritage for his own protection. Surely, many Americans would not have been so accommodating.

Often, I thought about how one prejudice – such as homophobia – was related to others, such as racism, anti-Semitism, or Islamaphobia. The very nature of discrimination is to undermine the value of this specific person based on your own preconceptions of the larger cultural group. Too often, the individual is held accountable for the actions of their politicians, their government, or their religious leaders. In all good conscience, how could I possibly show any malice to this young man?

Injustice anywhere is a threat to justice everywhere.

"So, how did you like Key West? It must be so very different from home?" I said, trying to change the subject and keep him from becoming too self-conscious.

"Yes, it was great. It must be so wonderful to live here."

We conversed on and off over the next few miles. I identified some of the water birds standing in the shallow waters. I explained the history of Flagler's railroad and how its construction led to the 42 bridges that connected many of the Keys. When we arrived at Bay Point, I pulled off onto the shoulder to let him disembark. I would be turning onto Bay Drive, and he needed to continue up US1 towards Miami.

"You live here?" he asked, pointing to a small house a hundred yards away.

"Oh no. We are building a house about a half mile up that road." I offered.

"You and your wife?" he asked nonchalantly.

"Oh no. Me and my boyfriend, Joe." I decided that I would disclose since he asked.

"Your boyfriend?" he echoed with mild curiosity. There was no sense of shock in his demeanor. "Well, you sure are lucky to live in this beautiful place." He shook my hand again and thanked me. He retrieved his backpack from the bed of the truck and gave a wave and smile as he resumed his roadside hitchhiker stance.

I arrived home minutes later and started making my breakfast. I couldn't help but think how difficult it might be for Ali to keep his core identity as an Iranian secret for fear of reprisal. This was, of course, not so different than those of us who kept our sexual orientation hidden in a society that would judge us unfairly or inflict harm. Sitting down with my coffee, I wondered why a Muslim man would not have been more shocked at my coming out as gay. Smiling to myself, I realized that my own bias was in play. It may well have been that Ali came to Key West specifically because of its openness and gay community.

The harassment in the firehouse hadn't abated. While some of the men made derogatory comments about me when I was in earshot, most of the wisecracks were simply general slurs suggesting that gay men were weak and not 'masculine' enough to be a firefighter. Eventually, though, the men seemed intent on undermining my confidence about making it through the Fire College training.

"The pansy is going to *wilt*," one guy said. This set off a round of childish snickering.

"The silly little fairy will be running back home with his tail between his legs!" another guy said.

I had heard numerous comments about the challenges of Fire College. Several guys had failed in their attempts to complete the training. What I hadn't heard were hints about how to survive the ordeal. Al Rahming encouraged me. He informed me that many of the current firefighters in the department – and particularly those who were taunting me – wouldn't survive Fire College themselves. These guys were 'grandfathered' in by being hired before State certification was mandatory.

I decided that I had to prepare for Fire College. I started routinely going to the gym. Located on Duval Street, the facility was popular with gay men. I wasn't there for the eye candy, but it sure helped with my motivation. I focused my workouts on building muscle and increasing my body's overall flexibility. My daily running routine provided me with a cardio workout, building my endurance. What this gym offered was their recent installation of new Nautilus® machines that allowed the user to select muscle groups to be toned or strengthened. Then, there was the dry heat of the sauna.

Upon each visit to the gym, I would finish my workout with increasingly longer periods in the dry sauna. Always aware that I might overdo it, I was intent upon bolstering my ability to remain in the very hot environment without losing mental focus. I assumed that the Fire College training would place me in very hot fire scenes, testing my physical conditioning and my mental discipline. In raging fires, a firefighter must stay mentally sharp, focus on the task at hand, and resist the urge to panic. A firefighter who panics or freezes can either do something stupid or do something dangerous. Other guys would come and go from the sauna, unaware that I was silently chanting an inner mantra: *It will be alright...relax. You can tolerate another minute of this heat.* Once I thought that I had been in the heat long enough, I might challenge myself to "just a few more minutes." I knew there were challenges ahead and I wanted to be physically and mentally prepared.

I had also heard that Fire College would entail more than physical and mental challenges. There would be 'academic' content, though I had no idea what that meant. I was quite surprised when Jackie, our dispatcher, called me into his radio room one day. The very small room – his primary domain – contained the phones and radio equipment he used to keep everyone in touch during fire calls. Jackie was sure that no one else was close when he motioned me towards his papers.

"You might need this for Fire College," he said.

He handed me a copy of his cheat sheet of radio call signs used by dispatchers to communicate with officers responding to a call. Common examples of these standardized codes are "10-4" (acknowledgment) or "10-20?" or "What's your 20?" (What is your location?). The look of surprise on my face made him laugh.

"Boy," he said, "you are goin' to hafta pass Fire College if you want this job. They won't give you a second chance." I knew he was referring to the common practice of allowing a rookie two tries at the program. If you fail Fire College on the first go-round, you may be allowed to continue to work until the next training is scheduled. Two failures, however, and you are out of the department. I was thankful that he reminded me that the second chance was not guaranteed; I would be unlikely to get a second chance at Fire College after an initial failure.

Jackie may have been an alcoholic – may even have been drinking while on the clock – but he reached out to me anyway. Maybe he knew I loved firefighting. Maybe he admired my courage in returning to the firehouse each shift despite the harassment I faced. Perhaps, he just wanted to 'stick it' to some of the other firefighters for whom he had no love. Whatever his reasons, Jackie's small gesture was appreciated. He vigorously warned me about not confronting specific firefighters directly; he thought some of the guys would be dangerous and he didn't want to see me hurt. I think Jackie knew more about the nefarious activities going on behind the scenes than I could have imagined. I thanked him for his encouragement and assured him I would pass the Fire College training.

For the first few months in the Fire Department, I was bombarded with anti-gay slurs, inappropriate sexual innuendos, social ostracism, and minor damage to my truck and motorcycle. Still, there hadn't been any significant challenge to my job until mid-March 1982. The morning had been unremarkable. We accomplished our usual tasks of cleaning the fire truck and checking that the equipment was in good working order. After having my coffee, I was sitting out on the bench facing Flagler Ave reading a book. Without warning, Oneri burst out the door. His dark face was flushed, and he barked at me like a mad dog.

"The chief wants to see your sorry ass in his office now!" he said.

What could have him so agitated? More to the point, he seemed rattled. I closed my book and walked to the chief's office. It was a small room with two chairs facing the chief's desk. The office was located at the rear of the truck bay with a window that looked out into the garage. It seemed odd, but Oscar followed me into the office.

Chief Gates motioned me to come in. "Close the door," he said, speaking to Oscar. His voice was calm, though direct.

"Sit down," he said, "We have a problem to resolve."

Oscar remained standing at the side of the chief's desk, about six feet away from either of us. He seemed unable to stand still, shifting his weight from one foot to the other. I became keenly aware that my anxiety was mounting in response to Oscar's distress. Also, I was dreading what could possibly be the reason for my being in the chief's office. The chief appeared to be choosing his words carefully.

"Kevin, Oscar has accused you of some unacceptable behavior," he started.

"What? What do you mean?" I asked. I was truly surprised by the comment. I could already feel my face getting hot and flushed. I could recall nothing that would be considered inappropriate. Further, the irony of Oscar accusing me of inappropriate behavior was laughable.

"Oscar. Go on," the chief said, "repeat what you told me this morning." Oscar's facial expression clearly suggested that his level of anxiety had suddenly risen a notch or two. He nearly stuttered.

"Kevin has been touching me. Inappropriately touching me," he blurted out. He looked like a criminal trying to get his story straight after being brought in for interrogation. "When I am sitting down, watching TV," he continued, "he comes up behind me and brushes his hand against the back of my head. It is creepy. Whenever I go to take a shower, he is in the bathroom. I don't want no faggot looking at me. That kind of shit isn't right. He needs to be fired."

I was dumbstruck. I didn't respond because I was, quite frankly, speechless. *Where the hell is this coming from?*

"Anything more you want to add?" the chief asked.

"No. He needs to be gone today, chief," Oscar said. He had a sense of finality in the tone of his voice. I was thinking that Oscar had probably made a mistake by giving the Chief of the department a directive. It wasn't his place to talk to his superior officer in such a manner.

"You can go back upstairs," the chief said, "and close the door behind you."

My facial flushing that began with astonishment was now a sign of my anger. I knew that I had to stay calm. One of my useful internal mantras was to tell myself *I am in the midst of a storm, but the storm is not in me.* I momentarily closed my eyes and took a deep breath. Deep down, I was aching with the thought that this *"he said-she said"* scenario might be impossible to win. The chief could easily dismiss me from the department this morning. *How could I combat that type of accusation?*

The room was very silent with Oscar gone. I looked directly at the chief. His well-worn face suggested he had managed many personnel issues, but probably none like this one.

"You don't believe a word of that, do you?" I asked.

"Not for a minute," he responded. *Whew! Thank goodness!* Still, the chief seemed disturbed. "This puts me in a terrible bind, you know," he added. Again, the room was eerily quiet for a few moments.

"Chief, you know I have never lied to you," I said. I was particularly thinking about when I referred to the chief as an 'asshole' months ago. I was hoping that he recalled how I held myself accountable for that error in judgement.

"No," he said. "I don't think you had anything to do with Oscar blowing up like that. I am sure that the other guys put him up to this shit. They know how to work him to distraction." A great weight was lifted off me just hearing that he disbelieved Oscar's allegations. But why did the chief seem unsettled. "Kevin, these guys are getting worried because they thought you would be gone months ago. They were sure you wouldn't last very long. Your probationary period ends next week, and you become a permanent employee."

Now, I understand! I had not been watching the calendar. City employees serve at the pleasure of their supervisor for the first six months of employment. If they aren't let go, their job is secured. These guys were trying a last-ditch effort to get me fired before that magic date arrived. Now, I was really beginning to feel pissed off. I could not have expected the firemen to concoct such a libelous story just to get the gay guy dismissed from the department. An accusation like this against a gay man would, normally, have been a slam-dunk case; who would believe him over the sworn testimony of a straight man? It was common to side with the 'normal' guy being intimately assaulted by the homosexual who could not keep his hands to himself. Luckily, the chief knew Oscar well enough.

But there was more to it than that. Even if everything was going very well and there were no major conflicts, the chief could legally fire me simply for being gay. Neither the United States, nor the State of Florida, had antidiscrimination laws to protect homosexuals in their jobs, housing, or public accommodations. Some people mistakenly thought that being gay was 'illegal'; in 1981, the sexual acts between male partners were still punishable under the law but *being* gay was not against the law. However, if the chief decided my sexual orientation amounted to 'moral turpitude,' he could fire me and I would have no law to protect my job. I sensed that the chief wasn't done with me yet.

"I could fire you at any time, you know?" he said.

Yes, he could. I couldn't discern his intentions. His wrinkled face was blank. *Was he weighing his options? Was he unwilling to stand up for me? Had he reached his limit with the firemen's opposition to my being in the department?*

"Yes, you could Chief," I replied firmly. "And I could take you to court for it. And, if I lost the case, I would take it to a higher court. I would continue to the Supreme Court, if need be, to simply get justice. There is no reason why I shouldn't have a place in the fire department."

I do believe I saw him stiffen at my resolve. I meant every word and I think he could sense that I meant business. I was firm, but respectful.

"No. I am not going to fire you," he softened. "You are going to Fire College next week. If you don't pass, I cannot guarantee anything." He seemed satisfied that the ball was back in my court. He stood up, motioning that our meeting was over.

"Just be careful with these guys for the next few days," he said. The chief didn't shake my hand.

"Thanks Chief," I murmured. I kept to myself for the remainder of that shift, hoping that the men wouldn't learn of the chief's decision and start another conflict. I didn't feel that these firemen 'had my back' when it came to fighting fires. In fact, I thought they would do anything to make sure I messed up so they could argue that I should be fired. I had to be extra careful now. *Would I ever feel part of this team?* At the beginning of my next shift a few days later, I was transferred to Station 2 in Old Town to fill in for a rear-end man who was out sick (I learned much later that the transfer was planned to protect me from further interactions with the men on my own watch). My last work shift before leaving for Fire College was my scheduled Kelly Day. I spent the next few days with Joe, completing some projects at our house site. *Now, all I have to do is survive Fire College.*

CHAPTER 11: Fire College

There were three of us rookie firefighters that needed to complete the State of Florida Minimum Standards Training Course to earn our certification. Known as "Fire College", the 6-week training was provided by the State Fire Marshal's Office. Johnny, John, and I were to travel to Ocala, Florida in mid-March, staying at a motel for the training period. Johnny and John shared a room, and I had a room to myself. The rooming arrangement was no surprise. I am sure neither one of them would have felt comfortable sharing a motel room with 'the gay guy' for the next month and a half.

I barely knew John and Johnny, as we each worked on a different watch. Neither one talked with me about his plans for getting to Ocala. I think they traveled together. My partner and I stacked my motorcycle with everything I thought I would need for Fire College. I took a notebook and pencils, a variety of clothes, my personal grooming supplies, and a camera. I was quite nervous about the coming challenges. Joe, on the other hand, was excited for me and expressed complete faith in my abilities. On a rainy morning in March, I set out for the 8-hour drive. It rained the entire distance and I prayed that this was not an omen for the coming weeks.

I characterize Fire College as six weeks of 'boot camp' with burning buildings. The first thing Monday morning, 33 recruits from around the state met in the classroom for program orientation. The State Fire Marshall made a cameo appearance to welcome us to the facility. He highlighted the importance of firefighting to our communities and expressed his admiration for anyone undertaking the noble profession. This inspiring talk soon faded as the next speaker assured us that half of the 33 recruits in the room would be gone before the end of the program. This, I surmised, was intended to temper our jovial mood, and serve as a warning as to the rigor of the program. However, it aligned with what Chief Gates told us before we left Key West. The failure rate at Fire College was intimidating.

In this cohort, we had 32 men. The only woman in the group, Linda, was a Black firefighter from nearby Orlando. I couldn't help but think of her as a kindred spirit. She was facing an uphill battle for acceptance in the fire service. Furthermore, she was being tested alongside mostly white men in Ocala, a city known for its Southern 'pride.' In other words, this place was a hotbed of racist attitudes.

Some of the recruits were volunteer firefighters, a few of whom introduced themselves as 'Lieutenants' or 'Captains' or 'Assistant Chiefs' in their departments. It was apparent that this attempt to impress was not accepted well by the professional firefighters or the instructors. None of us were in Fire College to prove that we were better, or more experienced, than each other. We were there to learn scientifically sound and effective firefighting skills.

We each received training manuals that morning and an onerous reading assignment for the next day. We were warned that exams would be used to test our knowledge. There would be unscheduled tests. There was so much to learn about the hydraulics involved in firefighting, the unexpected characteristics of water in superheated environments, and the toxic nature of fires fueled by modern building materials.

I was feeling comfortable that I could master the academic material in the program. However, that first day we were asked the most basic of questions: "What *is* fire?" *Huh!? What is fire? Everybody knows what fire is…everyone has seen it.* One after another of us offered our guess as to the basic definition of fire, based upon our experience. None of us could provide an acceptable description. The instructor wanted us to know the scientific nature of fire. Admittedly, I have never considered the question. Apparently, neither had any of the other recruits.

We were enlightened. We knew that one needed to have fuel, oxygen, and heat to initiate and sustain a fire. But this lecture explained the vaporization of the fuel into small particles and the many chemical reactions that occur in the process. We learned why some parts of a flame burn brighter than others, some materials burn much faster than others, and why different kinds of firefighting techniques work in one situation, but not others. *Fascinating*! The scientific explanation gave me a new respect for the nature of our 'enemy.' We were learning fire science! Not all the recruits were as excited as I was to know that we had academic work to complete. Some simply wanted to 'fight fires' without the supplemental book learning.

Starting the next morning at 6:30 a.m., we began our day running laps around the sports track. Then, we donned our turnout gear for the physical training exercises. It was already quite hot and humid by 9 o'clock in the morning. Located in central Florida and far from the beaches, Ocala retains the heat. That first week, the temperatures were hovering in the mid-80s. This area of the state is also a national hotspot for lightning strikes. All outside activities would immediately cease if the conditions were right for lightning. The warning didn't concern me. It was more intimidating to stand in front of the 3-story, blackened concrete buildings that would be used to test our firefighting skills.

That first day on the field was physically tough. We retrieved rolls of hose and worked in small teams to hook up to water hydrants that were strategically placed on the training grounds. We were learning safe ways to carry and raise heavy ladders. We practiced using many kinds of firefighting equipment. A cardinal rule on any fire scene is to not wield a tool in a manner that endangers yourself or others. There were very few breaks in our training schedule and relatively few opportunities to drink water. The instructors would not allow us to stop and rehydrate. We learned to capture sips of water from our hoses without the instructor's seeing us.

We were exhausted by late afternoon. The last 'exercise' of the day was to lay out a 2.5-inch hose that didn't have the usual brass fitting on the end of it. I thought this was curious. Then, the instructor turned on the water. The end of the hose writhed wildly as the water gushed out. It was like a wet snake squirming in all directions. Our challenge was to take turns trying to wrestle the hose and gain control over its movements. As each of us attempted to control the untethered water serpent, the sheer power of the whipping action would land us in the mud, sopping wet. A round of laughter would follow as each of us failed. The instructor explained that this exercise was designed to underscore the danger to life and limb if one releases a hose without first completely closing the nozzle. However, I suspected that the real intention was to give the recruits a few minutes of fun at the end of a grueling day. In the Florida heat, I think we were thrilled to get wet in the exercise. We left the field laughing and looking forward to a good shower.

John and Johnny, my fellow recruits from Key West, had not engaged with me at all during that first day. They never mistreated me, they simply ignored me. I was just hoping that we all survived the next weeks of the training. Walking off the field, I heard many of the others discussing where to eat dinner that evening. Luckily, a few guys asked me to join them for dinner at a Ruby Tuesday restaurant that evening.

A recruit could fail the Fire College training for any number of reasons: failing to follow orders, unable to complete the tasks as instructed, or unprofessional behavior. By the end of the first week, we had already lost 7 enrollees from the original cohort, including both John and Johnny from Key West. To her credit, Linda was still standing strong. I had so many emotions. On the one hand, I was relieved that my fellow Key Westers were not going to be around. I felt no animosity towards either one, but I also felt no support from them as coworkers. I'd been concerned that they might inform the other recruits to my sexual orientation. I decided to not openly declare my sexuality in this setting, because I was concerned that the Fire Marshall's office might dismiss the 'gay guy' without first giving me the opportunity to prove myself. In this setting, I couldn't even imagine the complications that would ensue if they ejected me unfairly. I wasn't going to deny who I was either. I admit that I did feel a bit vindicated when John and Johnny failed. After all, the two straight guys from Key West were heading home with their heads hung low and the gay guy was still going. I couldn't imagine how they would explain it to their family, friends, and fellow firefighters. Still, I wasn't being cocky about my abilities. I seriously wondered how I would persevere alone in this rigorous training. As it turned out, I wouldn't be alone. Fito was heading to Ocala that weekend.

At the news that Key West had lost two of their men in the first week,

Chief Gates was given the opportunity to send one more recruit up to Fire College for the remaining five weeks. I received notice from the College secretary that Adolpho (Fito) Rodriguez was on his way to Ocala. Fito was a brand-new hire into the KWFD. We had not yet met. *Oh my god. I don't need another homophobic jerk to have to contend with during this boot camp ordeal!* Johnny and John had shared a motel room during their short time in Ocala. Now that it would only be Fito and me, I was informed that we would share my motel room. *How nervous was Fito going to be about such an arrangement?* I was pleasantly surprised.

I guessed Fito to be in his mid-40s and approximately 30 pounds overweight for his short stature. My first thought was that he was not physically prepared for this exhausting training. He looked so nervous when we met at the door of the motel room. I decided to be direct. The first evening he arrived, I sat him down and made it very clear that he should ignore anything he has heard from the other men. My being gay had nothing to do with firefighting. My goal, I explained, was to pass Fire College. If he was also there to pass, I added, then that is all either of us needed to know. He was in no 'danger' by sharing a room with a gay guy.

Fito was direct with me, as well. He was afraid that he would not make it through the next 5 weeks of the program. He told me how much he needed a stable job to support his family. Passing this program was important to him and he was intimidated that the others had failed during the first week. I offered that I would help him as much as possible. However, I would expect that he would exert as much effort and focus as he could muster. I summarized what we had learned during that first week. I emphasized the importance of following the orders of the instructors and adhering to any rules they set. I gave my personal opinions on why several of the recruits had already failed.

I assured Fito that I didn't want to go through the remaining weeks of Fire College alone. He would have to persevere through the physical challenges because I didn't want him blaming his lack of physical strength for failing. I explained that focusing on the task-at-hand would counter many of his fears. As we talked, I sensed that I wasn't the man he had been warned about when leaving Key West. Finally, I asked that Fito not discuss my sexual orientation with anyone in Ocala as it was none of their business. I wanted to complete this program on my merits and not be unfairly disqualified and sent home for being gay. He assured me that he would not breach my privacy. Fito, it turned out, was not what I expected; I was guilty of harboring unfair preconceptions.

I assumed a teaching role with Fito. Firefighters frequently use rope at fire or rescue scenes. We recruits were expected to tie different types of knots in the dark. So, that first evening, I taught Fito a simple bowline knot. I wanted him to start building his confidence by giving him a single task to master. Then, to simulate darkness, I had him tie the knot with his eyes closed. On Monday morning, we were given details on 15 different fire extinguishers. One contained foam as the active agent; others expelled dry powder, water, or chemicals. Which extinguisher is best to use on a wood fire? An electrical fire? What type of extinguisher is discharged in a structure fire without harming computer components or other electronic equipment? We were going to be tested on our knowledge the following week. *This was going to be a challenge!* I imagined that Fito and I would struggle to recall the academic material. I hung sheets of paper on our motel room walls; each had the details for one type of fire extinguisher. Each morning and afternoon, I drilled Fito on the specific details for one extinguisher at a time. He couldn't cheat by looking at the sheets on the wall. Then, he would challenge me. After dinner, we would do it one more time before going to sleep. Eventually, we both passed that exam. I thought Fito was really trying his best. Though we didn't become 'friends' over the course of the program, I was sure I had gained Fito's respect.

Each day, there was a focus on a different firefighting strategy. There were several large concrete buildings on the campus that were able to withstand repeated fires. The structure fires were sometimes fueled by burning combustibles like wood pallets. Other simulated fires were created with pumped in liquid petroleum (LP) gas. One day we would fight a simulated gas tanker fire and the next day we might battle a 3-story blaze in a make-believe apartment building. Each scenario was intended to teach us the dangers of a particular type of fire scene; each was also designed to test specific skills the instructors wanted us to demonstrate.

By the end of that second week, our cohort had suffered a total of 19 failures, 18 men and one female. *Darn! I really wanted Linda to make it through the training.* The remaining 14 of us had begun to lean on each other for support. Alliances began to form. I had made friends with another small-framed guy, Pete. He weighed as little as I did. We ended up spending so much time together that we were nicknamed 'Pete and re-

Pete.' We had a 'bromance.' Though not coined as a phrase in the 80s, we got along well. I was sure he sensed that I was gay; I suspected he was attracted to me.

Pete knew I was building a house with another guy. He knew that Joe and I would live in the house together. Perhaps, his apostolic Christian faith kept him from pursuing the matter with further questions or even facing his own feelings of attraction. No matter, it was great to have a buddy in the training.

Make no mistake, Fire College presented physically grueling challenges. At the end of the day on the field or in the 'burning' buildings, we would return to our motel room, shower, and collapse on our beds. Pulling hose, climbing ladders, and battling fires in the Florida sun required an extraordinary degree of stamina. Fire College, though, also required more mental discipline than most people are used to dredging up. Several times, I recalled my stints in the gym sauna in Key West that I had designed to manage feelings of panic when my body was fatigued from the high temperatures. The preparation paid off: I was often able to critically think and be creative during the challenging training exercises.

One day, we were exposed to a particularly hot fire in one of the concrete buildings. We had been given directions on what skills we needed to demonstrate during the exercise. The fire was particularly intense; one could not stand up as the super-heated air at three feet off the floor was enough to seriously injure or kill you. We had to crawl on our bellies – staying as close to the floor as possible – to approach the source of the fire. We had masks on our faces to breathe from the air tanks on our backs. I was the team leader of a small group of three men. I advanced with my nozzle opened to emit a broad fan of water that would provide some protection from the scorching heat radiating from the fire. One of my team was immediately behind me and the other two men a bit further behind for back-up. Once we had demonstrated the requisite set of skills, the task was complete. I motioned to my team that we could begin our retreat, backing out of the building. The guys in the back began slowly pulling the hose back towards the door. I needed to keep the 'fog' stream of water between us and the fire until we had moved far enough away to not be seared.

We had only begun to retreat when I noticed that the fireman behind me wasn't moving. Still holding the nozzle and directing the water stream, I reached back to physically motion him to leave the building. No response. *Oh, my god! This guy has passed out from the heat! What the hell do I do now?* I continued to move away from the fire until I was side-by-side with the guy. By this time, I decided that getting him out of the heat was my priority. I motioned for one of the others to take hold of the nozzle and maintain the necessary water barrier between us and the fire. I tried pulling my man towards the door. *Oh jeez! He is heavy!* I wasn't going to be able to move his dead weight. I thought for just one moment and chose an alternative strategy. I kneeled at the side of the guy and rolled him over onto his back. This was no easy feat because he was wearing the air tank on his back. I could hear clanking as the tank hit the floor and I continued to push. Over and again, I rolled the recruit like a log until he was out of the building. He was now awake and disoriented. *Probably heat exhaustion.* Two instructors were quick to move him into the shade, remove his turnout gear, and spray him with water. Then, the other two instructors turned to attend to me. After learning that I was all right, they burst out laughing! They had never seen such an unconventional way to move an unresponsive person. They congratulated me on the approach.

Each cohort in the Fire College had an assigned lead instructor. We were assigned to Jerry. He was a no-nonsense, hard-ass trainer with a paramilitary personality. He would bark orders and maintain discipline. True to the stereotypical leader in the Army or Marines, he could be harsh when demanding rigor. He gave clear instructions and screamed obscenities if one of us didn't follow them closely. He was immediately intimidating. "Firefighting is serious business," he would say, "and there is no place for screwing up!" Whenever he caught any of the men laughing – usually to reduce our heightened anxiety – he would strongly discourage our levity. I began, affectionately, calling him 'Sarge.' The first time I used the nickname, he laughed.

"My job is to be sure you all remain safe over these next weeks," he said.

On most days, one recruit was charged with arriving at the fieldhouse early to lay out the equipment and gear for the day's activities. On my first early morning assignment, I arrived at 6 a.m. There was a heavy mist in the early morning air. I guessed the day would be stiflingly hot. Soon, Sarge arrived and unlocked the equipment shed and directed me to move specific items out onto the field. We were chatting as I walked to and from the shed.

"So, you're from Key West, huh?" he asked nonchalantly.

"Yeah," I responded. "I've been living in the Keys almost 4 years now."

"Oh, not a Conch!? Ha! That's unusual, isn't it?" he asked. He seemed familiar with the emphasis that Key Westers placed being born on the island.

"Yep. But here I am!" I said. "Fito is a Conch," I added. I thought it only right to give my roommate his due.

"Key West has a lot of gays now, doesn't it?" Sarge asked. I hadn't expected him to raise the topic and, surely, not in such a nonchalant manner.

"Yeah," I offered, "they have built successful businesses and brought lots of tourists to town." I hoped that would be the end of this line of conversation. I could feel my heart racing. To keep him from seeing that I was getting ruffled by the topic, I focused on counting out the piles of gear I was preparing for my fellow recruits. However, he wasn't done with the subject.

"Well, I guess someday we will start to see gay guys coming up to the Fire College," he offered.

OK. The cat is out of the bag. He knows I am gay. I might as well be open and transparent.

"I guess my chief told you I was coming?" I asked. From his facial expression, I could see that he was baffled by my question.

"As a gay guy in the department, I assume that my chief told you about me?" I added.

Sarge's expression told me that he was blindsided. It was as if I had accused him of some terrible transgression. He struggled to respond.

"No! I was only talking! I didn't hear anything about you," he said. "So, you are gay?" He seemed authentically surprised by my coming out.

Then, in an unexpected expression of understanding, he offered some supportive advice.

"I suggest that you keep that to yourself here. They would just as soon kick you out if they knew," he said.

"Sure," I said, "there's no reason to bring it up."

He told me to finish my work and meet the recruits at the track for our morning run. I was shaking a bit. I wondered if this unexpected conversation would bring my Fire College experience to an untimely end. Once at the running track, I tightened up my shoelaces. Each day, I challenged myself to achieve my personal best time in the 1-mile run. To most of the other recruits, this was the worst part of their day. For me, though, running was an outlet. It gave me the opportunity to shut out most of the noise and focus on just my cadence. I was used to running much longer distances at a slower pace. Fire College was providing me an opportunity to increase my speed in the one-mile distance each morning. In the evenings, I tried to get in longer runs to keep myself in shape.

Sarge was already sitting in the bleachers writing in his notebook. My fellow recruits arrived on time for the 6:30 a.m. deadline and were loosely grouped at the starting line on the track. As the designated leader for the day, they were awaiting my signal. I raised my right arm and yelled "*Ready. Set ...*" Suddenly, I heard Sarge yell to me.

"Mallinson! Come here!" he said.

I motioned the cohort to stay where they were and walked up a few flights of bleacher seats, stopping about six feet from our instructor. He had a wide grin on his face and whispered so the others couldn't hear our conversation.

"Living in Key West for three years nearly *ruined* my marriage!" he said. Then, suddenly transforming into the Sarge we all knew and respected, he barked at me in his loud military tenor. "Get your asses out there and run!" he said.

I bounced back down to the start line and, again, raised my hand. I quickly glanced his way before repeating the standard kick-off phrase. He was smiling as if satisfied with himself. I returned to my task "*Ready. Set. Go!*" As I ran the first lap around the field, I tried to make sense of his revelation. *What did he mean...nearly ruined his marriage?* As I passed him on each lap, his expression provided no hint, no evidence at all for me to make meaning of his comment. As usual, he was yelling at the slower runners to pick up their pace. I relaxed considerably after Sarge's titillating disclosure. He seemed to be countering my private disclosure with one of his own. I picked up my pace and had a personal best for the mile: 8.5 minutes.

It was almost a week before Sarge had a private space to expand on his enigmatic comment. He had been in the Keys for an extended assignment with the Fire Station at the Naval Air Station on Boca Chica Key. He and his wife had military housing in the Sigsbee community. Apparently, his wife came home one day and found Sarge in bed with a male sailor. Yet, a couple of decades later, they were still married. Relationships are complex. At this point I had no more concern that Sarge would betray my confidence.

The daily exercises were increasingly challenging and dangerous. The firefighting scenarios required us to be strong, flexible, and mentally focused under increasingly difficult circumstances. The instructors needed to be sure we weren't injured in the training. They watched our every move and offered guidance on how to complete maneuvers effectively and safely.

One day, we set up a 50 ft high ladder against the 3-story smoke tower. Each of us had to climb the ladder to the top and back. *Easy peasy!* While climbing a ladder may seem basic for a firefighter, the further a ladder is extended, the bouncier it becomes. At this great extension, our ladder was wobbling up and down with my weight alone. Of course, we were wearing our heavy turn-out fire gear in the hot Florida sun. Once I had completed my turn to the top and back, I thought the challenge quite simple. *Too simple.* Sure enough. Once each of us had completed our climb, Sarge increased the difficulty for the next stage of the exercise.

"OK. Let's up the stakes a bit," he said.

We couldn't imagine what was coming. Two of the assistant instructors stepped forward and demonstrated for us how one firefighter can be descending a ladder while another ascends the same ladder. As the two approach each other mid-way, the ascending fireman had to swing his body around to the underside of the ladder and use his legs to help keep himself from falling. He had to position his hands at the sides of the rungs so the descending firefighter can have a spot to land his feet as he passes. Once the descending fireman has passed, the ascending man had to swing around to the topside of the ladder and proceed up to the top. It may look easy, but you are doing this while 20 feet above the ground. It was bad enough to think about doing this maneuver without hearing the foreboding instructions from the Sarge. He made it clear, in no uncertain terms, that we could be seriously injured if we didn't focus and adhere to the steps that were outlined by the instructors. I was quivering at the idea of hanging upside down off a ladder and thought the heavyset recruits were equally terrified. In my usual manner, I offered to go first. Before I knew it, I had completed the task and was back on the ground! *That wasn't so bad?* The other recruits were praising my skills and bravery, but they all passed.

I was seeing how a high-stakes environment like the Fire College could forge bonds between recruits. We were getting to know each other through our actions and ability to work as a member of the team. In the (eventually) all-male environment, I expected many more anti-gay jokes. Surprisingly, it was not the homophobic and hateful atmosphere I had feared. There wasn't a sense that we were competing against each other. There was no need to disparage any of our fellow recruits. We had a goal in common and we each were challenging ourselves to do our best. All of us were afraid of failing the program and being sent home in disgrace.

The increasingly dangerous exercises left no room for making stupid mistakes. I began to understand why the instructors were quick to fail recruits who were not strictly following their orders or who couldn't physically keep up with the rest of the cohort. The physical and psychological challenges before us each day were designed to test our resolve. The instructors had years of experience designing fire scenarios to test our courage. For example, there was a large vehicle on the field that simulated an overturned oil tanker truck. Underground gas lines allowed the instructors to set it alight with the flick of a switch. Even as a simulation, the fire was dangerous and potentially deadly. Approaching the inferno was terrifying, but one has to trust that the tactics for remaining safe will work. It built my confidence!

I think that being exposed to maneuvers that threatened life and limb brought out the best in each of us. During those first few weeks at Fire College, I thought the point was to 'break' us as individuals so that the weaker recruits would fail the training and be sent packing. Over the second half of the training program, however, I became increasingly aware that we needed to depend upon each other – and to trust each other – if we were to remain uninjured. I realized that Sarge and other instructors broke us down to rebuild us as a team. Firefighting is a team effort, not an arena in which individuals display their bravery or seek to be heroes. Unfortunately, I was unlikely to have the same kind of mutual trust and back-up in dangerous situations when I returned to the KWFD.

Our ability to work as a team came in handy off-campus as well. Most evenings during the week, we would go out to dinner in small groups. The Ocala area had a variety of homestyle food restaurants. One evening, we were driving back to campus when a car came up from behind in a precarious manner. The female driver was repeatedly blowing the horn as if in a panic. She brought the careening car to a stop next to us at the red light. It seemed only a nanosecond before a couple of the firemen in our car jumped out to render assistance.

The woman's husband was having a cardiac arrest and she was frantic to get him to a nearby hospital. It took only seconds for someone to take charge. One of our guys, 'Peanut', jumped into the back seat of the car and began performing CPR on the husband. Someone else took the steering wheel and moved the wife to the passenger's seat. The driver of our car knew the area and we sped off, leading the other car towards the hospital. We used our headlights and car horn to warn other drivers to pull aside. It was a few exciting minutes before we pulled into the emergency room entrance. As soon as Peanut reported off to the receiving healthcare team, we were back on the road towards home. *This is why we were professional firefighters.* We worked as a team with a singular mission. Everyone assumed their role in the urgent situation without question. As is often the case in firefighting, we never heard how the husband fared. We didn't know if he lived or died.

In Week 5 of Fire College, the exercises to test our resolve continued to challenge our greatest fears. This one day, we were to repel off the roof of a 3-story building. I would not have expected this to be in the firefighting skillset. I don't think I ever imagined performing such a feat. We were given clear instructions on how to tie the rope, forming a rescue harness around our groin. Each of us had to demonstrate the correct way to hold the rope in our left hand to maintain vertical positioning while using our right hand to control our descent. After some instructors demonstrated a controlled descent (including a stop midway down), it was our turn. Pete and I were eager to take on the challenge. We climbed the stairs past the third floor and out onto the roof. The recruit just ahead of me, Tony, was the usual show-off in the group. He viewed himself as a tough firefighter and a lady's man. I've never been impressed with the kind of bravado that has no substance. Sarge was providing a final check to be sure that we knew what to do. As he reminded us, there is no safety net once you lean back and start to descend the outside wall. When it was time for Tony to go, he froze. Sarge encouraged him and gave assurances that he could do it. Tony couldn't seem to pull himself together. Some of the guys started taunting him.

"Don't be such a pussy!" one guy said.

"Don't wimp out like a little faggot," said another.

Suddenly, Sarge pulled Tony away from the edge and removed the rope from his hands. He directed him to stand aside and let someone else go. Sarge glanced in my direction. "Nope. No room for wimpy faggots," he said. "Mallinson. You go." I am not sure, but I think he winked at me. I stepped forward and positioned my rope as I had been instructed. Though I have never been afraid of heights, I was a bit wary about repelling. *Kevin, if you have ever done anything in your life before, do this now!* I didn't want to show any hint of hesitating. I leaned back and started to bounce down the side of the building.

"Man!" I yelled on my way down, "this is great!" Mirroring what the instructors had done, I stopped about halfway down. "Hey Sarge," I yelled, "am I doing OK with this?" I could see him smiling broadly as he motioned me to keep descending. As soon as I disconnected myself from the ropes, I watched as Pete came down. He, too, seemed confident and having fun. Both of us immediately began climbing the stairs to have the chance to repel again! Tony eventually completed the exercise.

It didn't take long before the Ocala area lived up to its reputation as a hotspot of racist attitudes. One evening, four of us went out for dinner. As usual, we headed towards a family-friendly chain called Shoney's that was likely to have a variety of calorie-rich, fat-laden meals. As a vegetarian, it never bothered me what others ate at the table. Invariably, I could find something to eat in most restaurants, even if it was a plate of overcooked vegetables.

Upon entering, I noticed that an older Black couple was standing on the side of the host's stand. He looked to be about early 60s with his gray-streaked short hair. She looked a little older but dressed nicely enough to suggest going out for dinner was special. Assuming that they were in line waiting for a table, I spoke to the husband.

"Oh, a bit busy tonight?" I asked. He nodded. Moments later, a hostess approached me.

"Table for four?" she asked.

"I'm sorry," I responded, "but these folks were here before us." I motioned to the man and his wife. The husband appeared appreciative, and I was sure they were ready to be seated. The hostess quickly glanced at the couple and then turned her back to them.

"Oh, honey," she said loudly enough for all to hear, "you come before N*ggers do." She extended her arm, motioning us to follow her to a table.

Had I heard that correctly? In my momentary disbelief at the blatant display of racism, I saw the dejected look on the faces of the couple. Instantly, I surmised that they were used to this kind of behavior in public. They displayed no shock. They offered no protest to an action I considered outrageous and repugnant.

"That's disgusting!" I blurted out. I turned quickly to the couple and spoke in a softer voice. "I'm sorry," I said.

Turning to leave, I found my three fellow firemen frozen in place. The blank expressions on their faces suggested that they were also used to hearing these kinds of derogatory comments. They were, perhaps, used to being seated before Black patrons? Whatever they were thinking, it was clear they were not expecting my reaction.

"I'm not eating here. *We* are not eating here," I said. I was adamant.

Two of them were telling me not to make an issue out of it.

"Relax," one of them said. *Relax?!* Pete didn't say anything. He may have been surprised by my response, but he wasn't advocating to stay and eat.

"We can find another place," I said. I offered no hint of acquiescence. "I wouldn't eat here if they paid me."

As we drove to another place, I continued to explain to the guys that such racism and discrimination was unacceptable. Knowing that they were 'God fearing' Christian folk, I suggested that the Almighty purposely put a variety of people on this earth and He wouldn't approve of such inhumane, immoral behavior. I thought about expounding upon how bigotry leads to dehumanization and violence towards minority groups. However, I decided that lecturing wasn't going to accomplish any more than my actions had that evening.

Finally, the six weeks of Fire College were over and the 14 of us had survived; the other 19 recruits had failed. We were coming off the field on the Thursday afternoon of that last week when an office assistant met me at the gate. She handed me a Western Union telegram. *Telegram?* I was nervous as I stepped aside and opened it up. It was short and to-the-point.

> Congratulations, hon. I am proud of you! I knew you would make it! Love, Joe.

I was overwhelmed with emotion. How wonderful that the man I loved would be so thoughtful and confident in my abilities. I had been feeling quite lonely at Fire College and I really needed the boost that came in that telegram.

April 16, 1982. My fellow Key Wester, Fito, was beside himself with pride – and he deserved it. He had worked hard. He had managed to complete every difficult exercise the rest of us had to endure. He had lost some weight and gained a boatload of self-confidence. We dressed in the best clothes we had and proceeded to the Fire College classroom for our 'graduation.'

The Fire Marshall came to the ceremony to congratulate us. He spoke briefly about the importance of professional training to assure that we fought fires and rescued the public without hurting ourselves in the process. Another State Fire Marshall official stood and spoke to our discipline and bravery. It was good to hear someone verbalize that firefighting was more than brute strength. Firefighters had to be calm under pressure. Surely, this Fire College training had been designed to test our self-control, critical thinking, and willingness to act in a manner that wouldn't get us killed. He warned us that 'playing the hero' tends to get firefighters hurt.

We were beginning to get antsy. We were eager to get home to our loved ones. The Fire Marshall returned to the podium. *Will this ceremony never end?* He explained how each cohort at the Fire College showcased recruits from across the State of Florida. At the end of each training, it turns out, the field instructors evaluated each recruit's performance. Throughout the weeks, they had been taking notes on our strengths and weaknesses. We were also graded on our academic performance in the classroom activities.

"This year's number one, all-around recruit, finishing in First Place, is Kevin Mallinson from Key West!"

I was dumbstruck! There was no wooden plaque or certificate, but the whooping and hollering of the recruits and instructors was more than enough for me. The Fire Marshall came over and shook my hand and assured me that my Chief would receive a formal letter noting my outstanding performance. *Now, let those guys back home chew on this!* Although two Key Westers had to return home a month ago, I was coming back feeling very proud of my achievements. I was also pleased that Fito had passed the training program and secured his position in the KWFD. Sarge came up to congratulate me. I could see the pride in his eyes. I thanked him for being such a mean, loud-mouthed 'hard-ass' because it made me work harder.

"You know, some guys have to work twice as hard just to be accepted," he said. I knew exactly what he meant. I knew that I had worked to exceed the expectations of our instructors. As a gay man, I always felt that I had to overachieve just to be perceived as *just as good* as a straight guy. He assured me that I had earned my first place standing.

Some of the men who lived relatively close to Ocala, like Pete, left for home immediately after the ceremony. I would be leaving the next morning for the 8-hour return to Key West. At dinner that last evening, it struck me as curious that not one of these guys had asked me directly if I was gay. These guys knew I was from Key West, a city known to have a large gay community, and that I was building a house with another man. They also knew that I planned to live in the house with Joe. Still, not one of them delved any deeper with their questions. Perhaps, they didn't want to know. Perhaps, they decided it wasn't important. Sadly, I would never see any of them again.

See these photos in color and more at: https://alarminthefirehouse.com

or

https://www.facebook.com/AlarmintheFirehouse/

Barbara Deming in her garden

Kevin (1982)

OWLS speakers panel: me, Phoebe, Joe, and Greg (not pictured Carmen)

Kevin at 'controlled burn' on Stock Island
[photo: State Archives of Florida]

Capt. George 'Viti' Vidal, Engineer Al Rahming, and Kevin

Maternal Grandparents: James Smith and Mary Morris Smith

(L to R) Pete, Kevin, and another recruit at Fire College 1982

Fire Station 1 after painting and landscaping (1983)

Fire truck for Wesley House playground

AIDS Quilt panel for Bill Burroughs

Newspaper clipping October 18, 1985

Heat put on gay fireman

Friday, October 18, 1985
Page 6

Oh, no! Not a vegetarian! It may have been almost difficult for the boys at the Key West Fire Station to accept that he was vegetarian as it was that Mallison, had one of the first openly gay firefighters in the country, joked Kevin Mallison with his typical good humor.

Mallison said a sense of humor is what got him through his nearly four years on the Key West Fire Department, while his fellow workers tried to get him to leave the job.

"I was too strong, I had too good a sense of humor," Mallison said.

With his curly hair showing giants of red and matching eyes of sienna, Mallison sometimes has an almost "impish" look about him, while at the same time being able to become quite serious.

Mallison said he wanted to be a fireman since he was "a little kid."

Mallison explained that his grandfather and his grandmother had been fire chiefs in England. He said that his grandfather had been fire chief of an English town and when in World War II all of the men in the town went to war, his grandmother took over his grandfather's position as fire chief.

"I've seen a picture of both, together, in fire department uniform," Mallison said. He said that when he told his parents he

had decided to become a firefighter his mother was "real excited," and his father "thought it was a good idea."

Mallison said that being a fireman was a "fantasy" for him, ever since he was young, like the fantasies of hundreds of boys. The difference is Mallison is gay, and not the type to "hide in the closet," he said. And to top it off, he was applying for a job at the southernmost point of the United States, in a department filled with "locals."

"It's a close knit group where many are related to each other either by family or marriage and it's almost as if you're going into a family there," Mallison said. However Mallison's entry into the department met with more than the usual family bickering.

"The first six months was real hell. They really wanted to humiliate me," Mallison said.

He explained that his "toughness" was tested by comments made by some of the other firefighters, when he would enter the room, such as "I think they should take all the faggots and shoot them...stuff like that."

"They would tell 'faggot jokes' in front of me," Mallison said. He dealt with the humor, Mallison said, by kind of throwing it back at them. He laughed and said that, he did, however, make a formal

request to have certain attempts at humiliation come to an end, and that was when someone began hanging articles about AIDS on the bulletin board everyday. "Some of them would have real derogatory remarks made about gay men dying of AIDS," he said.

"Most of time I could avoid it, but the more people that got sick, the harder it got," he says.

"Finally I made a formal request and it be brought to an end. The Chief, Assistant Chief, Fire Marshall and Captains have always been super. "I think he did his job very well. I found him to be...a very

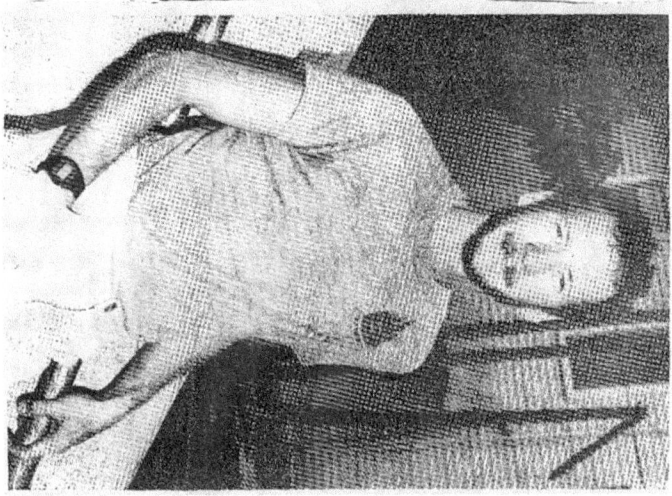

El Siboney Inn fire August 1985 [photo: State Archives of Florida]

El Siboney Inn fire August 1985 [photo: State Archives of Florida]

CHAPTER 12: Two Different Worlds

It felt so good to get back home. After the trials and tribulations of Fire College, it was comforting to be safe in the arms of the man I loved. I had lost nearly 10 pounds and was in the best physical shape of my life. Joe had made significant progress with our house. We resumed an aggressive schedule for framing out the house, despite the inclement weather. April was even hotter and more humid in the Keys than it had been in Central Florida. Luckily, our lot included 60 feet of waterfront on the canal. So, after working hard each day, we would jump into the water to cool off. Occasionally, we would see my fellow firefighter out in his yard, but he rarely engaged in conversation with me.

In the spring of 1982, Key West and the Florida Keys had been in a tug-of-war with the U.S. Border Patrol after an immigration roadblock had been established in the Upper Keys. In a tongue-in-cheek publicity stunt, Key West 'seceded' from the United States, declared itself the *Conch Republic* (hereby, a sovereign state), and applied for $1 billion in foreign aid! The antics, spearheaded by Mayor Dennis Wardlow, brought national attention to the effect of the border policies on tourism in the Keys. The tomfoolery spread quickly, and everyone seemed to be enjoying the widespread silliness and frivolity.

No one could have guessed that the establishment of the Conch Republic would allow for a degree of solidarity between the Conchs and the gay business leaders. Of the handful of gay individuals that contributed to the success of the marketing ploy was Dennis Bitner, a good friend of mine who was the owner/manager of the Club Key West on Truman Avenue. Dennis was one of the gay business owners who could envision a day when the locals and newcomers, even gay newcomers, would be living together peacefully on the island. Ironically, while the mayor was collaborating with my gay friend on the tourism prank, his two firefighter brothers – Billy and Dickie –were determined to have me fired from the fire department.

As hoped, the Conch Republic 'uprising' brought unprecedented notoriety to the Keys; there was an immediate boost in tourism and businesses prospered. Eventually, the official Fire Department badge we sported on our uniform shirts was redesigned to integrate a conch shell, an image of the Florida Keys, and embroidered with 'Conch Republic.'

Back at Fire Station 1, not much had changed. Although Chief Gates congratulated me for my first-place performance in Ocala, it was never publicly mentioned to the firemen nor acknowledged on the radio or in the newspaper. The letter from the State Fire Marshall was never added into my personnel record. The only thing that Capt. Stephenson and the others on my shift knew is that Fito and I had passed the training. It wasn't long before we fell back into our banal routine. The taunting continued where it had left off. The social ostracism kept me out of even the most casual conversations. Surely, I didn't feel like this was the 'team' I could count on when fighting fires.

For the month and half at Fire College, we wore our turnout gear daily. Despite attempts to have it cleaned, my jacket and pants always reeked of smoke. In fact, Joe mentioned that I still smelled like smoke even after a shower! There were some fires that required a closer attack pattern that, invariably, coated our hair with soot and permeated our gear with a lingering stench of burned residue. Whenever I came home after a fire, Joe enjoyed reminding me that the reality of living with a gay firefighter surely didn't match up with his fantasies!

Still, I was enjoying the profession. *Sure, I admit that sliding down the fire pole was exciting.* Jumping out of bed and sliding down the pole got the adrenaline pumping. The uncertainty about what we would find at a fire scene was one of the elements of the job that I enjoyed. The sudden "up and running" action, though, was in stark contrast to the usual sedentary routine of our firehouse. Most of the time, we responded to one or two calls per day. Between fires, and on days with no fire calls, the guys usually sat and watched television. They often watched baseball. By tradition, it seems, each firehouse claims a team for whom to root. For some unknown reason our firehouse had adopted the Chicago Cubs as our team. Watching those games was one of the few experiences I could share with the guys without being socially shut out. Though I lacked knowledge of the finer points of the game, the players, or the statistics when I joined the department, I quickly adapted. It wasn't long before I could yell about a home run as passionately as any of the others.

I suspected that none of the firemen had attempted to maintain the grass around the firehouse while I was at Fire College. Even if our building was a concrete, utilitarian, municipal structure with nondescript architecture, the guys could have maintained the lawn. Some were adamant that the city was responsible for maintenance and that firefighters shouldn't take on new duties. I had heard that the City of Key West had hired a landscaper in the Public Works department. After some searching, I contacted Kathy Wolf and asked her to come by the firehouse to work on a plan to improve the surrounds.

Kathy brought a survey map showing the placement of the building and borders of the property. She also had blueprints for the building. Kathy rolled out the plans on the dining table while I made some coffee for us. She asked me what my overall plan was for the land.

"Ha!" I burst out with a grin. "I have no plan yet." But I was just thinking to myself *Now, how would a gay boy do this*? We laughed. I added, "I love plants, but I'm not a landscape architect." It turned out that Kathy and I worked well together. She had a penchant for planting varieties of bushes and trees native to the Keys which would require no fertilizer and minimal watering. I was in total agreement. I wanted to recommend to Chief Gates that we paint the building, so Kathy and I kept that in mind when deciding on the plantings. Two of the firefighters, Raymond and Louis, were huddled in the TV room, about 12 feet away from Kathy. They were talking in low voices, so I thought they were just making their usual unsavory comments about females. I ignored their behavior and after giving Kathy her coffee, we proceeded to discuss how she could produce a rendering which showed options for painting and landscaping. I was optimistic that if the chief and other stakeholders could agree on changes, we would have small projects that the firemen could work on during the periods between fire calls.

After about twenty minutes, Capt. Stephenson pulled me aside and told me to wrap things up and escort Kathy out of the building. I was taken aback and a little perturbed at his demand! I reminded him that the chief had already given permission for me and Kathy to conduct these initial meetings. Then, he explained my impropriety.

"We cannot have a woman in the firehouse. It is forbidden," he said. "You need to get her out of here before anyone finds out."

"She is a city employee," I said. I was advocating for common sense. "What's wrong with her being here to work on a city project?"

Undeterred, he insisted that Kathy leave the building. When she and I got back to her vehicle, I apologized for the absurdity of the policy, and we planned to meet at a later date. I came to learn that there had been a history of Key West firefighters bringing women into the sleeping areas for sexual activities. It was one of the blemishes on their professional reputation that had resulted in the administration's ban on females in the firehouse. The irony was that I was the gay guy! Honestly, of all the firefighters, who was least likely to misbehave with a woman?

Over the next few months, we completed our plans. My fire station was not located in Old Town and, therefore, did not have to align with the Victorian architectural style that makes Key West so unique. Rather, it was a contemporary building whose modern design could be emphasized rather than denied. My first project was to paint the exterior block walls an off-white base color. Then, using the horizontal mortar lines between the blocks as guides, I painted a chocolate brown stripe around the firehouse, starting at about 10 feet above the ground. Then, the stripe assumed variable heights to highlight the stratified levels in the building's multi-level design. Immediately underneath the brown stripe was a secondary stripe in an ecru shade. The city provided us with the paint and necessary supplies. Per our request, the Department of Public Works sent a painter to design and paint the 'Fire Station 1' lettering above the truck bay opening.

Once the building was painted, we began the foundation plantings. We planted larger scaevola and silver buttonwood shrubs near the walls.

Then, we planted smaller and more colorful dracaena, aralia, and firecracker plants in front to add a layer of interest. Finally, we planted two gumbo limbo trees and several coconut palms that would, eventually, add the significant height necessary to complement the modern design of the firehouse.

Initially, my fellow firefighters scoffed at the improvement project. They complained that it was the City's job to complete the work on the firehouse and maintain the yard. They were resistant to doing work that they felt should not be their responsibility. I countered by suggesting that when we take pride in our firehouse property, we demonstrate that we are good citizens, and this type of activity might improve the department's reputation in the eyes of the public. If we grabbed the public's attention in a positive way, there might be pressure on the city administration to improve our fire equipment, provide additional personnel, and raise our salaries. Though my appeal fell on deaf ears much of the time, there were several firefighters from different shifts who began to assist with the landscaping. One would mow the grass while others raked the yard. Even more assistance came when we decided to add a nautical touch by digging holes and 'planting' wood pilings bound with thick, hemp rope. We left an opening in the roping so that one could easily walk to the flagpole for the traditional raising and lowering ritual each day. Finally, I used 4x4 wood posts and cross boards to create a sign for the station. One of the firefighters used his router to permanently carve the letters into the wood. Once the sign was painted, the improvements were complete. I was beginning to think that I had made some inroads into becoming a member of this firehouse 'fraternity.'

Over the month with Kathy, I learned of struggles she was experiencing as a female 'outsider' (non-Conch) working in the Public Works department for the City of Key West. When she offered recommendations or made requests for support, she was frequently ignored. She found that the nepotism in hiring led to ineffective workers who were ill-equipped to do the jobs for which they were hired. She found that the 'Bubba system' allowed many to have a virtual 'job for life.' Relatives and close friends were unlikely to ever be fired for laziness or inappropriate behavior. As with me in the KWFD, Kathy struggled to work with ineffectual city employees.

Kathy was also a trailblazer in 1980s Key West. Her motivation to improve the island's environment aligned well with her social consciousness. She had principles to which she adhered. A teenager had been ordered by a judge to complete 100 hours of community service; Kathy was to supervise him. She learned that he was the son of a city official. The guy had been arrested for a gay-bashing incident that left the victim badly injured. The young man had been arrested and admonished by the judge, but he expressed no remorse for his violent attack. He thought he was justified in his attack on the 'faggot.' After hearing the guy's incorrigible attitudes, Kathy requested that he be reassigned to someone else for the remainder of his community service. Over time, Kathy and her husband became good friends of mine, and I was glad to have their support for my position in the KWFD.

The Fire service is a 'fraternal' profession; you can go almost anywhere and visit a firehouse and get at least a cup of coffee, if not a meal. *You are one of us, you are welcome.* One day, a firefighter from Chicago drove up to our station. After a brief tour of our truck bay, we offered him coffee. Four of us sat down with him at the dining room table to discuss our equipment, challenges, and notable fires. Finally, one of the firemen asked him "So, how do you like Key West?" The guy mentioned Key West's beautiful architecture and fascinating history.

"Gee, though," he said, "you seem to have a lot of faggots here."

My fellow firemen froze. They knew that I was going to have a retort to that derogatory comment. I was sure they were terrified that I might 'come out' to this visitor and 'embarrass' them all. I leaned forward and put the palms of my hands on the table to emphasize my point. I leaned as I responded. *Keep to the issues, Kevin.*

"You know what?" I said. "We have a pretty good relationship with the gay community in this town. They provide a lot of financial support, and they advocate for us before the City Commission so we can get better equipment."

The visitor looked somewhat surprised but was quick to apologize. "Oh no, sorry," he said, "I can understand it's important to have the community behind you."

"Hey, let's go downstairs," Oscar said quickly. *I was sure Oscar was trying to get the visitor out of my presence before I said anything more!*

My KWFD work schedule was quite flexible. I decided to volunteer for the 24-hour crisis line service in Key West. The HELPLINE organization was underfunded and depended upon volunteers to provide crisis referral and basic counseling. The volunteer training sessions included skills-building in therapeutic communication, active listening, and empathy. I familiarized myself with the long list of referral resources available to individuals and families in the Lower Florida Keys and Key West. I could never have guessed how much I would learn by listening to anonymous callers in crisis. I learned so much about the lives – and the secrets – of the people in my community. People were in crisis because of drug and alcohol addictions, unstable relationships, sexual activity, interpersonal violence, and financial struggles, to mention a few. The calls not only revealed incredible strengths in women, but the many frailties of men. My many hours answering crisis calls opened my eyes to how much stress, loneliness, and interpersonal violence people in our community lived with on a daily basis. I was left feeling grateful for the many good things I had in my life!

In some ways, I was living in two very different worlds. In the firehouse, I was frequently on edge, careful not to say anything that would set off the homophobes. I was careful not to discuss politics in their presence. In the most casual of conversations, much of my private life was off-limits for fear of being subjected to hateful rhetoric, giving them fodder for further taunting. The firemen who harassed me seemed to think that my entire existence centered around being gay. They were, apparently, unable to see me as just another man finding his way in life.

Once I was off duty, I was a normal person again! I was free to resume the activities that made me complete. I was spending considerable time volunteering as the Race Director for the Southernmost Runners Club. The club would hold events throughout the year, raising funds for various charity organizations. It was great to see so many different sectors of our community come out to participate in our events. The road-running events attracted runners from far and wide, so we had a lot of planning to do. We worked year-round to obtain commercial funding and distribute ads to attract nationally known athletes. Our largest annual event – the *Last Resort Marathon* – usually began with a 1-mile Fun Run for the kids, followed by a 10K run for the casual runner. Simultaneously, we offered the more fit and adventurous runners either a half marathon (13.1 miles) or the full marathon distance of 26.2 miles. The marathon course was meticulously laid out and measured so that a runner could use the course to qualify for more prestigious events such as the Boston Marathon. After expenses were paid, the remainder of our profits from the entry fees were donated to local non-profit groups. Over the years, we supported high school sports leagues, programs for developmentally challenged kids, and a shelter for abuse victims. While engaging in these activities, I didn't have to think about being gay; it didn't matter. It should not have mattered in the KWFD either, but the men kept making a point of my sexual orientation. They wanted to reiterate that I didn't deserve to have a position in the department.

One day in the firehouse, I mentioned that Joe and I had gone fishing with my friend Jan and her boyfriend, Richard. For a couple of the firemen, it seemed beyond their comprehension that a straight couple would spend a day on a boat socializing with a gay couple. There were times when their preconceptions were so ridiculous that they didn't deserve a response. Their stereotypes of gay men constrained their ability to see us as well-rounded human beings. They couldn't seem to grasp the idea that gay men enjoyed scuba diving, catching lobsters, or spearfishing for hogfish snapper. *It would blow their mind to know that some of my friends were sports fanatics!* It was sad that they couldn't imagine gay men engaging in such 'normal' behaviors, least of all socializing with heterosexuals.

Many Conch women were responding differently to me than Conch men. My community activities allowed me the opportunity to collaborate with local women on issues they found important. We honed the crisis line services to better meet the needs of Spanish-speaking residents. There was long-term planning for reducing substance abuse and domestic violence on the island. Some of the Conch women were related to the firemen who were trying to get me fired. Yet, I don't believe they cared one bit about my sexual orientation. They were focused on the issues at hand. I could only have hoped that some of their family discussions led to increased understanding and acceptance of gay and lesbian persons.

CHAPTER 13: GRID and AIDS

Joe and I had no idea that our world was about to fundamentally change. It was a hot summer day, and I was laying the metal roof panels for our house on Bay Point. On this type of stilt home, the roof was completed before the walls were built. We had stored the metal roofing on the main house level, about 10 feet above the ground. Joe would lift the panels, one at a time, up to me. I was another 10-15 feet up on the roof deck. The sub-roof had been laid, covered with roofing paper, and topped with furring boards onto which the metal panels would be laid. Once each panel was aligned properly, I would secure it in place. This was an exhausting process, but an exciting next step towards an eventual move into our new home.

We were listening to the radio while working. At one point, a newscaster was describing a new disease – a 'gay cancer' – that had been diagnosed among men in New York City and San Francisco. *That's ridiculous! There is no such thing as a 'gay' cancer.* Apparently, half of those diagnosed with this new disease had already died. Most, though not all, of the men were characterized as having been previously healthy, young homosexuals.

"Luckily, we don't live in New York or San Francisco," I said to Joe. There wasn't the slightest inkling that this new disease would be a problem for us in Florida. At the time, I thought this 'news' to be nothing more than anti-gay propaganda. Then, over the following months, newspaper reporters and television anchors would refer to the emerging health crisis as *Gay-Related Immune Deficiency* (GRID) or the 'gay plague.' It was so frustrating to hear the erroneous terms being thrown about and not being able to have a venue in which to expose the inherent homophobia behind their use. This was not a gay disease and labeling it as such only encouraged more stigma and discrimination against gay men. Finally, by the Fall of 1982, infectious disease experts coined the name *Acquired Immune Deficiency Syndrome* (and its acronym: AIDS) to properly describe the nature of the illness. Thankfully, this new name did not imply that only gay men were being affected.

Kip was the first person I knew to be diagnosed with this new terrifying disease. I heard that he had been diagnosed with a cancer of the blood vessels called Kaposi's sarcoma (KS). I was ignorant about the illness and dreaded the idea of going to see him. I was also not sure what to say to him. The diagnosis surely meant he was going to die. Kip was in his early 30s. Kip's partner, Dale, was also not feeling well. However, Dale seemed to have just diarrhea and not the AIDS-related KS or the *Pneumocystis carinii* pneumonia that confirmed an AIDS diagnosis. After three weeks of wrestling with my conscience, I finally decided to call Kip and schedule a visit.

The guys had a beautiful small Conch house with a lovely backyard of palms, ferns, and assorted flowering shrubs. Kip's mother met me at the door and brought me through the house to the back garden. Apparently, his parents had moved down from up North to provide care for him and Dale. Kip and I sat around a white wicker table outside in the garden; the sunlight was streaming down through the palm fronds. This is paradise.

Never in my life had I been so scared to be near someone. I read that the disease was sexually transmitted and not likely through casual contact. The face and neck of this handsome young man were peppered with dark purple bruises. Some were raised and some were flat. Overall, his face was swollen and pale. Apparently, the lesions were interfering with his blood flow back to the heart, resulting in the edematous aftermath. The swelling only accentuated his sickly appearance. The only thing that put me at ease was that we were sitting a few feet apart from each other.

His mother served us breakfast. Kip was quite open, talking about his AIDS diagnosis. He was filled with optimism about surviving it. He laughed about how the lesions on his face and neck would keep him from pursuing a modeling career. While I laughed with him and acknowledged the unprecedented amount of fear and stigma around the illness, I felt myself to be a hypocrite. I was so scared of what I saw. Yet, on the other hand, I could see that his distorted external façade didn't alter Kip's personality. Despite his abhorrent appearance and fatal diagnosis, this was Kip. We talked about my struggles working in the Fire Department. He was interested in how city politics were changing as the result of the influx of gay men and lesbians. Kip helped me think more about how the stress on the Conch community led – directly or indirectly – to the homophobic actions of the firemen. He worried about how AIDS might, eventually, have an impact on the island community. To be honest, I couldn't imagine the devastation that was coming.

Then, it happened. I experienced something that would change the course of my life. Kip's mother came back out to the garden to gather our dishes. Holding them in her right hand, she put her left hand on her son's shoulder. *She is touching his shoulder?!*

"Do you boys want some more coffee?" she asked.

"Sure, Mom. That would be great," Kip answered.

His mother bent over, pulled her son close, and kissed him on the cheek! As she pulled away, she spoke to him, lovingly. "OK, honey. Just a few minutes."

I was flabbergasted. *Do his parents understand that Kip has AIDS? Isn't she afraid of dying?* But then, almost immediately, I realized that I had witnessed an incredible exemplar of a mother's unconditional love. For her, it wasn't a matter of potential infection. She needed to express her love for her son, especially now that his life was being seriously threatened. I began thinking that if his mother could hug and kiss him, I sure as heck shouldn't be afraid of touching him. After we finished our visit, I reached out my arms and gave Kip a bear hug. Astoundingly, I didn't experience the fear I thought would overwhelm me. To this day, I thank his mother for ridding me of my reticence to touch people living with HIV infection or AIDS.

Over the next few months, both Kip and Dale succumbed to the new disease. Their deaths shocked me. Grief was a new experience and I didn't know what to feel. I began to perceive AIDS as a potential threat to my health and well-being. It would be another year, though, before I dedicated myself to the fight against AIDS.

CHAPTER 14: Dangerous Times

I had been in the Fire Department for a year now. My partner, Joe, had transferred from an outdoor construction position with the cable TV company into a studio position. He was charged with developing a line of local programming to serve the needs of the community. Joe's experience with radio broadcasting prepared him well for this new endeavor. I was pleased that he found such a change in his career path challenging and exciting. Our house construction was moving along well, and we were looking forward to moving into our new home in a year or so.

Not much had changed since I returned from Fire College. The workplace harassment continued. Clearly, the emotionally dysfunctional men on my shift thrived on demeaning each other with wisecracks about each other's wives. They teased each other about their (alleged) sexual prowess, marriages, and manhood. The adolescent banter seemed to be mostly in good humor and not meant to be taken seriously. However, when I was harassed, it seemed much more personal. When I was the butt of their jokes, their attacks seemed intent upon offending me.

There were still days when I was shocked, and saddened, by the inane conversations that took place in the dining room. One day, two of the firemen began bickering about a recent trip to Miami – without their wives – during which they 'shared' a prostitute. Horrifying images came to my mind upon hearing this banter! However, it was like watching a B-grade movie with poor acting: you just cannot seem to turn away without finding out how it ends! I wanted to interject with a psychological debrief about what it might suggest that each of them watched the other have sex with this woman. *Yikes! That conversation would go south quickly!* Or, I could have convinced them that the purely sexual objectification of this woman for their personal pleasure was immoral and inhumane? *No, that kind of feminist critique wouldn't go over so well either!* I could also have educated them about any number of sexually transmitted infections they could have picked up in their encounter. *I don't think they would have believed me.* As they continued quibbling about monies paid for their hour of sexual service, I walked out. I was never ashamed of being gay, nor embarrassed by what I did in my sex life. However, I was not in the habit of letting other men know what I did with whom. It struck me as crude – and quite odd – that these firemen would share specific details of their sexual activities with each other.

There were times when the men tried to intrude into my personal life, aiming to cause me stress. I had a friend visiting from New York City. David was a tall, well-built ex-Marine. He was blond and handsome. He was vacationing for a week in Key West and, after settling into his guest house, drove over to the firehouse in a rented red convertible. David and I sat on the bench outside the firehouse, catching up on our lives and recent adventures. He was particularly interested in my experiences being openly gay in the firehouse. In his various military and paramilitary positions, he understood the need for straight men to protect their sense of masculinity and project an air of dominance. He couldn't imagine having been open about his sexuality over the course of his career.

After an hour or so, we decided to meet for breakfast at his guesthouse the next morning after my shift ended. I walked back upstairs to the TV room to face a barrage of questions from one of the guys.

"Who was that guy? Does Joe know about him?" he asked. The others seemed unusually interested as well.

"You mean David? A friend. Of course, Joe knows *about* him," I responded.

"You screwing this guy?" he continued, "I don't think Joe knows about this guy. Why don't I call Joe and tell him about your tall blond friend?" *It never ceased to amaze me how they spent time imagining what I did in bed and with whom!*

"Okay," I countered, "...go ahead and call Joe." I felt like I was back in high school with this adolescent banter. He seemed like a dog with a bone, continuing to provoke me. He was trying to make me panic that Joe might find out about David. They understood so little and assumed too much about my relationship with Joe. I admit that the taunting was starting to irritate me. I reached over to the wall phone and quickly dialed the number for the TV studio. His assistant answered.

"Hey, can you put Joe on the phone?" I asked. I could see the shocked expression on the fireman's face. The other guys were whooping it up as I escalated the dare. "Hey Joe," I said, "there's a fireman here with a question for you..." I handed the handset to the fireman. He clearly wasn't expecting that. He didn't put the receiver up to his ear. He panicked.

"Oh, shit!" he stammered. He slammed the handset back onto the wall. "Can't you take a fuckin' joke?" By this time, the two other guys were jabbing the fireman in his ribs, teasing him about looking so foolish. I turned and walked away.

Later, Joe told me that he regretted not having the opportunity to concoct a fantastical story to play with the fireman's imagination. Joe's nature was always to 'fight fire with fire.' Though I admit that I fantasized getting revenge in such ways, it wasn't my approach. Luckily, Joe didn't act on his simmering anger towards these fools.

Only once did the guys suggest that they might harass Joe at work (or *hurt* him). The threat seemed real enough. So, I went to Chief Gates and made it clear that my partner was off-limits! I told him that there was a point at which the Fire Department needs to be accountable for the conduct of its employees. I assured the chief that I would get a lawyer and sue the City of Key West if anything happened to Joe. That small bit of advocacy seemed to have squelched any additional threats towards my partner.

There was a significant difference between the firemen trying to disrupt my relationship and them trying to get me killed. Over those first months in the department, I adjusted to the childish verbal taunts and acts to isolate me from the team. Occasionally, one of the men would make a side comment about me not being right for the job; they would allude to me having to leave the department because of being hurt at a fire scene. Those comments were intended to intimidate me. A central tenet of working in the Fire Service is that you look out for one another. You are 'brothers' on the same team and should 'have each other's back' to be sure everyone gets out of a fire safely. One of my mistakes was not sensing that their comments were indicative of actual threats to my safety.

Soon, though, it became obvious that some of the firemen were trying to put me in danger at a fire. The first incident arose when we responded to a house fire on Johnson's Lane, a narrow street near the city cemetery. As the lead firefighter, I was taking the nozzle into the front door of a house engulfed in flames. The flames were incredibly hot, and the house was full of smoke. In those situations, it is possible for a roof rafter to fall on you or for the floor to give way under your weight. At first, two of my fellow firemen were immediately behind me, helping to advance the hose. Unbeknownst to me, the two firemen soon began backing out of the structure, leaving me on my own. A captain from Station 3 had arrived with his company to fight the blaze. While his men were hooking up their hoses, he quickly scanned the fire scene and noticed the men retreating.

"Who is leading in there?" the captain asked the two firemen. He was concerned that they had abandoned one of their colleagues who was advancing into a burning structure.

"Kevin," one of the guys responded. Reportedly, the captain was furious at his flippant attitude. He yelled at them to get back to their post and provide me with back-up support. The captain was so outraged by the unprofessional behaviors of the firemen that he reported the incident to my captain and Chief Gates. Apparently, he said "Gay or not, Kevin should not be put in danger." It was weeks before I knew all the details of the Johnson Lane incident. However, neither Capt. Stephenson nor Chief Gates ever spoke with me about it. I withheld the story from my partner, Joe, because I didn't want him to worry about my safety. I thought the actions of these two firemen to be a fluke and unlikely to happen again. That, it turned out, was a mistake.

In retrospect, I should have officially reported and documented these types of incidents. At the time, I felt that if I reported everything that happened, I would not be believed. I also felt that I would be blamed for 'creating' the problem by simply being homosexual. Finally, I didn't want my fire department personnel file to contain so many incidents that I appeared to be whining about every little transgression I suffered. I was willing to risk my life to fight fires in our community, but surely did not want to have my life purposely put in danger by homophobic coworkers.

On August 4, 1982, four months after graduating from Fire College, both Fito and I were officially promoted from Recruit 11-1 to Firefighter 13-1. In addition to a slight raise in pay, it solidified my standing in the KWFD. It was clear to everyone now that I wasn't planning on going anywhere. I didn't have much opportunity to work with Fito as he was stationed in another firehouse. But one day, our company was driving around testing fire hydrants when we stopped to visit Fire Station 3 on Grinnell Street. While the captains were chatting in the kitchen, the rest of us were hanging around the bay doors just 'shooting the breeze.' Most of the discussions seemed to focus on municipal politics. A hot topic was Richard Heyman's campaign to become the city's mayor. The prevailing belief was that electing a gay mayor would lead to the destruction of their cherished Key West and, apparently, the demise of Western civilization as we knew it. At one point, Henry Delvalle, made a nasty comment about *faggots* and motioned towards me.

"And what do you think, punk?" he asked. Yet another slur to refer to my sexual orientation. Fito shifted his body towards Henry quickly. He was clearly pissed off.

"Don't you say a damned thing about Kevin. I would never have made it through Fire College if it hadn't been for him!" he said. It was out of character for Fito to be so confrontational. I think it took us all by surprise. *Wow! Fito stands up for me!* I appreciated his support, but there was more to his story than just my motivating, mentoring, and pushing him through the training.

"Fito, you earned that certification," I said, "You worked hard for it."

Amazingly, Henry shut down. He glanced away, as if not to care, but I think he was honestly impacted by Fito's heartfelt support of me. It seemed to take the wind out of Henry's sails. It felt so good to have one of the firemen stand up for me like that. *Thanks, Fito, for speaking your truth*

CHAPTER 15: Captain Vidal

It was rare, but not unheard of, for a captain to be temporarily placed at a station to replace one who was sick or taking vacation time. I was surprised to arrive at the firehouse one day and find that Captain George "Viti" Vidal was in charge. I had encountered the captain several times over my first year in the department. I estimated him to be in his mid-50s or so. The only thing I had heard from the other men was that Viti had been a professional baseball player in his younger years. He always seemed to be in a good mood, jovial; he was known for telling hilarious stories. He was also strong. Upon meeting, he shook my hand with such conviction that I knew he was being forthright and welcoming. Within minutes, he had me laughing. He seemed to be dedicated to professional firefighting and expected the best of the men under his command.

On that day, we went out to practice fire 'hydrant landings.' Once he found a hydrant at which to practice, the engineer (driver) had to position the truck close to the hydrant. A rear-end man would retrieve the hydrant wrench and remove the large cap; the threads on this part of the hydrant were identical to those on the hose coupling. Then, the rear-end men could remove the heavy, hard suction hose, connect it to the truck, and direct the driver to maneuver the truck so that the hose would line up exactly at the opening of the hydrant. Once connected, the hydrant valve would be opened to provide water to the truck's pump. I had learned that practice is crucial if you are expected to do this in the middle of a crisis – or the middle of the night – and lives were depending upon your speed and accuracy for the timely delivery of water.

It was clear that Oneri and Louie were not interested in practicing that day. I could see Louie roll his eyes (in clear disrespect) when the captain told us to get ready for some drills. Yes, it was a hot, humid day. This was Key West. Did we expect to practice only during moderate temperatures? It seemed like a toss-up as to who was performing worse: Oneri or Louie? During the practice runs, Viti was loud, direct, and certainly 'in charge.' At one point, he turned to me to explain what was – or was not – going well with the exercise. Then he laughed and exclaimed loudly (so the others would hear him) "Oh, what am I telling you for? You completed Fire College!" He was implying that my serious approach to our practice session was more professional than the others. Viti seemed to be proud of my accomplishments in the department. When we got back to the firehouse, I made Cuban coffee for everyone. Viti took a sip and smiled.

"Not bad at all, Kevin," he said. Then, he pulled me aside. "I would take you over any of these fuck-ups!" he added. I knew then that this was the beginning of a wonderful friendship.

The second day that Viti was substituting for our captain, we started the morning with a practice session on the snorkel truck the city had purchased for the department. This specialized fire truck has an articulating boom that raises an aerial platform high above a fire scene. Water is pumped up through a pipe on the boom to a nozzle securely attached to the platform. The firefighters in the elevated 'basket' can direct a water stream over great distances without becoming fatigued. Capt. Vidal made sure that each of us had an opportunity to climb into the basket and operate the controls to raise, maneuver, and lower the boom safely. It was great having a captain who truly enjoyed his job and took the responsibility to teach his team firefighting skills.

After a break for coffee, the captain told us to prepare for a drive around the neighborhood. Oscar walked downstairs and started up the engine of the fire truck. I grabbed my turnout gear and boots and was waiting by the rear of the pumper. Viti walked up to me and paused for a moment.

"How much experience do you have driving?" Viti asked.

ALARM IN THE FIREHOUSE

"Me?" I replied, as if it were a joke. "None."

As the engineer position – also called the drive or Lieutenant – was a higher rank than the rear-end man, there was never an opportunity for me to drive the truck. Once or twice, I received some informal training from Alex or Alan about running the pumps at a fire scene. The apparatus was relatively complex and, clearly, there was no way that I could effectively operate the delivery of water to the fire hoses without more experience. What was important to me at the time was that these professional firefighters thought it worth their time and effort to prepare for me to assume the job of engineer someday.

Viti smiled widely and, with a good-natured laugh, offered "Well, it's about time you did!" He told me to grab my turnout gear and throw it up into the cab. The look on Oscar's face was priceless when the captain informed him that I would be driving the truck and he should ride as a rear-end man! There was considerable hemming and hawing, but eventually Oscar vacated his usual position and moved to the back. Though a little overwhelmed with excitement about driving this massive truck through the streets of Key West, I also wanted to be sure I wouldn't screw up. I quickly scanned the dashboard to familiarize myself with the dials, knobs, and buttons.

"Where to, Captain?" I asked. He seemed to arbitrarily point out a direction.

Once out onto Flagler Avenue, I began to feel comfortable managing the massive fire truck. The street had two lanes in each direction, separated by a grass divider. We headed east, away from downtown. Following Viti's directions, I took a right turn onto S. Roosevelt Boulevard. Also known as Route A1A, the road circumscribed the southeast corner of the island. *Look at me!* I was driving a fire truck along the edge of the Atlantic Ocean! It was a thrill to have this opportunity! It was a bright, sunny day and the clear water was glistening.

"It's so nice out, Captain," I said.

"Then, keep it out. Doesn't bother me!" He quickly responded. He then burst out laughing. I couldn't help but laugh at his sexual innuendo. He must have sensed that I was feeling tense in this initial opportunity to drive the truck.

"Now, doesn't that feel better?" he asked. "You're doing a good job."

After a mile or so, we started taking the turn back in toward the center of the island. At the first left, we turned onto Atlantic Boulevard. I pointed out to Viti the CBS (concrete, block, and stucco) apartment buildings on the corner.

"That's where we first lived when I came to Key West," I explained. Somehow, I wanted him to know something more personal about me.

"And now you are living on Bay Point?" he inquired.

"Yeah. We're building a house on a canal-front lot we bought a couple of years ago," I added. I was enjoying this exchange.

"Who is your contractor?" he probed. It was such a new experience to have an officer that seemed interested in conversing with me.

"Oh, no contractor. Joe and I are building the house ourselves," I answered. Then I explained that when our plumbing passes inspection, we would obtain our Certificate of Occupancy and be able to live in the house. I described how we purchased antique wooden Bahamian louvers to install in the kitchen and dining areas. On the opposite side of the house, we inserted sliding glass doors in both the living room and bedroom to catch the view over the water and the stunning sunsets. Our home was beginning to take shape. Although our Airstream trailer served us well, it was a cramped space for two men.

We halted our conversation briefly as I needed to slow the truck and carefully maneuver around a large van on the shoulder. Rather than talk, I tried to 'feel' the movement of the massive fire truck, sensing how it responded to turns of the steering wheel. Still watching my driving, the captain picked up the handset of the radio and called to someone in Spanish. After a brief conversation, he put the microphone back in its saddle. We crossed over White Street and past the West Martello Tower, a historic military outlook from the early 1800s situated at Higgs Beach.

"You ever been in there?" the captain asked.

"Sure," I responded, "the history is fascinating, and the gardens are just incredible."

Higgs Beach was a popular spot for tourists as it was a perfect spot for swimming and snorkeling. Its sand had been brought in by truck to create a beach on an island made of coral rock. Key West had little to no natural sand on its shores. Families would find a place to settle in with their blankets and umbrellas so that their children could safely play in the shallow waters. Next to the parking lot was the obligatory snack shack. However, the outstanding feature was a wooden walking pier that extended about 500 feet or so into the Atlantic.

The Higgs Beach pier was the 'gay beach' in 1982. Approximately seven feet wide, it had enough space for sunbathers to lie on the right side while leaving enough room for people to walk out to the end and back on the left side. There were two wooden staircases descending into the clear waters, making it easy to take a dip when the sun was too hot. By the early afternoon in tourist season, the pier would be covered with people enjoying the weather. The vast majority of those on the pier would be gay men and their friends. As we drove by the beach, it was clear that tourists had already begun to stake out their place on the beach. Even the pier sported a dozen or so sunbathers. Viti pointed at the pier.

"Oh look. The *dick-dock* is filling up this early in the morning!" he said.

"Captain!?" I reacted as if surprised that he would know that nickname for the pier. Oh course, he lived on this island and would know the reputation of the gay landmark.

"Would you prefer *queer-pier*?" he quipped. He burst out laughing and I joined in on the fun.

"No, captain," I offered, "dick-dock will be fine."

The captain was showing me that my sexual orientation was not threatening to him. He wanted me to know that we could laugh about such things. It felt wonderful to have someone at his level in the department that I felt I could trust. But, oh, Viti's fun was not over yet. After a few turns, we were on Grinnell Street heading towards Fire Station 3.

We pulled up in front of the open bay doors of the firehouse. This was the oldest of the three firehouses, circa 1907. Built to house the wagons that would have been pulled by horses, the garage openings were barely wide enough for the modern fire trucks. Despite its age and lack of regular maintenance, this firehouse reminded me of our profession's history. Throughout the building were vestiges of its many iterations.

Remnants of call bell systems harkened to days when there were no telephones for dispatching fire trucks to specific areas of the city. The old floorboards reeked of the soot that had fallen off the boots of generations of firefighters.

Viti jumped out of the cab of our truck and bounced across the street to greet his counterpart, Capt. Charlow. Climbing down, I caught a quick glance of two firefighters – Alan Vidal and Henry Delvalle – coming out of the truck bay with expressions of surprise? Shock? Disbelief? I knew instantly that my temporary position as driver had been unexpected. Without acknowledging my presence, Henry began to goad Oscar for his 'demotion' to rear-end man. He wanted to humiliate Oscar. It was apparent that his teasing was having the desired effect. I was thinking to myself *"Is this what Viti had wanted? Was he purposely embarrassing Oscar and Louie by having me drive the truck over to visit colleagues at Fire Station 3?"*

I was ignored by the other firemen. After a few minutes of being socially ostracized from the conversations, I started roaming around the truck bay, examining this station's fire trucks. Alan Vidal approached me and started talking about the specifications of the water pumps. He congratulated me for completing the Fire College training program. He continued with some history of Fire Station 3 and noted that his family had a long history of service in the KWFD. It turns out, Viti was his uncle. During this engaging conversation with Alan, I felt almost welcome as a fellow firefighter. I wasn't sure of his motivations for speaking with me, but I had a sense that I could trust him. He was so much more professional than the men I had on my watch.

On the way back to Fire Station 1, Viti explained that I would need to relinquish the driver role back to Oscar once we arrived. With my lack of experience, assuming the responsibility for all the tasks expected of an engineer at an active fire scene would be foolish. Viti's actions that day did, however, break a barrier I had been facing. Up until then, there had been very little effort to orient me to the fire truck's water pumps. Eventually, I would be given opportunities to build my driving skills and learn the basics of the engineer's role.

CHAPTER 16: Life Saved, Lives Lost

The New Year started out well enough. In January, Al Rahming, Alex Vega, and Alan Vidal were all promoted to driver-engineer and Alex's father, Frank Vega, had been promoted to captain. Capt. Eddie Castro had now become the Assistant Chief of the department. My encounters with these men convinced me that they were more professional than the men I worked with on my shift. In my estimation, these promotions would contribute to a more effective department.

It never ceased to amaze me how lazy some of my fellow firemen could be. In 1983, the Key West firefighters were not responsible for running medical rescue calls; there was a separate, private ambulance service funded by the city. However, we were all trained as 'first responders' who could stabilize someone while waiting for the paramedics to arrive on the scene. Between the occasional calls to fire scenes, we had periods of relative nonactivity in the firehouse. I would usually pass my time reading or working on the landscaping. This day, though, we were sitting watching a baseball game on television. Suddenly, I heard our door slam open and a young kid yelling behind me. I jumped up and turned around to find a boy of 10, maybe 12. He was quite upset. I encouraged him to slow down and explain what was wrong. He said another kid had been injured in the football field next to the firehouse.

"How bad?" I asked.

"Real bad! He fell," he said.

I quickly turned to Jackie and asked him to dispatch an ambulance. The guys remained sitting on the couch. The captain was upstairs taking a nap. I didn't have time to think. I turned to the boy and motioned him to return to the field.

"Show me!" I said. As I rushed out, I heard Oscar yell after me.

"We don't run rescue. The City pays for rescue!" he said. *Oh my god, he is such an asshole!*

I followed the boy downstairs and around the side of the building. There was a high concrete wall between the football field and the firehouse property. The young boy somehow jumped up and climbed over. *There was no way I could jump over that wall.* Then, I was joined by a fellow firefighter. I think it was Jerry. He motioned me to the truck bay. We unhooked the ladder from the side of the truck and used it to scale the wall.

There was the boy, also about 10 years old, laying on the ground and surrounded by adults and kids. I made my way through and told Jerry to push everyone back. Someone was explaining to me that the boy was climbing on the goal post horizontal bar when he fell. The boy wasn't responding, he wasn't breathing. As quickly as I could, I squeezed his nostrils closed and attempted to give him two full breaths through his mouth. *That was not easy.* Then, I realized that the football outfit he was wearing was tight and constricting. I tore open his shirt and unraveled the string that crisscrossed down the front of his chest. Once released, I checked again for breathing and a pulse. After finding no breathing, I attempted another two breaths. Almost immediately, he vomited in my mouth. *Oh my god, this is a nightmare!* On a good day, hearing anyone vomit was enough to make me retch. I was struggling to keep my lunch down when I heard Jerry whisper in my ear.

"Don't throw up on him, Kevin. Throw up on the grass," he advised. *Thanks for the advice.* I really appreciated his support and his ability to keep the onlookers out of my way. I'm not sure how, but I was able to avoid vomiting. I had to start chest compressions and supplement with mouth-to-mouth ventilation until the ambulance arrived. I could only hope that it was enough. After I was assured that someone had contacted his parents, Jerry and I headed back to the firehouse. I let Jerry explain everything to the captain while I went upstairs to clean up. Unexpectedly, in the midst of my shower, I vomited. I guess I hadn't realized how much the experience had traumatized me. I never could forgive the firefighters for sitting there watching TV rather than respond to an emergency.

In the Spring of 1983, I had become so habituated to hearing the anti-gay slurs and homophobic insults that they ceased to catch my attention. Some conversations in the firehouse were so inane that I didn't need to listen. The guys bantered around absurd fantasies and conspiracy theories about gays taking over the island. Nearly every other word was 'fuck' or 'motherfucker.' At times, I think their vocabulary was so limited that they couldn't think of the appropriate words to clearly express themselves and curse words were simply used to fill-in where needed.

One morning, I arrived for my shift to find a makeshift 'scoreboard' posted in the dining area. It referred to the newspaper reports that 500 Americans had died of this new disease: AIDS.

AIDS	Faggots
500	0

I was overwhelmed with emotion. Up to this point, I had been managing the grief of losing several friends and acquaintances to AIDS. However, being confronted with this horrific display of homophobia suddenly brought it all to the surface. The disrespect for human life – the lack of compassion and outright display of hatred – was not only despicable, it was unprofessional. My initial sadness quickly turned to anger. I walked up to Capt. Stephenson to express my outrage. It was fine, I explained, if they wanted to tease me with their adolescent jeers. However, mocking the deaths of people is unbecoming and unacceptable.

"It's not like they are dying of *cancer*," the captain responded. I couldn't believe that came off his lips! He continued to defend the firemen's behavior by claiming that 'boys will be boys.' I reminded him that these 'boys' were approaching middle age and that he, as captain, was their superior officer. *I expected that he would demonstrate the leadership needed for a professional work environment.* I expected too much. I couldn't tell if the captain agreed with the antics of his men or if he was just unable – or unwilling – to demand some degree of professional behavior. I suspected it was a little of both.

I was having some difficulty managing my grief. When it came to my needs for emotional support, my partner was less than helpful. I was not able to deny – or suppress – my feelings and it was painful. The mounting deaths from AIDS made me fearful, surely, but also uncertain. There was no test for the HIV virus, so there was a constant dread for who might be next to be diagnosed. Much of my support came from Tom. He was a friend who lived in Old Town Key West. He had a strong affinity for Eastern philosophies, natural foods, and meditation. Tom's peaceful, calm demeanor provided me comfort; his willingness to listen to my concerns was crucial when the firemen were so cruel and inhumane. With Tom's support and love, I was able to find a peaceful, thoughtful space to debrief such encounters. Sometimes, the right person is there when you need him to be.

More than once, some of the firemen tried to get me hurt in the line of work. At a house fire one day, we were ordered to have one hose in the front door and the other into the attic space. The team from Station No. 2 was already setting up for the frontal assault. Two of us got our ladder from the truck and moved to the side of the house. We could see smoke seeping out of the rafters, but no open flame at the roofline yet. We set up a ladder on the side of the house to access the attic window. I climbed up the ladder first, holding the empty hose over my right shoulder. The firefighter behind me on the ladder handed up a pike pole so that I could safely break the glass out of the window. Immediately, thick brown smoke began pouring out. We motioned for the engineer to pump the water. As soon as the hose filled with water, it weighed more than one man could manage. I had learned in Fire College how to entwine your legs around the rungs of a ladder so that you wouldn't accidentally fall off, even if you were rendered unconscious.

The hose suddenly became heavy and the fireman below me was effectively carrying some of the weight. I slowly opened the hose and directed the stream in through the attic window. It was only a couple of minutes before I felt a huge gush of water hit me. If my leg had not been locked onto the ladder, I might have been knocked off balance and fallen nearly 15 feet to the ground. Looking over, I saw the guys on the other hose line laughing. Apparently, they thought it funny to aim their hose stream at me. They tried to knock me off that ladder! The expression on my face must have communicated how angry I was about their assault. *I will deal with this later*. Focusing on the task at hand, I was able to maintain my hose stream until the fire was under control.

Once on the ground, I didn't confront the firemen. I was sure that their captain had seen the offensive behavior. As we were packing up the truck to leave, one of guys not involved in the assault came up to me. He was stationed at the other firehouse, and I barely knew him. He muttered an apology.

"That just isn't right," he said.

"It was a hell of a lot more than *not right*," I responded. "It was downright dangerous. Thanks."

The next day, I knocked on the door of the chief's office. Assistant Chief Castro was there. I wasn't sure if he had witnessed the incident while at the scene of the fire. I told him how the firemen from the other station had purposely put my life in danger. I warned him that I would be advising my partner and family to sue the city and the Fire Department administration should I be seriously injured or killed at a fire scene. I wanted him to know that 'enough was enough' and I would demand accountability. It was only much later that I learned that the two firemen had been reprimanded for their actions. However, their captain never came to me with an apology.

On the other hand, there were brief moments of hope that helped to sustain me. We were the second truck to arrive at the scene one day. I had just jumped off the truck, gave the coupling of my hose to the engineer to connect to the pumper, and stretched the hose down the street to the scene of the fire. Another firefighter took the nozzle from me. He was quickly joined by his rear-end man. There wasn't much left to do at this point. My captain told me to ask the first captain on the scene if there was something I could do to help. The fire was being quickly suppressed, so there was little that I could contribute now. As I walked over to the captain from Fire Station 2, one of the guys called me a 'maricón'.

"*Pendejo!*" I responded. I was really muttering the curse word [asshole!] to myself, but the captain heard it as I approached. I could see surprise on his face.

"Oh, captain," I said, "I didn't mean you!" I had learned my lesson about swearing at your superior officers. He laughed.

"I just didn't know you spoke Spanish?" he said. "Relax. You did fine." Then, he moved closer to me and spoke in a sincere, almost concerned, tone of voice. "Hey, how are things going for you?" he asked. "The guys can be pretty rough." *Wow! Was I really getting genuine concern and support?* This was unexpected. I assured him that I was doing fine and thanked him for his concern. I told him that the insults were the least of my concerns. It left me realizing how the older, more experienced officers seemed to appreciate my passion for fighting fires. They were much less concerned with what I did in my private life. I guessed that the older one gets – the more experience one has in life – the more they can appreciate the diversity of human abilities, human desires, and human sexualities. Maybe this captain had a relative or friend who was gay or lesbian. Whatever his motivation, I appreciated his expression of concern and willingness to check in with me.

CHAPTER 17: The Man or Woman?

It never ceased to amaze me how often the firemen brought up the topic of homosexual sex acts. Of course, they were not supposed to have any experience with gay sex, so they would direct their curiosity towards me. One day, I had been upstairs in the bunk area reading a book. I walked down to the kitchen for a cold soda. Oneri was sitting in the dining area with one of the other firemen. Capt. Stephenson was standing with his back to them, looking at the TV in the other room.

"Hey! I got a question for you?" Oneri yelled. I turned around, not particularly wanting to engage in discourse with him.

"What?" I asked.

"Are you the man or the woman?" he shot back. His devious expression couldn't hide his insatiable interest. The other fireman was silent, but surely interested in how I was going to answer. The captain heard the question and turned on his heels to look across the room at me. I did my best to appear baffled by the question. Admittedly, it came out of nowhere.

"The man or the woman? What the hell are you talking about?" I asked. He was not deterred. I could see he was determined to provoke me.

"You know, when you are *doing it*, are you the guy or the girl?"

I stopped moving and tilted my head a little to the left as if perplexed by the idea. I looked at the captain and then the other fireman for a second before looking back at Oneri.

"You mean, I have to *decide* to be one or the other?" I asked, innocently. "No one told me that I had to make a choice?!" I could see the smirk on the captain's face, suggesting he was pleased with my answer. They all should have appreciated the irony of the moment. They had seen my partner, Joe, in his construction gear and they see me as a fireman doing the same job as themselves. *In their estimation, which of us is more 'masculine'?* The fact that they had to ask the question suggests that the inquiry was laughable.

"Hey Captain," I said, "it seems these guys have nothing better to do than fantasize about my sex life? It strikes me as odd." And then, as if I had something new to ponder, I walked out of the kitchen murmuring to myself. "Huh, imagine that? I have to make a choice?"

It had seemed absurd to me that our society labels professions as either 'masculine' or 'feminine.' Firefighters are masculine and nurses are feminine. Who made these rules? To me, there was no difference between my skills in crocheting an afghan and my wiring the electrical outlets in our new home. Yet, somehow, our society suggests that there are female and male activities in all aspects of our lives. This limited worldview conceptualizes sexual relationships only in heteronormative terms. These firemen were only able to imagine a sexual encounter that involves masculine and feminine roles. The unspoken assumption, of course, was that the feminine role was the naturally inferior role.

I think that, to these firemen, I was emasculating myself by having sex with another man. They were baffled with how a man could, willingly, denigrate himself by being submissive to another man. *Here, I believe, is the crux of the matter. The men's homophobia is rooted in the belief that a sexual partner is submissive to the 'man.' I agree with many feminists that misogyny is the underlying issue at play here.* There is an erroneous belief that when a gay man engages in sex with another male, he is acting out a female role. I believe it is based on the presumption that a woman is, somehow, to be dominated when having sex with men. Men often talk about conquering women. There is an implication that men *do it to* women, as if their penis was a weapon. Consider the subtle message conveyed in the most common swear words or phrases used by straight men to inflict insult: *Fuck you!* (my penis in you); *Suck this!* (as if forced onto my penis); or *Up yours!* (entry by my penis as if by force). There is an implication that men enjoy sex when they dominate their partner. This is not to say that partners cannot enjoy mutually-agreed upon role-play in which dominance is an element of their fantasy. But if it is only to please the 'male' partner and not be a mutually satisfying act, where is the equity and respect for the 'passive' partner? Why should being the 'receptive' partner suggest that one is submissive? Why is a woman who pursues sexual encounters labeled a whore while men are just 'playing the field?' Why is it shameful to enjoy getting fucked or desiring to suck a penis? So, when considering sex between two men, is there an assumption that one man is being 'victimized' by the other when having sex? Is a man any less masculine for seeking a more equitable sexual relationship in which each partner enjoys pleasing the other?

I think that the desperate need for men to cling to male dominance as an essential element of their masculinity contributes to homophobia. As early as the 'beat' generation, writer Allen Ginsberg *questioned why there was a negative connotation to getting fucked*; why was a receptive partner being debased for their position in bed? After all, sex is beautiful, by its very nature. Throughout history, women have written of the spiritual nature of having their partner 'inside' them, connecting in a deeply intimate manner. Because men have a prostate gland that is stimulated during anal intercourse, they can derive extraordinary pleasure as the receptive partner. However, even in the male gay community, the man who portrays himself as the 'top' man (erroneously referred to as the *active* partner) who inserts his penis during anal intercourse is regarded as more 'manly' than the man who receives the penis in the role of 'bottom' man (the *passive* partner). In real life, a bottom partner may be anything *but* passive. If both partners are engaging in sex for mutual pleasure, why make any distinction at all between relative positions in bed?

In our society, it is the illusion of masculinity that must be preserved, especially by firefighters. The male firefighter is to be tough, virile, and courageous. Traditionally, these are not the adjectives used to describe gay men. I think that when I joined the department as an openly gay man, some of my coworkers found it difficult to adjust. How could I demonstrate bravery, strength, and resilience in my job and go home at night to sleep with a man? If I am doing the same job they are doing, what does that say about their 'masculine' facade? Getting to the root causes of homophobia is crucial if we ever hope to eradicate it. No way in hell, though, was I going to have this kind of sociopolitical, philosophical discussion with these firemen. *It would be casting pearls before swine.*

There were times when I was my own worst enemy, it seems. It has always been in my nature to question assumptions, think critically, and initially look at things with an open mind. My desire to know more about the world around me, and share it with others, was in my nature. However, it was also threatening to some of the firemen. One hot summer day, we had been practicing different positions for holding a fire hose. I demonstrated a few strategies we had learned in Fire College that allowed greater control and lessened firefighter fatigue. Although the captain seemed receptive, it was clear that others were not happy to learn something from me. Once we parked the fire truck back in the bay, two of the guys muscled me up against the concrete wall.

"You think you are so fucking smart, don't you?" one said, nearly spitting in my face. If he was trying to scare me, he was doing a good job. I was unwilling to show it, but I feared that this would be the first physical attack from the firemen.

"I don't think you'll be so clever, faggot, when the fire is burning your dumb ass," the other guy added. "There won't be anyone there to save you. You think I would risk my life for a little faggot fairy like you?"

I kept quiet. My mind was racing. How would I manage to escape if they started beating me? They had moved in so closely and I couldn't imagine getting away without a struggle. I was hoping that they wouldn't risk hurting me here in the firehouse, while on duty. Luckily for me, their anger diminished quickly, transforming into mockery. One pulled away and began feigning an effeminate boy lisping and prancing.

"Oooooh, pleeeease! Don't hurt me!?" he teased. Honestly, he looked ridiculous. I suppressed the urge to say how <u>well</u> he impersonated the stereotypical gay boy. The other guy had now backed away from me as well. I took a breath and scanned the surroundings. There was no one else in the truck bay.

"Get the fuck out of here," the other guy barked.

I started moving slowly. I didn't want him to think that he controlled my every move with his demands. Rather than escape to the relative safety of the second floor of the firehouse, I walked over to the truck and began wiping it down. The two firemen were still within 20 feet of me. It wasn't that this menial cleaning task was the best thing to do at the time. I wanted to show them that I wasn't running away in fear. Besides, a rear-end man was expected to wipe down the engine. I attempted to appear calm, despite being scared to death.

After they left, it took another half an hour for me to calm down. I kept imagining the pain I would feel had they struck me. *Would they call an ambulance if I had needed it? How scared and angry would Joe be when he found out?* Although they didn't strike me, it had been terrifying to see just how much anger they held. If they had hurt me, I would have pressed charges and the past two years of assaults would come out in the newspapers. It was then that a terrible thought entered my mind. Some of these guys had friends that they could call upon to beat me up at some locale other than the firehouse. It would be nearly impossible to track the attack back to the firemen. I tried not to think about some thugs showing up at our house and roughing me up. *Why was I such a threat to them?*

Eventually, I learned to reign in my comments. My ideas about how we might improve the ways we fight fires was of no interest to these guys. I decided to stay out of most firehouse conversations. I was judicious in what I decided to share with the firemen. This, of course, is no way to build teamwork and camaraderie. It made life in the firehouse isolating.

I wasn't getting the support I needed at home, either. Joe was quick to anger when I described the assaults by the firemen. He would have struck out at them physically if need be. He might have devised ways to get revenge and cause them distress. That wasn't a road that I was willing to consider. What I needed from Joe was an empathetic sounding board to help me release my stress and develop constructive strategies for responding to these traumatizing incidents. It was not my intention to 'fight back.' Although Joe tried his best, he could not be there for me, it wasn't in his nature; he was quick to give me advice on what he would do in the situation. This was less than helpful to me.

In June 1983, an article appeared in the *Miami News* about police officers and firefighters in Miami Metro Fire Department being issued rubber gloves to protect them from contracting the AIDS virus when treating injured persons. At the time, there had been fewer than 120 cases of AIDS in Florida, yet the fear was mounting exponentially. Key West had a significant number of the state's AIDS cases. I had already known 5 guys to die of AIDS, so I was aware that we all had to be careful about blood exposures. Even though we didn't run medical rescue calls, we had first responder obligations. Still, I was relieved that my coworkers were unaware of the growing number of persons with AIDS in our city. It would only have sent them into a panic. The firemen didn't ask if I knew anyone with AIDS and I, surely, didn't volunteer that information. I was unaware that this very issue would soon jeopardize my position in the KWFD.

CHAPTER 18: Mayoral Race

In the fall of 1983, the political environment in Key West was becoming highly charged. Richard Heyman's campaign for mayor was in full swing. I believed that his professional demeanor would bring increased respectability to the Office of Mayor. He was spearheading a call for accountability, ethics, and transparency in municipal operations. He had been an outspoken critic of the 'Bubba system' that allowed for rampant nepotism and financial mismanagement in the city. I was pleased that he was supportive of the Fire Department, recognizing that the lack of adequate personnel and outdated firefighting equipment was undermining our ability to protect the city. If elected mayor, he promised to work with the Florida Keys Aqueduct Authority to replace water lines and non-functional hydrants, assuring we had more resources to do our jobs. Richard had specifically aimed to get more Black persons and women into the police and fire departments. I could foresee that the KWFD would benefit if Richard was elected.

The city was abuzz with excitement, and heightened anxiety, as the elections neared. Richard Kerr, Heyman's opponent in the mayoral race, billed himself as a 'family man,' a veiled attempt to make Richard's sexual orientation a central issue for Conch voters. His fear-based campaign insinuated that a gay mayor would bring an end to morality in the city. He suggested that Conchs would be forced out of their jobs and have no choice but to move off 'their' beloved island. Kerr's nasty campaign spewed inflammatory speech and innuendo, furthering homophobic stereotypes in an attempt to persuade Conchs to vote for the 'decent' candidate.

Many of the firefighters, like brothers Billy and Dickie, seized any opportunity to spread mistruths and incite unnecessary panic in the community. They pontificated about gay men but didn't take the time to talk with gay men. It seemed cowardly that the brothers would instigate actions to have me fired, yet neither one ever engaged in a conversation with me. Unfortunately, though, my presence in the Fire Department provided the brothers with 'proof' that the local's way of life and traditions were at risk of being eroded. Many of the firefighters assumed that Richard and I knew each other. To be honest, we barely knew each other, and I don't believe that Richard even was aware that I was an openly gay firefighter. The anti-gay vitriol ratcheted up as election day approached; the tensions in the firehouse mounted and the potential for physical violence towards me was nearly palpable.

There were unethical shenanigans in the mayoral campaign. Some of Kerr's supporters distributed false flyers that made ridiculous accusations against Heyman and his campaign, attempting to discredit him. The rhetoric and misinformation were blamed, in part, for verifiable threats against the lives of Commissioner Heyman and his allies on the City Commission. Some of the firemen would try to 'bait' me into arguments about the election of a gay mayor. When I was in earshot of their gossip and hatemongering, I would be taunted with questions such as *"You think a faggot mayor will change our uniforms to tight-fitting shorts, pink shirts, and construction boots?"* I emphasized that the campaign was not a matter of sexual orientation. Rather than fall into their trap and engage in inane banter, I stuck to the issues facing the KWFD and city.

"I think *Mayor* Heyman would get us proper air tanks and functional water hydrants," I offered.

"Oh no," another guy said, "a faggot mayor would have us in black leather vests and chains. Ha! Hey, what is it about you gay guys and leather?"

Admittedly, holding my tongue was challenging. I didn't want their adolescent provocations to lead to open arguments that would serve no good purpose. What some of the firemen weren't saying is that having an 'outsider' running the City Commission might put them at risk. A properly functioning municipal administration might uncover any number of illegal activities that were commonplace in 1980's Key West: drug smuggling, embezzlement, and corruption. Some of the men in the KWFD were involved in illicit activities that, if caught and prosecuted, might put their jobs at risk. If Commissioner Heyman became the next mayor, he would have no tolerance for firefighters who were drinking or smoking pot while on duty. It had also occurred to me that some of the firemen had a side business or second job that may have depended upon lucrative contracts with the City. Heyman was keen on eliminating the long tradition of nepotism in Key West that benefited the Conchs while erasing opportunities for others, particularly Black contractors.

Just weeks before the end of the campaign, the sitting mayor (Dennis Wardlow) was asked to speak to a high school social studies class. It was reported that he began his talk with an angry personal and political attack against Richard Heyman. Both students and the teacher thought it to be inappropriate and unbecoming of a sitting official. The incident didn't surprise me because I never felt that the mayor's two brothers in the KWFD had ever shown much professionalism in their behavior, let alone personal restraint. The brothers expressed only contempt for me, though they knew so little about me.

In November 1983, Richard Heyman was elected for his first term as Mayor of Key West. This was a historical milestone for the island city. In fact, Richard was the first elected openly gay mayor in the United States! He received congratulatory notes from around the globe. In my day-to-day world, however, the anti-gay attacks went unabated.

CHAPTER 19: A Fundamental Shift

It was also in the Fall of 1983 that I was transferred to a new watch. When I first heard of a possible transfer, I had an overwhelming sense of dread. It had taken me two years to adapt to this sorry group of firemen. Now, I would have to start all over again with a whole new team. As luck would have it, this was the best thing that could have happened to me!

As it turned out, I wasn't the only one being transferred. My new assignment was to work under Capt. George 'Viti' Vidal. He was the older Cuban-American captain that treated me so well the previous year and was now at Fire Station 1. Also, I would be working with Alex Vega as my driver! Even Al Rahming worked me on a more regular basis. I began to share more shifts with Alan Vidal (the captain's nephew). It seemed to me that I had been transferred from the lowest scoundrels of the department to the most professional firefighters! It was almost too good to be true. I now enjoyed going to work each day. With these firemen, I felt more comfortable bringing personal items to work with me. I continued bringing my drafting board to draw blueprints. I was able to complete plans for two houses, one on the Saddlebunch Keys and the other on Cudjoe Key. The firemen on this new watch even took time to review my work and offered suggestions that helped me improve the designs.

The change in watch assignment, however, didn't put an end to the anti-gay harassment. Nearly every day I was on duty, there would be some homophobic transgression from men at other firehouses. I would receive phone calls on the private line that were intended to annoy me.

"Cocksuckerrrr..." an anonymous caller would snarl.

"You say that as if it was a *bad* thing?" I replied.

It struck me as so sad that some of these men had nothing better to do with their time than to try agitating me. They were more interested in my sexual orientation than I was! One morning, I left the station after my shift. I hadn't washed our antique Ford pick-up truck in days, so it was covered in coral dust. As I approached it, I noticed that someone had crudely scribbled *"Fagot"* on the side door with their finger. Instinctually, I turned to look up at the glass doors of our dining area to see several firemen watching for my response. I slowly shook my head to communicate that I were so disappointed in this juvenile graffiti. Then, I carefully used my finger to add an additional 'g' to correct the spelling. *"Faggot."* Honestly, *I never could tolerate poor spelling.* Days later, when I returned for my next shift, the men could see that I had not erased the slur from the side of the truck. After discussing it with my partner, Joe, I decided to let the graffiti remain until I made my point that such childish behaviors wouldn't crush me or make me quit the KWFD.

Again, once away from the firehouse, it was easy to 'forget' that I was gay. My life was full of activities that did not center around my sexual orientation. When building our house, for example, I installed plumbing, electric, and sewer systems. Not once did my being gay have any impact on the construction process. I continued to volunteer on the HELPLINE staff. The 24-hour crisis line had hired a new Director, Larry Szuch, to streamline the organization and boost the cadre of volunteers. In helping to orient new volunteers, I realized that I had learned so much about counseling anonymous callers through their crises.

Slowly, but surely, the emerging AIDS epidemic was creeping into my life. My friend, Dennis Bitner, had been an architect of the secession of the Conch Republic from the USA. He invited me to a fundraising dinner to raise money for people with AIDS. It was at this event that I met my hero, Leonard Matlovich. I relayed how I used the *TIME* magazine cover in college and thanked him for challenging the military's unfair policy of discharging gay and lesbian service members. His brave actions motivated me to resist oppression and injustice. And of course, I briefly described my experience as an openly gay firefighter.

In response to the growing AIDS crisis, I chose to enroll in the training for the initial cohort of 'AIDS educators' for the American Red Cross. By 1983, the scientific community had identified the HTLV-III retrovirus as the causative agent that led to the collapse of one's immune system and a subsequent AIDS diagnosis. However, there was not yet a test available to identify who was infected. Therefore, our educational programs focused on what we did know; we taught about HIV prevention, seeking care for symptoms suggestive of AIDS, and reducing fear and stigma in both the affected communities and the general population. As gay men, Joe and I were at risk for acquiring this new disease. I knew I had to contribute in some way. Surprisingly, I found that engaging in AIDS work reduced my fear and anxiety about the emerging epidemic.

One day, I received a call from a television producer in New York City. He had heard that I was an openly gay professional firefighter. He told me Charles "Charlie" Cochran had been the first NYC police officer to come out as gay in 1981. He helped establish a new organization called the GOAL (Gay Officers Action League) to provide a support system and guidance for fellow police officers who were gay or lesbian. The producer invited me to be interviewed alongside Officer Cochran for a segment to be shown on a NYC cable television public access channel. The trip was a great opportunity to meet Charlie and discuss the similarities and differences in our experiences. The interview gave a boost to my confidence and gave me hope that there was a future for sexual minority individuals to serve their community without bigotry.

The transfer to Viti's shift had, fundamentally, altered my KWFD experience. I was now working with firefighters who were dedicated to their profession. Now, I came into a firehouse that was full of laughter. Captain Vidal didn't tolerate bad behavior or harassment on his watch. Rather, he set the tone by making his signature dish: bread pudding filled with guava paste! He was proud of bringing a smile to the faces of the men on his shift. Viti told me stories about his 11 years as a pitcher with professional baseball teams in Florida. He felt that in both baseball and firefighting the best teamwork comes from appreciating that every member brings something unique and valuable to the table. His optimistic outlook and an infectious laugh made work a pleasure.

As a rear-end man, I would occasionally be transferred to one of the other two stations for a shift, as needed. At this point, I had been on the KWFD for more than two years. Still, so many of the other firefighters knew little about me. My transfer to their station for the day was often filled with periods of awkward silence. My attempts at engaging them weren't always welcome. One day, I was sent to work at Station 2 at the corner of Angela and Simonton Streets in Old Town. Despite being a part of the City Hall building, the firehouse was outdated and in desperate need of renovation or replacement. I began by reporting to the captain, letting him know that I had arrived. The captain was anything but warm and inviting. There were a couple of firefighters sitting at the table that I had never met. The captain did not tell me their names. *It will be an awkward shift if I don't even know the names of the men on my fire truck!* I proceeded to put my fire gear on the truck. The two firemen quickly followed me into the back of the truck bay. It was such a small, cramped space that my back was pushed up against the wall.

"I could beat the shit out of you, sissy boy!" one of them said. He was doing his best to be physically intimidating. He was taller and heavier than me, so he had certainly filled me with fear.

"Of course, you could," I said, "You are much bigger than me." I was simply stating the fact. Staring straight into his eyes, I tried to show no emotion, no panic, no fear for my well-being. Nothing could be further from the truth. *I was terrified.* But I didn't want the two of them to get any sense of my fear. Though I had been assaulted like this in my own firehouse, this was more frightening. *I don't know these firemen or what they are capable of doing.* Luckily for me, it was only a moment or so before the captain walked into the truck bay. Immediately, the two guys moved away from me, as if nothing had happened. It was clear to me that the captain sized up the situation. He knew that these two were threatening me. Yet, he simply walked away without speaking to me. I knew then that I would not be assured protection in this firehouse.

I had other interesting experiences when visiting either Station 2 or Station 3. As both firehouses were in Old Town neighborhoods, I would know some of the gay men and lesbians walking or biking past. Frequently, my friends would stop and chat. One day, I was sitting outside of the firehouse on Simonton Street. An elderly man who lived across from the station crossed the street and came up to greet me. It was Sir Philip Burton (father of the actor Richard Burton). He was a well-known resident of the island. I had known Philip for a couple of years and sometimes worked on projects around his property. We chatted about various things before he left to shop at *Fausto's Food Palace*.

"Don't tell me he is gay?" said one of the firemen.

"OK. I won't tell you," I responded. I stood and walked upstairs. *Why wouldn't Philip be gay? Because he was nearly 80 years old? Because he was famous?* Some of these guys hadn't a clue.

Sometimes, the firemen eavesdropped on my conversations with friends. *Did they think that I was going to say something 'gay' or outrageous? What did they think they would hear?* As with Sir Philip, my friends usually discussed work, hobbies, or their time at the beach. I hoped the firemen were learning that gay people also talk about the most mundane of subjects. It struck me, though, that they probably never had much opportunity to 'engage' with gay people.

There were also opportunities for me to be a role model for gay men who were living secret lives. One day, a panel truck pulled into the driveway of Station 2. This was not legal parking (a fire truck may need to exit at a moment's notice), so they must have known a fireman. It was a carpentry crew whose boss wanted to chat with his friend. As the three guys got out of the truck and approached us, I saw Raúl. He was a closeted Conch man that I met when he spent the night with a friend of mine a couple of weeks earlier. I provided no hint that I recognized him. Still, I could see that he was immediately uncomfortable. I engaged one of the other carpenters in conversation to alleviate any fear Raúl might have that I would speak to him directly. I also wanted him to know that I wasn't going to avoid 'normal' conversations with guys visiting the fire station. *It must be so hard to be a gay Conch.* I could only hope that Raúl would find his way to a happy and fulfilling life without the need for clandestine encounters or living in fear of being 'found out.'

Things were looking up since I joined Viti's shift. It was exciting to work with firemen who were thinking about how to advance the department and improve our relationship with the community. Alex Vega appreciated the role that firefighters could have in promoting fire prevention among the public. He also knew that community relations could impact how the City Commissioners perceived the department. After years of news reports about illegal activities and disruptive behaviors of the firemen, a little positive input couldn't hurt.

With Joe's help in the TV studio, a few of us began creating fire prevention PSAs (public service announcements) to be shown on the local TV channel throughout October (Fire Prevention month). It seemed ironic; while some of the firefighters were harassing me about being gay, some others were collaborating with me (and my partner Joe!) to create TV spots that brought good publicity for the KWFD! Some of the firemen seemed proud of me when I was acknowledged by the Key West Citizen for providing fire prevention tips for readers of the newspaper.

Out of the blue one day, I got a phone call from a representative of the Key West Jaycees. Actually, I didn't even know what the Jaycees represented. I learned that, in 1983, the civic organization's mission was to encourage men, particularly businessmen, to develop personal and professional leadership skills through service to others. The caller informed me that I had been selected by the Key West chapter's membership to receive the *Outstanding Young Firefighter* award for my actions in performing CPR on the injured boy. They were also aware of my work with the Southernmost Runners Club and HELPLINE crisis call center. Someone had done their homework.

I received the award at a casual dinner meeting in their meeting hall on Flagler Avenue. I was sure that some of these folks were dyed-in-the-wool Conchs that had heard of my reputation in the KWFD. Amazingly, I sensed no trepidation with them giving me the award. I know they were hoping that I would join as a new member of the Jaycees, but my life was chock full of other obligations at the time. Strangely, though they had taken photos with me accepting the award from the leading officers, there was no mention of the award presentation in the local newspaper, the *Key West Citizen*. This was unusual in Key West as everyone wanted good publicity. I was quick to let Chief Gates and Assistant Chief Castro know that I received the award.

CHAPTER 20: The Black Hats and the White Hats

In the first few months of working on Viti's shift, I began to learn so much more about the overall department. Since joining the KWFD, I had regularly worked with firemen who were taunting and terrorizing me. Now, I was assigned to a watch of men that were funny, engaging, and respectful. In my struggle to understand what made one group of firemen so different from the other, I began to distinguish the men with the *'black hats'* from the men with the *'white hats'*.

Through this metaphoric lens from American cowboy movie lore, the men with black hats bullied the townspeople, rustled cattle from the lonely widow's ranch, and instigated barroom brawls for the fun of it. They needed to be seen as 'powerful' because, deep down, they felt powerless in their lives. As with the archetype in films, anytime a fireman bullied me, he rarely acted alone; he had to have at least one other collaborator to witness his 'masculine' acts against me. Even if one of his confederates found himself struggling with the morality of the unprovoked assaults, he would not feel free to speak up for fear that he would become a target himself. When I listened to banter among the *black hats*, I noticed that they frequently used obscenities, as if they lacked a rich vocabulary with which to express themselves. When they were bored, they would annoy each other with disparaging comments, goading one another for no reason. They would badger their colleague with the express intent of provoking an outburst. Unable to tolerate the pestering anymore, the 'victim' might scream obscenities or throw an object against the wall. This would usually result in raucous laughter and the malicious taunting would cease for a while.

The *black hats* were married to "bitches" (their term) who regularly took their paychecks and "gave me just enough for a couple of beers." They complained that their wives were the reason that they couldn't go fishing, hunting, or otherwise 'have fun' when they wished. Taking time to be with their kids seemed to be a burden. There were times when these men would come to work in wrinkled uniforms that relayed disrespect for their position. It seemed to me that the *black hats* weren't proud of their past, discontented with their present, and uncertain about their prospects for the future. There always seemed to be someone else to blame for their shortcomings; they didn't hold themselves accountable for their sad circumstances. And, if they couldn't be happy, why should anyone else enjoy themselves? Occasionally, the *black hats* brought shame and embarrassment to the KWFD. Honestly, these men were not cartoon cut-outs; they were complex individuals with strengths and weaknesses. Unfortunately, they were consistently demonstrating their weaknesses.

The guys in the white hats, on the other hand, I conceptualized as the good cowboys. True to that movie characterization, these firemen were affable and collegial. Sure, they liked joking around, but having fun never came at the expense of hurting someone else. The *white hats* were the ones who loved being a professional firefighter (for all the right reasons). They were the ones who mentored rookies on how to handle hoses without injuring ourselves or others. They practiced their skills and tried to think of better ways of fighting fires. The *white hats* were the firefighters that the public sees as honest, trustworthy, and dependable.

The *white hats* seemed more secure in their own skin. They expressed love for their wives and kids. These guys were excited to go on vacation with their families. They never claimed to 'know it all,' and it was not uncommon for them to ask others for advice. As they got to know me, they asked questions they thought I could answer. As there was no Internet in the 1980s, I learned a lot by reading books. My few years of college had provided me with a great foundational knowledge of math, art, anatomy, and psychology. The *white hats* weren't timid about asking questions about health or science. As I had an inquiring mind, I would often go to the library and bring back an answer.

The guys in the white hats were curious and I believe they trusted my insights. Some of them were intrigued by my volunteer service at the HELPLINE crisis call center. Maybe it helped them to know that other people struggle – like we all do – to manage life's stressors? Several times we talked about loss and grief management; I had a wealth of anecdotes that provided opportunities for them to reveal their own sad stories of family members and friends. One of the most unexpected questions came one day when three of us were sitting at the dining table. One of the guys mentioned that his wife was in the clinic for 'bleeding.'

"Do you mean a heavy period," I asked, "or some abnormal kind of bleeding?"

"I don't know," he said. It was a tentative answer. I thought maybe he hadn't asked his wife enough of the right questions.

"What is a period?" he asked. "I mean why?" By the look on the faces of these two young men, I could see that a woman's period was a mysterious unknown. I pulled out a piece of paper and drew the essential components of the female reproductive tract and explained the menstrual cycle. Anatomy and physiology of sex organs was one of the subjects I studied in college. Imagine the irony of having the gay guy explaining this material to straight men. I was so glad that they asked.

Of course, there were many more men in the KWFD that I didn't know well enough to put them into the black hat or white hat category. In fact, I would have needed to conceptualize a few more additional groupings to account for the diverse range of personalities. Some of the men never spoke to me; others were cordial, but distant. Some seemed to enjoy seeing me be taunted while others appeared disturbed by their colleagues' unprofessional behavior. I was curious, though, how the *white hats* managed to engage with me freely at the risk of being guilty by association. It was risky for any straight man to stand up for the gay guy; he would be 'suspect' by advocating for me in front of the bully. It isn't much different than calling a White person a 'n*gger lover' when they spoke up after seeing Black persons being mistreated. Bullies don't want dissention in the ranks; they don't want their behavior to be openly challenged. *I wonder what kind of sideways comments the white hats got from the black hats for treating me as a legitimate fellow fireman?*

It never ceased to amaze me how people assume they can spot a gay person in a crowd. It didn't annoy me, though, unless they were expressing homophobic attitudes. One beautiful day, we were meeting up with firefighters from the Naval Air Station Fire Department for joint practices. There were times when we worked together to fight fires, so it was prudent to be familiar with each other's protocols. This particular exercise simulated an accident in which persons trapped in a car had to be safely extricated from the mangled vehicle and transferred onto an ambulance. The car doors had been crushed and could not be manually opened. It was my first experience with using the 'Jaws of Life' tool. *Man! This sucker is heavy!* I found it fascinating how the hydraulic mechanism was used to cut through metal and expand an opening with ease. As the next fireman took his turn with the tool, I moved back into being an observer. I was standing aside with one of the KWFD guys, Pic, when a Navy firefighter started talking to us.

"Hey," he said, "I heard you have a gay guy on your department now?"

"Yeah, we do," I answered, "Why?"

"Oh, nothing much," he said. "How's that working out?"

"I think just fine," I responded. Then, I turned to Pic. "Don't you think it's going OK?" It was hard to tell from Pic's facial expression if he was embarrassed or stupefied. He was speechless. I turned back to the Navy firefighter and offered my hand.

"Hi. My name is Kevin," I said. "I think I'm doing OK." It took him a minute to piece together what had just happened. He realized that I must be 'the gay guy.' I was pleasantly surprised that he shook my hand, wished me the best, and nonchalantly changed the subject.

This AIDS epidemic was beginning to rattle the American public. In the Fall of 1983, an article in the Miami Herald newspaper admonished a hospital in Gainesville for an unnecessarily transferring an AIDS patient to California. Even hospital administrators and medical professionals were afraid to have AIDS patients in their facility; they were expressing irrational fears based on misinformation and homophobia. These kinds of incidents contributed to further stigmatization and discrimination against gay men. It wouldn't be long before the firemen would bring the AIDS hysteria to roost on my doorstep.

Sadly, after two years in the KWFD, my fellow firemen and I were not friends. I was never invited to social events or barbeques. Key West is a small island. I occasionally encountered firemen with their wives when shopping in town. Most of them would not acknowledge my presence; others would be gracious enough to greet me and introduce their spouse. If Joe were with me, I would respond with introducing him as my partner in a nonchalant manner. It was my hope that these brief interactions would normalize our relationship.

I was now working with a more engaged group of firefighters. They showed interest when the Key West Citizen published photos of Mayor Heyman engaging with local community members for social events and fundraisers. The firemen were becoming aware of how the [gay] Mayor supported local activities of interest to the Conch community: high school sports teams, civic organizations, and military and veterans' groups. He appeared with Jimmy Buffett at the opening of his Margaritaville store. They even mentioned when the newspaper covered me (as Race Director of the Southernmost Runners Club) donating proceeds to benefit their kids' activities. I was hoping that these articles presented us as the 'normal' citizens we knew ourselves to be.

There were historic fires that made of us proud of our profession. On the evening of December 29, 1983, we were dispatched to a fire at the Fountains Restaurant at 1108 Duval Street. The large structure was an architectural beauty with rounded-corner porch turrets and a grand, decorative facade. Built in 1917, it was commonly called the *Old Cuban Club*. For decades, the Cuban Club had been the center of socialization and special events for Cubans in Key West. I guessed that many of the firefighters had fond – if not cherished – memories of celebrations in the building. Even as a non-native Key Wester, the thought that this unique historical edifice could burn down was gut-wrenching.

On our way to the scene, we could see the smoke and red glow of the fire from several blocks away. We positioned our American LaFrance pumper on Duval Street, just a little south of the fire scene. After connecting the pumper's intake hose to the fire hydrant, we ran to manage the fire streams. I was directed to take one hose up the side of the building to provide water to a different face of the fire. It was terribly hot, and the noise of crackling wood was unusually loud. Despite the difficult conditions, we continued to deliver streams of water until ordered to retreat considering the growing fire. This fire was so large and potentially disastrous that it required the use of the snorkel truck from Firehouse 1. It was several hours into the night before the fire was extinguished. No matter our rapid response, the building was a total loss. However, we prevented a conflagration that could have destroyed dozens of old buildings in that section of Old Town.

Sadly, the Cuban Club fire was another scene at which the *black hats* attempted to injure me while battling a blaze. Luckily, I managed to avoid being knocked down by yet another a stream of water from another team's fire hose. The fact that the firemen felt they could jeopardize my safety meant that the commanding officers had not communicated clearly that such attacks on me were not to be tolerated. A couple of the firemen on the scene were disturbed by what they witnessed and reported the incident. Although I learned that Chief Gates was informed of the assault, he never spoke to me about it. I am sure he didn't want to expose the city to a potential lawsuit. At that fire, I suffered a back injury, unrelated to the adolescent behaviors of the other men. The pain and discomfort plagued me for the next three months and reminded me that simply pulling hose lines at a fire scene can cause injuries.

CHAPTER 21: White Boy Running...

I really enjoyed long-distance running. I had been the Race Director for the Southernmost Runners Club for the past two years. Many days, when my shift at the firehouse ended at 7 a.m., I wouldn't drive directly home to Bay Point. I would change into my running gear and 'hit the pavement' around the island. Key West is only about a mile wide and 3 miles long. So, if I were on a 10-mile run, I could cover a lot of ground. My runs allowed me to see all the nooks and crannies on the island. I became very familiar with various neighborhoods.

My running routine served me well as a firefighter, too. The island has dozens of small lanes and alleys that aren't easily located on a paper map. They had names like *Poorhouse Lane, Shaver's Lane, Baptist Lane,* or *Wong Song Alley.* If there was a house fire on one of these lanes, we would have to know how to find the address and if our truck would fit down the tiny street. We would also have to know how to locate the nearest fire hydrant. Many of the Key West firefighters gave directions by referring to places with personal or historical significance: "You know, you pass the old cigar shop on the corner and take the next left..." Unfortunately, with all the gentrification occurring on the island, some of those landmarks didn't exist anymore. So, my running allowed me to note recent demolitions and the progress of ongoing building projects. One day, we had a surprise quiz on the location of specific streets, lanes, and alleys on the island. I was able to score a 100%, much to the surprise of my fellow firefighters.

"Kevin even knew where to find Baptist Lane!" the Assistant Chief said. This small lane was off Petronia Street in the neighborhood known to Key Westers as 'Black Town.'

"Man, I haven't been down there in years!" said one of the firemen. That comment didn't surprise me; they had little interest in visiting the Black neighborhoods. One day, I was talking with a Black man who had worked for the Public Works Department for many years. I began to explain "I am a firefighter" when he interrupted me.

"I know who you are," he said, "You are the White boy that runs through our streets. We all know who you are. We were thinkin' …what you doing in our neighborhood?"

A little surprised by that revelation, I explained the method to my madness. I told him that I wanted to be familiar with the area in case a fire broke out.

"Ain't many of those firemen that could run like you!" he laughed. Then, he revealed a perspective on my experience in the Fire Department that I had not considered. He was aware that the KWFD had not been welcoming to Black men. But he also told me that the City workers knew who the 'gay' fireman was; they would see me at various locations around town as the fire truck went by their work sites. He seemed to admire how I resisted the Conch pressure to quit the Fire Department and I appreciated the support. Again, I was reminded that there should be no real expectation of privacy when living on a small island.

After many months of intense training, I ran the Orange Bowl Marathon on Jan 7, 1984. The course wove through several of Miami's beautiful neighborhoods. I finished the 26.2-mile course in 3 hours, 42 minutes; the pace was respectable (top third of the men running) for a first-time marathoner.

Later that Spring, I traveled to Orlando to run in Florida's *Firefighter Olympics*. The games invited firefighters from across the state to engage in friendly competition. The trip to Orlando was nearly 7 hours on the road. I asked my friend, Tom, to come along. We arranged to stay at a well-known gay hotel in downtown Orlando. The *Parliament House* had a pool, dance club, and entertainment bar that was popular for gay men and lesbians in Central Florida. Aside from this oasis, there were very few safe places for gay people to meet and party in this part of the state.

It was a beautiful morning for a road race, and I was excited to see firefighters from so many different corners of Florida. At about 7 a.m. hundreds of us were gathering near the starting line for the 10-mile race. I saw no female firefighters. As runners tend to be a friendly sort, and firefighters tend to be fraternal, we were in small groups introducing ourselves. I was the only Key West firefighter there (no big surprise). We were exchanging information about how many personnel and the kind of fire engines we had back home. There was a mixture between professional and volunteer firemen among us. One of the guys turned to address me.

"Where are you staying?" he asked.

"At the Parliament House on Orange Blossom Trail," I responded without hesitating. By the curious glances, it clearly was not the answer these guys were expecting to hear. The fireman thought a moment before continuing.

"The Parliament House? Isn't that a gay place?" he asked.

"Yes. It is," I replied. My nonchalant response seemed to baffle the group.

At that very moment, the race official raised his bullhorn and shouted: "*Runners: On your mark. Get set. Go!*" And we were off... We all started out at about the same pace, waiting for the very fast runners to assume the lead positions. Then, I began to pick up my speed. During my training, I had used a SONY Walkman cassette player to listen to specific songs that set the rhythm for my optimal running cadence. The new song by Matthew Wilder, '*Break My Stride*' was playing in my head. I was running alongside the firefighters in my small group. They seemed to be having a brief discussion and, almost in sync, they glanced over at me. I smiled back at them. The underlying message of the song in my head seemed appropriate today: the chorus was that 'no one was going to stop me from reaching my stride.' After a mile or so of this moderate pace, I decided to speed up and leave the group in my proverbial dust. After a quick wave to them, I reset my cadence by dredging up a quicker melody, Christopher Cross' classic '*Ride Like the Wind.*' Of course, I was intending to outpace these guys in the race. I wanted them to know that the firefighter they had just met from Key West was a serious contender. I kept my strong pace and didn't see the guys again for the remainder of the race. I wasn't going to win any trophies, but I did record a personal best for the 10-mile distance.

At the end of the race, each finisher was provided a commemorative t-shirt and *Gatorade* for rehydration. I saw one of the guys I had met earlier. He seemed unsure about striking up a conversation.

"Did you have a good run?" I asked. I think he was surprised that I spoke to him.

"Yeah, great. Have a safe trip back to the Keys," he responded.

"Yeah, thanks," I responded. "See you next year!"

By January 1984 more than 1,000 Americans had died from AIDS. The anxiety around AIDS was becoming omnipresent. There were reports of hysteria across the country as the 'average' American became concerned that rabid homosexuals with the disease would try to purposely infect them with the HIV virus. Some restaurant patrons were refusing to have salads because they thought gay waiters would spit on their food. Celebrities and artists were beginning to die of AIDS. The fear of this illness was giving new life to an already homophobic environment. There had been just over 25 reported cases in Key West by this time. I had already lost five friends to the disease. One day, I read an article in the *Miami Herald* reporting that firefighters in California were refusing to learn CPR skills with mannequins for fear of getting the HIV virus. *Jeez! I sure hope the Key West firemen are not reading this article.*

Throughout the country, firefighters had a reputation for being engaged with their local community. Usually, this meant showing up with the fire trucks for special occasions or giving support to kids with cancer or other life-threatening conditions. We didn't do much of that. The firemen were best known for raising money to support the Drive for Muscular Dystrophy held each New Year's Day.

One evening I had dinner with my friend Joy. She was the Director of Wesley House, a daycare/learning center for children on the island.

Thinking about how kids love fire trucks, I had an idea.

"We could build a fire truck for the playground," I offered. "The kids could climb all over it and pretend to be firefighters."

Joy loved the idea and I got to work on designing it. After getting the chief's permission, we began building the wooden structure in the back of the open truck bay at Fire Station 1. As the station had no bay doors, it would be easier to transport the structure when completed. Initially, there wasn't much enthusiasm for the project. However, as the fire truck began to take shape, a couple of the guys jumped in and contributed to its building and painting. Unbeknownst to me, one of the 'good' guys went to the chief to receive his assurance that none of the 'bad' guys would damage the fire truck while it was under construction. He told me later that it might have been vandalized if he had not taken his concerns to the chief.

The 'truck' had to be sturdy enough to hold several children at a time jumping up and down on it. It also had to be securely cemented into the ground so that it would remain in place for times when the occasional hurricane blew over the island. Luckily, we finished and painted the truck without interruption from any of the malcontents in the KWFD.

When delivery day came, one of the firemen loaned his pick-up truck for transport. Alan Vidal and I, along with three other firefighters (even the President of our union, Buddha), showed up to help with the heavy lifting. I made sure to have a photo of the playground addition appear in the *Key West Citizen* newspaper. When a fire department depends upon the community for its support, good publicity never hurts.

Life was going well. I was in great physical shape. We were living in our new home, enjoying the luxury of a queen-sized bed, spacious kitchen, and living room with a view of the sun setting over the mangroves of the Saddlebunch Keys. I started most days with an early morning 5-mile run through our Bay Point community. Joe's work in the cable TV studio was going quite well; he had created a host of local shows to highlight the most interesting topics in Key West and the Lower Keys.

I was now really enjoying being a firefighter. On Capt. Vidal's watch, we continued to engage in exercises to hone our skills, learn new strategies, and improve our communication. I had opportunities to drive and was learning how to 'land' the fire truck near the fire hydrant so that the intake hose could be attached to the pumper intake. This would be important for me to master for when – and if – I earned promotion to Engineer (driver). We practiced drafting water from ponds or the ocean. We trained on how to lay hose down a lane or alley that was too small to accommodate the fire truck.

Our firehouse was busy enough with small house fires, car fires, and even brush fires. And then, there were the more memorable events for which our training had prepared us. One Saturday morning, we got a call that a plane had crashed into a house in the 'new town' section of the city. It wasn't unusual to see Air Sunshine aircraft from Miami fly in low over the island in preparation for landing at the Key West airport. Even in April, the plane would be filled with tourists. My mind raced as I jumped into my turnout gear and grabbed ahold of the truck. As we screamed down the street, I couldn't help but envision a horrible scene with multiple injuries, and possibly several deaths. *How many houses would be engulfed in flames? What would be the dangers of burning jet fuel? Would we have to check the houses for victims? How much blood and bodily harm were we going to encounter?* Due to the burgeoning AIDS epidemic in town, I had already seen several dead bodies. However, a plane crash could result in bodily mutilation and dismemberment. I wasn't sure how I would respond to finding the body parts of victims spread across a crash scene.

Fortunately, the site of the plane crash was much less traumatizing than I had imagined. Rather than a commercial craft that would have carried dozens of tourists, it was a small, private, single-engine Cessna that had crashed almost immediately after takeoff from the airport. Two adults in the plane, a couple from Rhode Island, had been the only two fatalities. There were no injuries among the three family members that were in the house when it was hit. The house had significant damage and was burning. The tailpiece of the Cessna was the only clear evidence that this had been a plane crash. The impact had also set ablaze a travel trailer that was parked in the yard next door. Initially, the scene was hectic with so many different people (firefighters, police, neighbors, photographers) running about. The property was littered with debris and our captain was particularly concerned for our safety. These were the times when firefighters had to listen to their captain carefully. We also had to be sure that our fire hoses weren't going to interfere with the investigation that others were trying to conduct at the scene.

We extinguished the obvious fires rather quickly. However, it took more time to sift through the rubble to assure that there were not 'hot spots' that could flare up after we had left the scene. By this time, there were city and county officials onsite, arguing about who had jurisdiction over the investigation of the tragic event. As we drove away, I couldn't help but think that all the property damage was really nothing when compared to the loss of life.

When we got back to the firehouse, the men recalled the details of this unusual fire scene. This is a common – and much needed – debriefing activity for firefighters. We needed to replay our actions to judge if there was something we could learn to respond better in the future. It was also, I was convinced, a way for us to reduce the potential traumatic impact it had on us, personally and collectively. The captain took the opportunity to point out what each of us did correctly. He wanted us to be proud of our willingness to face these kinds of tragedies.

On my own, though, I was thinking about death…sudden, unexpected death. A call like this reminded me that anyone could be struck down at any minute. *What if someone had been on that side of the house when the plane came crashing down?* There would be no chance to say 'goodbye' to loved ones. They would have no chance to put their affairs in order before being struck down. I wondered how long the pilot and his wife knew that they were in grave danger. *What were their last thoughts? Did they have the time to be scared?*

Strangely enough, these musings about sudden death gave me some comfort. My friends who had died of AIDS had taken weeks or months to die. They had the opportunity to hug their loved ones. They laid out plans for their own memorial service and the final disposition of their remains. By comparison with the plane crash, this seemed like a benefit. There seemed to be a silver lining in the very dark cloud that had been hanging over my gay community. The short time given to my friends before their untimely death was some slight consolation. *If one had to die, is it best to have time to wrap up the loose ends of life?* This was all too philosophical, of course. The reality is that the last days and weeks of my friends' lives were all too full of uncertainty, fear, and isolation. All too often, they also had intractable pain and suffering. It doesn't seem that I could choose any 'best' way to leave this world.

In Fire College, one of the scenarios we trained for was searching in a smoke-filled house for someone who may be unconscious or overcome by smoke. As luck would have it, that day came when we received a call to a house filled with smoke. There was grave concern that a 4-year-old child was missing. Two of us volunteered to enter to search for the boy. After donning our air tanks and securing facemasks, we entered on hands and knees, knowing that a body could be laying on the floor somewhere. We conducted a slow, methodical sweep of each room to assure that we didn't miss him hiding under a bed, in a closet, or other crevice. But training cannot prepare you for the terrible anxiety you experience, thinking that you might find a small, lifeless body at the end of it all. We exited the house after finding nothing. Much to our relief, the boy had escaped earlier and was located at a neighbor's house.

I admit that my own internalized homophobia occasionally surfaced. One day, our fire truck passed three gay guys on bicycles in Old Town. As usual in Key West, they were shirtless and appeared to be on their way to the beach. Moments later, we stopped at a red light. As they coasted towards the truck, one of the guys recognized me. He let out a catcall.

"Oooooh! Hello Mr. Fireman!" he yelled. He pretended to find me very attractive. It was much more humorous than salacious. Still, I was caught off-guard, embarrassed. I smiled, nervously, and nodded my head in acknowledgment, but couldn't think of anything to say. I had met him before but didn't know his name.

"Yum, yum. I just love a man in a uniform!" he continued.

Playing along, I assumed a 'masculine' straight-backed pose while the truck pulled away. One of the other guys let out a wolf-whistle. I managed to wave goodbye but was surprised that their silliness flustered me. They weren't sexually harassing me. They were being playful as young gay men on bicycles in Key West tended to be. Surely, the other guys on the fire truck had heard the comments. *Was I afraid that the gay guys' behavior would enhance stereotypes and open me up to further taunting?* By the time we returned to the station, I had decided not to be embarrassed by the 'gay boys' who were having some harmless fun. Amazingly, my fellow firefighters never mentioned the incident.

That wasn't the only time the firefighter uniform brought unexpected attention. One late night, we had responded to a fire in Old Town. After connecting our pumper's hose to the fire hydrant, I was posted on the corner of Greene and Duval Streets, directly across from the famous *Sloppy Joe's Bar*. It was after midnight and many people on the street were drunk or high, or both. Within the span of an hour, I was propositioned by both a man and a woman. Ha! I understand that people have sexual fantasies about men in firefighting outfits. To be honest, though, the weather was hot and humid. Underneath all the gear, I was a big ball of smelly sweat! Not much of a fantasy.

The long-awaited Copa gay nightclub had opened. The bar promised to be the *be-all-to-end-all* in gay dance club entertainment in Key West. Of course, straight people would be more than welcome in the club. I was on the shift that joined Fire Marshall Ralph Maribona in conducting the final walk-through before their grand opening to assure that the renovations met the Fire Code. At the far end of the dance floor, there was a main exit leading from the dance area to outside areas. I noticed immediately that the metal double doors were hinged to open inward! Exit doors, by code, must always swing outward. Firefighters know that this fire hazard contributes to an increased chance of death by fire and smoke. The most famous example was the 1942 Cocoanut Grove nightclub fire in Boston; nearly 500 patrons died when they were unable to escape the flames and smoke. The Copa's doors did not open outward and were in violation of code. I reported my observation and concerns to the Fire Marshall. Still, the Copa opened the following week.

A few months later, while in the crowded club for my first time on a weekend, I noticed the doors had not yet been reversed. On Monday, I mentioned it to the Fire Marshall. Months went by with no change. I eventually wrote an official letter of complaint to the Fire Marshall's office and dropped a carbon copy at the City Manager's office. He may never visit the club, but I hoped that my complaint might be taken as a serious risk management issue. Foolishly, I expected the doors would be replaced quickly. It took me writing three more letters before the owners finally hired contractors to reverse the door hinges for an outward swing.

On July 4, 1984, the Southernmost Runners Club held our 3rd annual Conch Republic Run. This year was the first time I noticed that some of the firefighters had registered to run. In the past, it was their wife or kids who were running. This was a rare occasion for the firemen to see me in a completely different role. As the Race Director, I used a bullhorn to welcome the runners, provide them with relevant information about the race, and hand out awards at the end. I couldn't help but think that some of these guys might begin to see me as more than just the 'gay fireman.'

Key West was, indeed, a small island. It was a challenge to keep your activities private. Year-round residents, *Key Westers*, frequently knew what car you drove; they could identify your bicycle. It wasn't unusual to be asked something like "I saw your car on Shaver's Lane last night. What were you doing in that neighborhood?" So, it shouldn't have surprised me to learn that I wasn't the only firefighter in the department who enjoyed the intimacy of another man.

After getting off work one morning, I drove over to have breakfast with Chuck, a friend who worked at a gay guesthouse in Old Town. Simonton Court was a men-only establishment located a block from Duval Street. From the street, it was clear that several historical cottages had been renovated and linked together to create the compound. The Key West gingerbread architecture had been meticulously restored. Framed with Christmas palms and colorful bougainvillea vines, the exterior of the guesthouse exemplified the best of 'gay' gentrification. Still, most visitors couldn't imagine the tropical beauty they would encounter when entering the back gardens. I took a seat at one of the small tables overlooking the swimming pool.

I could see Chuck moving around the open deckside bar area, making sure that breakfast was laid out for the guests. Once his duties were complete, he came out with two cups of coffee and a plate of fresh pastries. I stood to give my friend a hug and a kiss and settled back into my chair.

"How are you two doing?" I asked.

Chuck's partner had just been released from the Florida Keys

Hospital after being diagnosed with *Pneumocystis carinii* pneumonia, an AIDS-defining infection. Chuck knew that I had been keeping up with the available information on the recently discovered virus – called the human T-lymphotropic virus (HTLV-III) – that was identified as the causative agent of AIDS. I was sure that Chuck had many questions. *What was his risk for infection? How could he best care for his partner? How do you obtain the best medical care? How long does his partner have to live?* I answered each question to the best of my ability, but I knew what he needed most was nonjudgmental support.

As it got closer to 8:00 a.m., some of the men began to emerge from their rooms for coffee and breakfast. I knew that tourists would often stay out very late, enjoying the Key West nightlife. A couple of times, Chuck interrupted our discussion to tend to the needs of his guests. Though I had romanticized the role of guesthouse host at times, Chuck's attentiveness reminded me that his position required good communication skills, an ability to predict problems before they surfaced, and more patience than I could imagine. Still, working in this tropical paradise must be some consolation.

As I was waiting for Chuck to return to our table, I saw a guest coming out of his room. I pegged him as the average gay male tourist to the island. He was in his early 30s, quite attractive, and wearing a simple, white, sleeveless t-shirt and tight shorts. *Well, will wonders never cease!?* The second man emerging from the same room was a Key West firefighter! It seemed the two had spent the night together.

OK. I wasn't expecting that. As they walked past my table, the guest offered the customary 'good morning' greeting. He seemed to do a double-take and I realized that it must have been an unusual sight to see a uniformed firefighter in a gay guesthouse. Then, it took only a moment for the fireman to realize that it was me sitting at the table. A look of shock – or fear or panic – flashed across his face. Staying as relaxed as I could, I smiled. "Good morning, guys" I said.

This was a firefighter I barely knew. We had worked together only occasionally, and he was always respectful. He never joined others in harassing me. I knew he was married. I would, of course, protect his privacy. I am sure he had a minor panic attack at first, but it was likely he knew my principles. He never spoke to me about the incident.

ALARM IN THE FIREHOUSE

Seeing him that morning made me think about the firemen who were harassing me. I don't think they understood bisexual behavior. They seemed to think that men were either straight or gay. If they had understood that male-male relationships ranged from sensuality to sexuality, they might have been more tolerant of the diversity in Key West. Decades earlier, Kinsey's research revealed that nearly one third of male respondents admitted to having a sexual encounter with another male to the point of orgasm at least once in their lifetime. Surely, some of those encounters were brief, anonymous, and clandestine. But there are men who couldn't sleep with another guy unless they were romantically involved. And, of course, some men enjoyed the company of women as much as they enjoy male partners. Key West was so small, I guessed that the firemen were aware that some colleagues were having these same-sex trysts.

One day, Alan Vidal and I were raking the grass in the front of the firehouse. The traffic light on Flagler Avenue had just turned red and a pick-up truck with three teenagers in the front came to a stop. One of the kids was pointing in our direction.

"Are you the faggot fireman?" one of the kids yelled. I was sure it was Oneri's boy.

"No, I responded. Pointing in the direction of Old Town, I added "He's working at the 3 station today." The teens looked perplexed and a possibly even embarrassed. They had to be thinking to themselves *"For sure* I thought that was the gay guy?" They drove off.

"You are _so_ bad! Alan exclaimed. He was laughing.

"You know, if they are unable to tell who the gay guy is, it is their own fault," I said.

The political environment had only heated up after Richard became mayor. One of the City Commissioners, Joe Balbontin, had become his main adversary. Balbontin was a self-aggrandizing blowhard who purported a conspiracy theory that gay people wanted to rid the island of Conchs. He was vehemently anti-gay and anti-outsider. Balbontin owned a plumbing company and was repeatedly accused of unethical practices by obtaining lucrative municipal contracts on projects that he voted to support as a city commissioner. Mayor Heyman's initiative to bring transparency to city functions was a threat to Balbontin's usual way of doing business. Balbontin put the 'nep' in nepotism. After a couple of years of political controversy, a new City Charter was finally approved; it clearly outlined equitable procedures for granting municipal contracts and the hiring and firing of city employees.

Balbontin would stop by the firehouse on a regular basis, spewing his rhetoric to glean support from the firemen. It was clear that he knew me to be the gay fireman, but he never spoke to me. He did, one day, start on a tirade against gay men and – while looking at me – said that Key West needed "red-blooded American men and not pansies." What is this absurd idea that gay men are not 'red-blooded American men'? My partner and several of my gay friends were Vietnam Veterans who served their country as well as any heterosexual. Balbontin found it so easy to demean and devalue gay men and not be challenged by his peers.

Despite attempts to reduce violence in Key West, gay-bashing had not been eliminated. One evening, my friend Dan Stahley and I were waiting in line to enter the Copa nightclub. Dan owned the Curry House guesthouse on Fleming Street and one of his guests had joined us for the evening. As we stood in the queue talking, a big guy walking along the sidewalk reached out and punched Dan's guest in the face. "Faggot!" he yelled. The attacker just kept walking. There was suddenly blood everywhere. The poor guy was screaming in pain. Dan ran inside to call an ambulance while I stayed with the victim. Our night was spent in the Emergency Room. The blow had shattered the man's eye socket and he had to undergo two surgeries over the following months to repair the damage. The assailant could just as easily have hit me or Dan. Those who think that gay-bashing is simply 'boys being boys' don't realize the serious damage that can result from one blow. That kind of incident traumatizes everyone involved. Do they think we will 'stop' being gay because of their attack? *Why are gay men such a threat to these guys?*

It was late December of 1984 when I was sitting with Capt. Viti having coffee at the dining table. Suddenly, he told me "Stay there a minute." He bolted out of the room and climbed the stairs to the sleeping quarters. A few minutes later, he returned with a piece of newspaper in his hand. He told me that he had been reading the Miami Herald and an article about firefighters caught his eye. The article described a fire incident in a railroad tunnel in Yorkshire, England. The Fire Department spokesperson being quoted was Ralph Mallinson.

"Isn't that crazy, a firefighter with your last name?" Viti said.

"Captain, my parents were raised in that part of England. 'Mallinson' is an old Yorkshire family name," I said.

Then, I proceeded to tell Viti how my maternal grandfather, James Smith, had been the Fire Chief of the small town of Morley during World War II. When the bombing of London was at its worst, James and his fire company were called to London to assist with fighting fires and rescuing victims. In his absence, his wife, Mary Morris Smith, was recruited to lead the fire service for the town. So, like many Conchs, I also descended from 'firefighting stock.' The captain asked me why no one knew that fact about me.

"No one ever asked," I responded.

I also described my mother serving as a 'nurse's aide' before World War II and then a radio operator at a Royal Air Force base near London during the war. At the beginning of our next shift, I showed the men on my watch the photos of my grandparents (each in their fire uniforms).

CHAPTER 22: City Safety Committee

Occasionally, we drove the fire truck over to the City garage at Garrison Bight for minor repairs or maintenance. One day, one of the women who worked there pulled me aside and whispered: "They are after your job. They are trying to get you fired." I knew she was a lesbian and was trying to help me out. She explained that a group of the firefighters were petitioning the City Safety Committee to have me fired because I posed a risk for spreading HIV infection in the firehouse. The standing committee was composed of representatives from various departments whose charge it was to protect municipal workers from occupational dangers. She told me the date and time of the meeting.

I spoke with a KWFD official who was particularly sympathetic to my cause. When I asked about this sneak attack, he claimed that he had not been made aware of it and, perhaps, it was the union leadership who were behind the petition. Apparently, there was no intention to have me present for the committee meeting.

As the day approached, I realized that I would be working my usual 24-hour shift at Fire Station 1. The City Safety Committee was meeting that evening in City Hall, adjacent to Fire Station 2. It was unlikely that I could defend my job without being at the meeting. Surprisingly, an official transferred me to Station 2 on the day of the meeting. He assured me that I would be able to attend the meeting, though I would have to leave immediately should there be a fire call.

This was, perhaps, the greatest threat to my position so far. I was nervous. When the time came, I told the shift captain that I was attending the meeting. To my surprise, he smiled, shook my hand, and said "Good luck" in a tone that seemed genuine.

The City Hall chamber was large with a crescent-shaped dais for the members of the committee. On the right was a microphone on a stand for the public to provide comments. The audience seating was terraced up and provided seating for over 100 people. One entered the room from the top of the small auditorium and walked down towards the dais. The meeting had already started and most of the audience of about 40 people had found their seats. Four firefighters were seated in the first row. They didn't turn around when I entered. I quickly scanned the room and was relieved to see no other firefighters were present. *The fewer, the better.*

After the committee had discussed some mundane topics, they acknowledged the representatives from Local 1424 of the International Association of Firefighters (IAFF). Indeed, these men were not speaking for the Fire Department; they were petitioning as members of the union. Two of the men stood to present their petition. Clearly, they were nervous. They started with my hiring in 1981; they felt that the KWFD should never have hired a homosexual. Then, in a manner that was as inappropriate as it was offensive, they discussed my relationship with my partner, Joe. *How dare they talk about my partner in a public forum!? Now, I was more pissed off than nervous.* The firemen expressed their disgust with my sexual orientation. They claimed that my 'lifestyle' did not meet the moral standards of the community. Without claiming that I had ever acted inappropriately, their case was built on the presumption that I would do so. Their hypothetical scenarios were based on stereotypes and designed to foster fear and dread among the committee members.

"Can you imagine how you would feel if you were showering in the firehouse, knowing that a homosexual man is leering and trying to catch a glimpse of you?" one offered.

In the end, though, their intent was to petition for my discharge from the department based upon their distorted beliefs and unfounded fears about the HIV/AIDS epidemic. They complained that exposure to this new disease threatened their health and safety at work. Their argument can be summarized as: "He is gay. He must have the HIV virus. He will spread that virus to us through the dishes, bunks, showers, and fire equipment.

Then, we will take it home to our wives and children." They sat back down to receive pats on their backs from the other two firemen. I realized that such assertions could easily sway the committee members who didn't understand the finer points of HIV transmission. It was shrewd how they began with linking all gay men to HIV and finishing with the hackneyed refrain that a gay man is somehow a threat to the heterosexual family unit. My hopes were sinking. My face and neck were hot and flushed with anger. My legs were shaking. I was trying to organize my thoughts quickly so that I could take my place at the podium and present my side of the story. Unexpectedly, a member of the audience was already standing and adjusting the microphone to speak. I braced for the worst. *There's no telling how the anti-gay rhetoric might ratchet up!*

Then, the real fun began. The chairperson thanked the firemen for bringing their workplace safety concern forward to the committee. Then, seeing the woman standing at the podium, he motioned her to speak.

"Good evening," she began, "some of you know me. I have tried to provide my expert guidance for this committee. I'm Bev. I am a registered nurse with considerable experience with AIDS." Beverly was a Nursing Director at the Florida Keys Memorial Hospital on Stock Island. She spoke in a measured and confident manner.

"I can't just sit here and listen to such ignorance and intolerance," she continued. "As we do not yet have a test for the HIV virus, you don't know if this firefighter even has the virus. If he is in a monogamous relationship, he may not even be infected. This is a serious epidemic. But there is no reason to let our fears lead to irrational or unfair behavior."

Wow! It was the miracle I hadn't expected. Surely, the firemen had not foreseen this turn of events. For nearly an hour, Ms. Smith answered questions from the committee members. *How is the virus transmitted? Is it likely to spread through the firehouse as suggested? Is there a reasonable risk to these firefighters?* She had a gentle, informative approach that allowed her to provide the necessary knowledge in a nonjudgmental way; she was neither condescending nor patronizing. Ms. Smith had no idea how relieved I was to have her on my side of this contentious issue. The firemen must have been feeling terribly deflated by the time she concluded and returned to her seat. There was no rebuttal from the firemen. Now, it was my turn. I walked down the stairs and took my place at the public podium. I turned to look at the four firemen.

The expressions on their faces were priceless! They had no reason to believe that I would be attending this meeting. They nervously whispered to each other as if in a panic. I adjusted the microphone and addressed the committee.

"Good evening and thank you for the opportunity to speak this evening. My name is Kevin Mallinson. I am the firefighter about whom everyone has been speaking." I don't think the committee expected me to be there either.

It occurred to me at that moment that I was standing before the committee and audience in my KWFD uniform, looking freshly pressed and professional. The firemen representing the union had come in street clothes and looked much less official. I began by thanking Beverly Smith for her expert insights and guidance for the committee. The tide had certainly turned in my favor. I was feeling more confident, though the outcome was anything but guaranteed.

The first thing I told the committee was that I had wanted to follow in my family's tradition and serve the community as a firefighter. Then, I outlined my exemplary service to the KWFD to date. As evidence of my dedication to professionalism, I noted my first-place finish at the State Fire College. I mentioned that my captain had recently evaluated my performance as 'above average.' In 1983, I had been recognized as the Outstanding Firefighter of the Year. To round out my contributions to the community, I briefly mentioned my volunteer service to the Key West HELPLINE crisis call center. I wanted them to know that I involved myself in the Key West community.

Attempting to hold back my anger, I turned my comments towards the unfair and blatant discrimination I faced. At one point, I challenged the firemen's presumptions about my relationship with my partner Joe and the impropriety of it being openly discussed in a public City Safety Committee meeting. This seemed to unsettle some of the committee members who suddenly looked less composed, less comfortable. Perhaps, I was striking a chord with their conscience? I took another step to make my point.

"Can anyone tell me about the wife of this firefighter? What does she do? How would you describe their marriage?" I asked, pointing at the fireman closest to me. "Or this guy's wife?" I added, directing their gaze to the one in the next chair.

"No. You can't," I continued, "you don't even know if this guy has a wife. That's because your private life is not a criterion for being a professional firefighter. Just like these guys, I don't have a *lifestyle*...I have a life." I wanted to emphasize that knowing someone's sexual orientation tells you nothing about the way they live their life.

"I wholeheartedly agree with Ms. Smith when she said that this committee has no right to be examining the private details of someone's life in a public meeting." I suggested that the only reason these men felt empowered to invade my privacy was because I was gay; that was not sufficient reason to deny me respect. "There is no reason why my job should be in jeopardy simply because of who I love," I said. "What is the next step? Do you want to go through the City rolls and fire anyone who is gay or lesbian?" *Then, of course, you would have to oust our openly gay mayor!* "Where would it stop?" I ended my defense by boldly asserting that the City should enact a non-discrimination law to protect individuals from being fired on the basis of their sexual orientation. With this, the city lawyer (sitting as advisor to the committee) spoke up.

"Another law on the books?" he blurted out, as if exasperated. "Don't we have enough laws? It seems I can't get out of bed in the morning without breaking a law!" I smiled.

"It's funny, but it seems *I can't go to bed* at night without breaking a law!" Many of the people in the audience laughed at how I turned his phrase. It was hard to tell, but I think some of the committee members seemed to be enjoying themselves. I summarized my argument for the committee to reject this request for my dismissal from the KWFD, emphasizing some of the points made so well by Beverly Smith. I was so thankful that the knowledgeable nurse was willing to advocate for me.

All committee members, except one, voted in my favor; the firefighters petition was dead in the water. As I left the chamber, I was becoming more apprehensive about the aftermath I would face in Fire Station 2 that evening. Surprisingly, the four firefighters did not come up into the living quarters to debrief. Maybe they were not in the mood to explain how their argument didn't hold up to scrutiny.

If the City Safety Committee had voted in favor of firing me from my position in the KWFD that evening, I would have fought the decision in court. In a lawsuit, the City of Key West would have been primarily responsible for the actions of its employees. However, the firemen who presented the petition were representing the Local 1424 of the IAFF in that meeting. They likely were not acting with the approval of the union membership; if a vote had been taken among the firemen, any number of my supporters in the department would have informed me. If I had taken my appeal to the courts, my suit would also have sought damages against the union, invariably involving the IAFF on the state and national levels. Such public scrutiny would have exposed the KWFD union to untold risk and unwanted attention. I was prepared to pursue the issue in court. As it stands, it was nearly another four decades before the U.S. Supreme Court would decide that employment discrimination based on sexual orientation was a violation of one's Constitutional rights.

Even at this point, I didn't really appreciate how 'earth-shattering' it was to serve as an openly gay firefighter in a fire department. The men hoped that the expanding AIDS crisis would give them the evidence they needed to have me fired. What surprised me was their unrelenting opposition to my employment. In their shameless attempt to seize on the public's heightened anxieties about HIV transmission, they tried to get me fired. I wasn't yet done with the Local 1424 of the firefighter's union.

CHAPTER 23: Local 1424

The AIDS epidemic was continuing to ravage the gay community on the island. One evening, I received a phone call through the fire dispatcher's line. A patient at the Florida Keys Memorial Hospital had asked a nurse to call "Kevin in the Fire Department." The nurse told me that my friend, Alan Scott, had come to the emergency room with probable pneumonia and was being admitted to the intensive care unit. As I was the only rear-end man on the truck that evening, I told the nurse that I would come by the hospital when my shift ended the next morning.

At 7 am, I drove to the hospital. Less than 10 minutes away, it was a relatively small facility with a 5-bed ICU on the third floor. Before I was in the KWFD, I had been admitted to the facility for minor surgery. I considered bringing Alan some flowers but remembered that ICUs don't usually allow fresh flowers for fear of spreading infection. I easily found the door to the nursing unit.

"Good morning," I said. "My name's Kevin. I am here to see Alan Scott."

"Hi. I'm Pat," the nurse responded. "If you can stay right here, I will go find his nurse."

The ICU seemed busy. I took a step back and stood against a closed door to be out of the way. Once inside the unit, the glass walls and doors allowed me to see activity in nearly every room. Pat seemed to find Alan's nurse on the opposite side of the bank of computer monitors. I could see her pointing towards me. Alan's nurse approached me.

"Can we speak outside for just a minute?" she asked. Once in the hallway, she looked around to be sure we had some privacy before continuing. "Mr. Scott died around 6:30 this morning, just before I started my shift."

"He died?" I asked, as if not believing her. "Wasn't he only admitted last night?"

It seemed inconceivable to me that this could happen so fast. I was shocked at the unexpected turn of events. The nurse explained how little she knew because she had not been on duty at the time of Alan's demise. My stomach ached, my breathing was shallow, and I couldn't focus very well. It was as if all the blood drained from me. I wanted to scream but knew it wouldn't be acceptable.

"Would you like to see him? He still in the room," she asked. "We will take his body to the morgue shortly."

"Yes," I responded. Looking at her name tag, I added "Yes, Ophelia, I would like to see him."

We walked back into the ICU and immediately entered the first room on the right. The curtains on the window had been pulled, so I wouldn't have thought it was a patient room. It was relatively dark in the room, with only a single fluorescent light fixture over the bed providing indirect light. Alan lay there lifeless.

To be honest, I didn't know Alan all that well. He was a 'fixture' at the Higgs Beach pier – the *'dick dock'* as Viti had called it during our drive that day. Alan was there most anytime Joe and I came down for a swim. His skin was always dark, but it was hard to tell if he was naturally brown-skinned or just spent too much time tanning in the Florida sun. We enjoyed chatting with him. He had served on Merchant Marine ships and, consequently, had seen much of the world. Alan was about 6 ft 6 inches tall, quite thin for a man in his 40s, and sported a thick, black mustache. He stuck out in a crowd. Alan was an intelligent, mild-mannered guy whose mysterious past seemed well aligned with the quirky nature of many 'transplants' who had moved to Key West. My instinctive response was to reach out and touch Alan's body. Dead or not, I wanted to have some connection with him. As my fingers glided over his bald head, they hit the headboard of the hospital bed. Realizing that his unusual height meant his feet were close to hanging off the end of the mattress, I smiled.

"Luckily, the bed was just long enough to hold him," I said. Ophelia didn't smile in response. In fact, she looked uncomfortable.

"How do you think he got it?" she asked.

"I'm sorry?" I was unsure what she meant.

"AIDS. How do you think he got it? Clearly, he wasn't a faggot," she said. The slur rolled off her tongue as if it were not a demeaning homophobic smear. However, I was sure I detected the hint of a sneer. *She knew what she was saying. Who did she think she was talking to?* Almost immediately, I realized that I had come directly from the firehouse and was standing there in my KWFD uniform. *Clearly, I was not a faggot.* I was a firefighter. Once again, my instincts kicked in and I responded appropriately to her indignant comment.

"Get out," I ordered, with all the restraint I could muster. My anger wasn't showing, but it surely was rising to the surface.

"What?" she asked, as if surprised at my reaction.

"I said '*Get out,*' I clarified. "I want to spend some time with Alan." This was the only chance I would have to advocate for Alan. I couldn't allow her to enjoy her moment of perceived superiority and privilege. It was shocking to me that a nurse would feel it appropriate to demean the deceased, least of all in front of a grieving friend.

By this point in the epidemic, I had already lost several friends to AIDS. Though I had attended funeral services with open caskets, this was my first time alone with a dead body. I felt more awkward than fearful. Though I was raised Catholic, I never believed in the existence of a higher power. However, I was aware of my spiritual nature. So, this was an opportunity for me to search for some peace amid an awful morning. Speaking softly, I told Alan that I was sorry he had died alone. I was sad that I hadn't known of his HIV infection. I regretted not spending more time getting to know him. *Why did he ask for me in his time of crisis?* There were so many unanswered questions about this epidemic that was devastating our gay community. Finally, I leaned over and, whispering in Alan's ear, swore that I would always respond to bigotry and intolerance with an unflinching advocacy for those who cannot defend themselves.

When I was done, I quietly left the ICU without talking to anyone. I knew Alan's next stop would be a cold slab in the basement of the hospital. Though he had asked for me to visit him last evening, I possessed no legal right to influence the disposition of his body. Still, I was trying to wrap my head around the idea that he could come into the hospital yesterday and be ready for the morgue in less than 24 hours? In my experience, a diagnosis of AIDS meant that you had a few months to live, not less than a day. I had much to learn about AIDS.

Soon after Alan's death, I received word that my friend Brian O'Regan was sick in Seattle. After losing his partner to AIDS, Brian had returned to his hometown and was living with his parents while looking for a place of his own. It was only a few months later that his parents called to inform me of Brian's death. At 29 years old, I was sobering up to the frail nature of our lives. Life, it seems, could end at any time. There was no blood test available yet to determine if one had the HIV virus. The evidence strongly suggested that the virus was sexually transmitted. *What if I were infected and didn't know it? What if I lost Joe to AIDS?* Between moments of panic about AIDS, I reverted to my usual coping style. I plan and I act. I decided that I had to do whatever I could to provide compassionate support for persons with AIDS.

Death wasn't finished with me yet. In November 1984, during a brief visit to Connecticut to see family, my mother died. My sister and I shared the stress of scheduling the viewing and arranging for cremation. Sue and I had always been close. Now, we were sharing the inevitable reality that to live is to suffer loss. Grief is painful and I needed to find better ways of managing its impact on me. Returning to the firehouse, I received no expressions of sympathy from my coworkers for the loss of my mother.

Despite being eligible to join the International Association of Fire Fighters (IAFF), Local 1424, Firefighters Union for several years, I was the only firefighter in the department not allowed to join. The men, purposely, would not inform me of when and where the meetings were being held. The union members had regular activities, the details of which were never given to me. Like firefighters across the nation, the union organized a fundraiser every Labor Day, collecting money for the Jerry Lewis

Telethon in support of the Muscular Dystrophy Association. For nearly three decades, the IAFF had supported the annual drive to support "Jerry's Kids." The firemen would stand in the city's major intersections, holding an empty firefighter boot in their hands. Drivers were encouraged to drop donations into the boot. I was never asked to participate with the others in this annual activity.

The IAFF Local 1424 also organized its own chapter fundraiser. Each year, they printed a KWFD Yearbook. Usually, the pages contained action photos from the more notable fires of the previous year, promoting firefighters as 'America's Bravest.' The pages also provided individual headshots of the firefighters, usually grouped by the watch to which they were assigned. Finally, the Yearbook would include more general photos taken at each of the three firehouses, or feature some of the 'sexy' equipment such as the *Jaws of Life* that had been purchased. The yearly publication raised funds by soliciting local merchants that placed advertisements to be peppered throughout the book. It was ironic that sponsorships often came from local gay or lesbian merchants. *Key West Fragrance*, *Key West Handprint Fabrics*, *Key West Aloe*, and *Fast Buck Freddies* were all frequent sponsors. Yet, during my years in the KWFD, neither my photo nor my name ever appeared in one of the annual editions of the Yearbook. If the firemen had thought strategically, they could have highlighted my status as a firefighter and, more than likely, increased their income exponentially.

Much to my surprise, I received an unexpected phone call at the fire station one day. I was sitting in the dining room, working a design on my drafting board. I was completing the plans for a house that my friends were going to build. The personal phone line rang, and the dispatcher told me to answer it. One of the firefighters working at Station 3 was calling. It was Louis, better known by his nickname 'Pic.' We had worked on the same shift occasionally over these years, but Pic rarely chose to engage me in conversation. However, he never taunted me. Pic was calling to inform me of the day and time that the men would meet at Fire Station 3 for the upcoming Local 1424 union meeting. Once he had communicated the relevant facts, his voice dropped to a near whisper.

"You aren't going to tell anyone that I called, are you?" he asked. I was thankful for his support. He was, after all, putting himself at some risk for divulging the details of the meeting. In all good conscience, I couldn't hang him out to dry.

"Oh, no," I assured him. "I am much too discreet for that. As you know, I am good at keeping secrets." He took a moment to respond.

"Yeah, thanks," he said.

When I hung up the phone, I couldn't help but think that I had initiated a shift in thinking among some of the firefighters, even those with whom I had little contact. Even if this guy had something to fear, he took a risk to call me. I respected him for that.

The day of the union meeting arrived. I was not on duty that day. So, I drove to Firehouse 3 and strolled into the truck bay. Most of the firefighters had already arrived. The truck from my firehouse was just arriving. I could see the surprise on their faces; they had not expected to see me there. My heart was racing. This was the largest gathering of the firemen I had ever seen. The meeting was to be held in the large open area on the second floor of the firehouse. I saw Henry, the membership officer, standing at the base of the stairs chatting with another firefighter. Although he was clearly aware that I wanted to talk, he finished his conversation and quickly turned to go upstairs.

"Henry!" I called out. "I'm here to become a member of the union."

"Sorry," he said. His tone communicated no sense of an apology. "The agenda is quite full for the meeting. We can't add anything more." He resumed climbing the stairs.

"That's unacceptable," I said. I was firm, but not aggressive. He was ignoring me. I decided it was time for a threat. I raised my voice considerably.

"I guess that I will have to contact Jack, our State rep to get in," I yelled. Indeed, in preparation for this meeting, I had called the central office of the Florida IAFF to be sure that I had Jack's name and contact information.

"No, you can't do that!" he said. I had captured Henry's undivided attention. He pivoted and quickly descended back to the base of the stairs. In a tone that communicated both fear and panic, he tried his best to shut me down.

"We don't bother officials with local issues," he said. "We are not going to bring you into the union because you keep talking about being gay. There's no place for that here."

"Henry," I said, "you guys are the ones who are always mentioning my being gay. Name just one time when I brought it up? I talk about fire equipment. *You* talk about my sexual orientation." I had assumed a rigid stance to support my in-your-face defiant attitude.

"In fact," I continued, "you guys talk about *your* sexual orientation all the time. Whether I want to or not, I am subjected to hearing about the women you find attractive. You talk about your escapades…whether real or fantasized. *You*, Henry, always seem have some kind of sexual innuendo coming out of your mouth."

I may have crossed a line by being so honest, Still, it was true. The firefighters often discussed the sexual acts they preferred. Some had pin-up photos and others had porno magazines in the firehouse. While they regularly kissed their wives at the door of the firehouse, they never once saw me hug or kiss Joe. They never even saw me hold Joe's hand.

As was my intent, our conversation had become so loud as to attract attention. Several firefighters were close enough to hear us confronting each other. Henry lowered his voice, offering what sounded like a small concession on his part.

"Look, you have to promise to never be open about being a faggot if you want to be a member of the union," he offered.

"Screw that!" I snapped back. I was intentionally louder to be sure the other men heard it. "You don't get to dictate to me what I can – and cannot – do or say."

At that moment, the President of the local 1424, Tim "Buddha", walked in. Henry, in a near panic, wanted to silence me so that Buddha would not get involved.

"Shhhh…..!" he implored.

OK, now is the time to really raise my voice.

"So, Henry," I said, "my only option is to call Jack and formally complain? He'd be interested in knowing why a firefighter hasn't been allowed to join the union after being eligible for years!"

This, I felt, was a turning point. Either we would begin to negotiate in good faith, or I was possibly about to be pummeled by an unruly mob of firefighters. My heart was beating wildly. My face was flushed. Still, I held my ground, maintained my composure. Henry, I could sense, was on the defensive and flustered. Without responding to me, Henry quickly grabbed Buddha by the arm, led him into the kitchen, and closed the door. Knowing that the small group of firemen still had their eyes on me, I leaned against the stairway railing with my arms locked across my chest in a confident and defiant posture. I surprised myself. I was feeling much more confident. Still, this wasn't over yet.

It only took a few short minutes before Henry and Buddha emerged from their private conversation. Buddha passed me and climbed the stairs without saying a word. It was time for the meeting to start and the other men had already begun to gather upstairs. Henry held up his palm to keep me from moving, suggesting that I should stay behind with him. I assumed he had something more to say. He moved in close, as if to keep others from hearing him.

"It will be up to the membership," he muttered. Begrudgingly, it seemed he was capitulating to my demand. "They will need to vote on it," he added. As he turned to climb the stairs, I took a slow, deep breath and followed. Walking into the union meeting that evening was scarier than I had anticipated. For the first time in my years with the department, I was seeing most of the firefighters together in one room. There were so many with whom I had never shared a shift or even had a conversation. They only knew me by what they had heard from the other firemen. Likely, my reputation was concocted from an uneven mixture of truth, confabulation, and hyperbole. This was going to be a challenge.

The union leaders started the meeting with some mundane updates. One made a snide remark about Mayor Heyman, suggesting that he was no friend to the department. To my surprise, Alan spoke up to say that Heyman had advocated for the KWFD to get some much-needed equipment; the mayor, he added, had spoken publicly about the need to increase salaries. *"Wow,"* I thought, *"a Conch who can honestly defend the actions of our gay mayor!"* But then, Alan was his own man.

Eventually, the topic of my entry into the union was raised. Initially, the room was quiet as Buddha brought up my unexpected agenda item. I knew that the men had never seen me at one of their union meetings before, so I was treading in new territory. I didn't know what to expect now that I had forced their hand on the issue. There was a rush of low whispers across the room. Attempting to not appear furtive, I looked around the room for friendly, if not merely familiar, faces that might offer some support. Yeah, there are the four guys that tried to get me fired in the City Safety Committee. *Grumble, grumble, grumble.* "Faggot!" somebody jeered. It was low, but still perceptible. *Was that Mike? At this point, I don't care.* Finally, one of the guys spoke up, saying "Kevin is a good fireman. What's the big deal? We can't keep him out of the union." To this day, I'm not sure who said it, but I think it was Alex. However, I was grateful for his fortitude. There was more grumbling.

"I don't want to be the one who has to sleep next to him," one guy shouted. He seemed pleased with all the laughter that came in response.

"I don't want to think some gay guy is looking at me in the showers!?" Henry joked.

Seeing that this group could become hostile quickly, I barked. "Hey!" My loud yell squelched the chatter and caught their attention. It worked. The room went silent, and they were all looking at me. Scanning the room quickly to be sure that they were all seeing me eye-to-eye, I ended up focusing on Henry. He quickly lost the smirk on his face.

"Honestly, guys," I yelled, "it's hard to believe any gay guy would look at you in the showers! If even *one* of you thinks you're attractive, raise your hand!" I emphasized my point by raising my arm. Not surprisingly, there were no takers.

"Yeah, it really isn't an issue, is it?" I caught the eye of the one fireman in the department that I found terribly sexy. Oh course, he had no idea how attractive he was in my eye. We had never worked together, nor exchanged more than a few words in passing. He was a bit more mature and had never joined the others in harassing me. He had a wry smile on his face that suggested he was enjoying my open challenge to the group. Still, I wasn't done making my point.

"I joined this department to fight fires and I do just that. It has been two and a half years since I passed Fire College. Either this union votes for me to join tonight, or I will file a formal complaint with the State office," There was silence.

"Buddha, I will be downstairs," I said. I turned around and saw the staircase in front of me. *Am I going to be attacked once I turn my back on these guys?* I hadn't been that scared in years. Some of these men barely knew me. Others had been outwardly hostile since my first day on the job. Rather than panic, though, I kept my composure and slowly exited.

The following week, the finance clerk at City Hall asked me to sign a form to allow union dues to be regularly deducted from my paycheck. Thanks to Pic, I finally became a union member.

CHAPTER 24: Firemen have no Balls

Shortly after arriving in Key West, Joe and I had met a Canadian nurse named Iva Stanley who was living in the Keys with her boyfriend, David Ethridge. They already knew my friends Jan, Barbara, and Jane. We were 'birds of a feather' with a liberal, progressive perspective and desire for peace and social change. Iva introduced me to the concept of hospice, a relatively new perspective on caring for persons with life-limiting illness. Recently, the Hospice of the Florida Keys had begun providing a wide range of professional nursing and volunteer support services to individuals who had been diagnosed with late-stage cancer, AIDS, and other debilitating conditions. They promoted an innovative palliative care approach. Iva suggested that I might be interested in becoming a hospice volunteer because of my previous work with the HELPLINE crisis call center and my compassion for persons living with AIDS.

A hospice volunteer was prepared to go into the homes of clients and provide an array of non-professional supports. The volunteer might assist a dying person (or one living with a life-limiting condition) by doing light household chores or bringing them groceries. Often, a volunteer might be asked to sit with the client so the family can have some respite from the emotional burden of daily caregiving. The volunteer training workshops provided a stimulating amalgamation of new and interesting skills: empathetic communication skills, non-medical symptom management, and strategies for talking about loss and grief. The hospice nurses and staff were some of the kindest people I had ever met in my life. Through the training, I met many other volunteers who had been suffering loss from AIDS. I felt I belonged in this little community.

As a new volunteer, the first patient assigned to me was a young man with AIDS. Tommy was about 10 years older than me. He lived alone in a small garden cottage in Old Town Key West. The staff informed me that his condition was advanced and that he had lost much of his body weight due to the associated wasting syndrome. He was physically unable to get out of bed because of his fatigue and muscle atrophy. I found the key to the door in the mailbox.

"Tommy," I called out. "It's Kevin. I am one of the volunteers." No response. *Could he be napping?* I called out again as I scanned the layout of the house.

"I'm in here," he replied. It was nearly a whisper.

I found his dark bedroom a few steps from the small kitchen. The house was decorated in a traditional Key West style. The wall colors were light pastels and the artwork reflected tropical flowers, sailboats in the mangroves, and conch houses with gingerbread balustrades. There seemed to be a lack of personal, everyday items that one usually finds in a home. Not knowing what to expect, I took a deep breath, entered the room, and sat down on the one chair next to the bed.

Tommy had all the characteristics of a gay man with end-stage AIDS. Though in his late 30s, the wasting syndrome had left him with sunken facial features. Still, I could tell that he had been quite handsome. His battle with HIV, though, had taken its toll. His mustache and beard were thinned and graying. Despite the seasonal heat and humidity, Tommy had a blanket covering much of his body. His bedside table was almost completely covered with medication bottles, leaving just enough space for a cup and saucer. I tried to imagine how hard it was for someone to manage the wide array of symptoms associated with AIDS.

Though Tommy's movements and speech were slow and deliberate, it wasn't difficult to engage him in conversation. In fact, he seemed eager to meet someone new and talk. I learned that he had been ill for a few months. Losing his job due to illness, and his apartment due to depleted finances, the hospice organization had found him this cottage at no cost to him. As he talked, I could see that he had only gratitude for the hospice staff and volunteers. I mentioned the beautiful gardens surrounding the house.

"I am going to die here," he said. His matter-of-fact tone of voice seemed more conciliatory than defeatist. He placed his right hand on two books next to him on the bed.

"Favorite books?" I asked.

"Photo albums," he corrected. "Can I show you?"

For the next 30 minutes or so, Tommy gave me the 5-cent tour of his brief career. He had served as a costume designer for the Ringling/Barnum & Bailey Circus. Slowly paging through his albums, he would stop at particular photos to explain the significance of the outfits. At times, he struggled to find his words or the energy to voice them. It never occurred to me how many different characters had to be dressed for the circus. In addition to the clowns, there were the trapeze artists, lion tamers, fortune tellers, harlequins, and the ringmaster among others. Tommy spoke of the awards he had won, described the textures of his fabrics, and the updates he made to contemporize traditional costumes. *I learned in hospice training how crucial it was to support reminiscing and listening to a 'life review'.* For me, it was a marvelous insight into a parallel world of which I knew little and a talented artist that I could easily have passed on the streets of Key West without a hint of his accomplishments.

I noticed that Tommy was now stumbling over his words, pausing to catch his breath, and looking pale.

"You look tired. How about some time to rest?" I asked.

"No. Not really," he said. "But I'd like a cup of tea? On the kitchen counter."

"Sure." I got up, took the cup and saucer from the side table, and walked into the kitchen. It took a few minutes to locate a pot to boil the water. The kitchen was brightly lit by the sunlight streaming in the windows. The view of the garden was lovely. The Christmas tree palms towered over the yellow hibiscus blossoms and red caladiums. This little oasis was a masterpiece of design with its differing heights, colors, and textures. Just as Tommy had labored over the specifics of his costumes, surely a gardener had designed this small bit of tropical paradise. I brought the tea back into the bedroom and placed it on the bedside table.

"I forgot, did you want milk or sugar?" I asked.

Tommy didn't answer. I thought he had gone to sleep. Then, by looking at the grayish color of his face and neck that wasn't there earlier, my mind flashed to seeing Alan's dead body in the ICU months earlier. I shook his shoulder and called his name. No response. I carefully checked for a radial pulse. *How embarrassed I will be if he opens his eyes and realizes that I thought him dead!* No pulse. OK, Tommy might have just died. I knew that there was no need to panic at this point. There would be no CPR performed and no ambulance to be called. He was in hospice care and the ultimate goal was to live fully and experience a peaceful death. Tommy looked peaceful. I sat at his bedside for some length of time before checking him again for some response. This time, I noticed that his muscles seemed to be even more flaccid and lifeless than when I had first come in the room. Convinced that he had passed, I sat for a few more minutes talking to him. *Thanks for giving me this gift, Tommy. I feel so honored to have been here today.*

I phoned the hospice office to alert the staff. The social worker came to the phone quickly and asked if I was alright. She said that a nurse would come over immediately and she was worried about me being alone with 'the deceased.' I assured her that I was relaxed and not anxious about being with Tommy. I would think back on that afternoon many times in the following years as a watershed moment in which I accepted the finality of death while cherishing the celebration of one's life. It helped me bring some of my KWFD experiences into perspective. *What is really important in life anyway?* For myself, though, I learned that I had the capacity – and the courage – to be compassionate to others with no expectation of reciprocity.

My time with Tommy had been so short; he gave me more than he could have imagined. Through this experience, I became even more convinced that most of the harassment I endured in the KWFD was pointless. Death has a way of putting things in perspective. Watching a young man die in the prime of his life helped me focus on what was important. I found that I had developed a fierce sense of independence over the past years. I wasn't going to lose my direction.

I had been volunteering at the HELPLINE crisis center for about two and a half years. Each Spring, we hosted a 12-hour Dance Marathon to raise much-needed funds to support the service. In March 1985, I collected the largest amount of donations and completed the dance marathon; this won me an all-expenses-paid trip for two to New York City for a week. Even some of my fellow firefighters were pleased to see my photo appear in the newspaper, shining a positive light on how firefighters contribute to the community.

It had now been 4 years since the first cases of AIDS were identified in the country. The president at the time, Ronald Reagan, had not even spoken the word 'AIDS' in public. I was outraged by the ineffectual government response to an epidemic that was disproportionately devastating America's gay communities. In the U.S., nearly 800 Americans had been diagnosed with AIDS and half of those had already died. There was a mounting panic spreading across the country. The television news programs that covered AIDS stories seemed intent upon stereotyping homosexual men. We were often portrayed as sex-hungry animals who cared little for our own welfare, never mind the safety and security of 'normal' heterosexual families who felt at risk. This only promulgated further stigma and discrimination. There was an overall lack of compassion for the human lives being lost in the epidemic. For gay men, it seemed that our only choices were to live in silence or to speak up. I chose the latter.

My self-perception was changing, as well. As I knew a lot about HIV and AIDS at this point, others were frequently turning to me for information and advice. My friends were, for the most part, older than me. Up to this point, I had unconsciously thought of myself as the 'younger brother' among those who comprised my 'family of choice.' Now, I found myself providing counseling, guidance, and support for my brothers. My knowledge of HIV/AIDS was extending beyond the basic HIV prevention I learned in the American Red Cross training. I was learning about nutritional support, symptom management, and end-of-life issues. In the hospice groups, we were exploring legal and ethical issues for gay men who were drafting their wills and expressing their wishes concerning life support or resuscitation. There was hope that the Food and Drug Administration would soon approve a blood test for the HTLV-III (HIV) virus sometime soon. A test would be extraordinarily important in identifying who was infected but would likely raise privacy issues. As an advocate, I sometimes felt like an older brother responsible for managing crises. This was not a comfortable role for me. I was maturing, whether I liked it or not.

I had been enjoying my work much more since being transferred to Viti's shift. In the Spring of 1985, I was encouraged by several KWFD officers and a few firefighters to take the examination for promotion to Engineer (driver). Some rear-end men had taken the exam more than once. I studied the few materials made available to me. With a score of 88%, I had passed on the first attempt. While I received praise from my supporters in the department, there were others who felt threatened. They were in a panic that I could be promoted and, consequently, be in a position to give them orders. My advancement would surely secure my spot in the KWFD structure. I learned that when Al Rahming first sat for the examination, he had been given an outdated manual to study for the test! He felt that institutionalized racism in the City administration was to blame. I don't doubt that his suspicions were well-grounded.

After nearly four years in the KWFD, I was still not 'friends' with my coworkers. I had no social engagement with the firemen. I had never been invited to a fellow fireman's house for a barbeque or other social event. When asked if the KWFD sponsored a traditional Firemen's Ball each year, I would laugh, saying "The Key West firemen have no balls because, if they did, they know I would show up and dance with Joe!" Though the guys talked of many fishing trips, I was never invited. They were not yet ready to accept me. If we had enjoyed social interactions, their myths about gay men would be debunked. As it stood, many of them had little idea of who I was and how I lived my life.

CHAPTER 25: Media Frenzy

As a tightknit community on an island, Key Westers took particular interest in keeping up on local gossip, politics, and news. The daily newspapers, *The Key West Citizen* and *The Miami Herald*, were popular. Less popular for the Conchs was the *Solares Hill*, a weekly newspaper that focused on political commentary, the arts, and environmental issues. Over the years, I had appeared in the *KW Citizen* numerous times for various activities such as teaching sign language, fundraising for HELPLINE, or hospice volunteering. The print media provided opportunities for the expression of minority opinion views and, unfortunately, thinly veiled hate speech. For example, after a group of anti-war peace demonstrators held a rally in town, a writer referred to the sponsor (Peaceworks) as 'anti-American.' I wrote a Letter to the Editor in response, making the point that America is strong because of its ability to avert war through negotiation. I encouraged readers to honor free speech as one of our most fundamental American rights. I was amazed how many of the firemen read that commentary. However, it was an article *about* me as a firefighter that caused more alarm in the firehouse than I could have imagined.

In April of 1985, I was invited by my friend Marilyn Volker-Yoblick to present a workshop at a conference in Miami. The *7th Annual Developing a Positive Gay or Lesbian Identity* conference was an opportunity for gay men and lesbians to develop effective strategies for combatting stigma and improving their mental health. My workshop was entitled *"Openly Gay on the Job"* in which I discussed my experiences in the KWFD and my strategies for managing the barriers I faced on a regular basis. A writer from the *Miami Herald* attended the workshop and published his summary of my presentation in an article on May 5, 1985. I believe that his synopsis of the presentation was accurate, albeit truncated. None of the firemen mentioned the newspaper article to me. I didn't realize that the shit was about to hit the fan!

Al Rantel, a local radio host in Key West, read the article and asked to interview me on his show. I agreed. Again, I thought that his interview was fair, and I kept a positive and respectful demeanor while providing honest answers to Al's questions. When I got home that evening, Joe congratulated me on the interview, but said "Holy shit! I hope the firemen were not listening in on that one! Maybe, because it's a weekend, they were not near the radio." I was surprised at his response. He explained that he didn't think the firemen would appreciate their 'dirty' laundry being hung out for the public to view.

On Monday morning, a mob was waiting for me at the firehouse. There must have been 20 or more firemen crowded into our living space on the second floor. The firefighters were enraged upon hearing the radio interview. Since that first day in the firehouse years ago, I was dreading an angry group like this one. Some of the guys were screaming obscenities in my face and threatening me with harm. My only recourse was to ask: What exactly did I say that upset them?

"You don't have to talk about being a faggot!" one guy yelled.

"I wasn't actually talking about being gay," I responded, "I talked about managing the harassment I am subjected to in this department *because* I am gay." Somehow, I knew the distinction was beyond them at this point. It disturbed me greatly that so many of the white hats – the guys I enjoyed working with – were present, though not particularly joining in the melee. However, Capt. Frank Vega was a man I respected and his expression of anger distressed me greatly. *Didn't he understand that I had every right to speak up about how I had been mistreated?*

"*You* are the ones who talked about me being gay," I continued, "from the very first day I walked into this firehouse. *You* are the ones who told your friends and family about the gay guy. *You* are the ones who tried to get me fired *twice*. And you think your behavior should be kept a *secret*?

I didn't say anything in that interview that wasn't true."

"You said that we were all Cuban, Catholic, and macho," another guy snarled.

"Actually, I said that this department is 'heavily' Cuban, 'heavily' Catholic, and 'heavily' macho," I clarified. "Is that not true?"

"It makes us look bad," he responded.

I raised my hand in the air as if to conduct a poll of all present. "How many of you are Cuban? How many of you are Catholic? Do you consider yourselves macho?" With each point, no one raised a hand.

"It's just when you put them all together that it sounds bad," the guy said. I did my very best not to laugh at that comment. I knew I couldn't explain that their Cuban culture provided them little tolerance for gay men. The Catholic Church was a major opponent to civil rights for homosexuals. And, of course, the very definition of 'macho' implied a strict adherence to 'masculine' behaviors that led to homophobia and the stigmatization of gay men. *Yes, I believed that all these elements contributed to their anti-gay behavior.*

There was no recognition of the 'good' things about the KWFD that I said in the interview. There were calls for me to quit or be fired. Others thought I deserved to "have the shit" beat out of me. It took at least another 20 minutes of yelling, taunting, and threatening gestures before the mob seemed to lose steam. Notably, the commanding officers did nothing to calm them down. At the earliest possible opportunity, I went upstairs. Once in the bathroom, I vomited. I was shaking all over. I wasn't sure I was going to be able to survive the next 24 hours. *Will this be the day that they will hurt me? Is this how my job comes to an end?*

I was amazed that they would attempt to make *me* feel responsible for their homophobia. These guys were the ones to gossip about me. I was sure they boasted to their family and friends that 'the faggot' wouldn't last a day; wouldn't last a week; wouldn't survive Fire College. Now, after nearly 4 years, how do they explain to those same family and friends how Kevin continues to be a professional firefighter, doing the same job that they are doing? How do these 'masculine' men maintain a reputation for being brave and strong when there is a gay guy performing the same acts of heroism? Worse yet, I had recently passed the engineer/driver examination; it was possible that I could supervise these men someday. I was quite sure that this was, in some part, a reason for their overreaction to the radio interview.

After all the harassment and assaults that I had endured, these men thought I shouldn't speak of their attacks? *Why should the victim be vilified for telling the truth?* This shifting of blame tactic has been used against Blacks who decry racism, women who charge sexual abuse, and immigrants who underscore how their rights were abrogated. As long as stigmatization, discrimination, and personal assaults remain in the shadows, they remain powerful. I had no regrets about presenting at the conference, nor being quoted and interviewed by the media. As painful as it seemed to the firemen, I spoke the truth.

Somehow, I did manage to get through the remainder of that shift. I thought deeply about how I was going to 'mend bridges' with the guys I respected in the department. *How was I going to help them see that the angry response was misguided and overblown?* When I arrived for the next shift a few days later, I was presented with a letter – signed by nearly all the firemen – condemning my comments in the media! Some of the men wanted me to retract nearly everything I had said, but I refused. I did, though, submit a letter to the Editor of the *Miami Herald* that was published on May 27, 1985; it read, in part:

> "I have seen some aggressive firefighters. Our [KWFD] members display courage, strength, and devotion in the performance of their duties. Much of our "Old Town" section would not exist if not for the experience and quick actions of our department."

Then, admittedly with a tongue-in-cheek comment, I closed with:

> "Our department consists of many individuals with various backgrounds, religious beliefs, and talents. It is this diversity, and the resultant cooperation, that enriches a department."

In the months following, there were only passing references made to the media fiasco. It was my hope that the professionals in the department would consider my comments in context of my experience. First, I was continually harassed since entering the department. Secondly, my fellow firefighters put my life in danger more than once *because* I was gay. Then, they tried to have me fired more than once. And finally, my consistently good performance over these years was evidence of my sincere dedication to firefighting. Despite this awful setback, I never once thought of quitting the KWFD.

So much happened in the summer of 1985. It passed by quickly for me. The explosive news in Key West politics surrounded the "Bubba" trial; the Deputy Chief of Police, Raymond Cassamayor, was indicted for crimes that included racketeering, cocaine distribution, and tax evasion. His son, Raymond, was one of our rear-end men. The trial was the hot topic of conversation for weeks. It uncovered the depth of the corruption in the Bubba system and highlighted the need to 'clean house' and bring honesty, professionalism, and respectability back to the Police Department. I think it sent a message to some of the firefighters that their activities might someday put them in jail.

The country was beginning to see an upsurge in openly gay men and women running for elected office. In June, America's first openly gay member of Congress, Rep. Gerry Studds (D-Mass), came to Key West to fundraise for candidates. It was my first time thinking about the tremendous policy implications of having gay and lesbian lawmakers in Washington. Although it was not the main reason for his visit, Rep. Studds gave a strongly worded rebuke of how the Reagan administration had been mismanaging the AIDS epidemic. The presentation interested me since I had been volunteering as an AIDS educator. I began wondering how to make a bigger impact fighting the epidemic. Another friend, Richard, died in May from AIDS.

It had only been three months since a test for HIV had become available in the country. The blood test was being offered by the Monroe County Health Department. Once someone had been counseled and a blood sample was drawn, it took two weeks for the results to come back. One day, I was asked by one of the married firemen if we could talk in private. He was clearly very upset. After I swore to keep our conversation confidential, he admitted that he had been having sex with another man, also a Conch, for the past year. His 'friend' had just been diagnosed with AIDS. *Yikes! I'm so glad that he felt comfortable coming to me for help!*

He was terrified. Even my mind was racing with the possible fallout for him and the KWFD if he, too, had become infected. I did my best to calm him down. I asked him to describe exactly what the two of them did in bed. I wasn't playing voyeur, I needed assess his level of risk for having acquired the virus. I concluded that his risk was lower than some, but definitely not zero, and I recommended he get an HIV test. He was terrified of losing his reputation in our small community. I explained that no names were required to get the test. I spoke with the public health nurse I had met in my AIDS training. We arranged for an evening blood draw that would allow him to get tested under the cover of darkness. I warned him that the waiting period to get the results was often excruciating and that I was available to talk with him at any time.

This was a firefighter who had never harassed me. I promised him that I would be available to go with him to receive his results; it wasn't good to have someone find out they were infected with HIV and have no support person at their side. Finally, the day arrived when he was to get his results. Again, I offered to accompany him to the clinic. He said that he had an in-depth talk with his wife the previous evening and revealed everything! So, his wife was going to the appointment with him. Luckily, he was not HIV positive. He thanked me for my compassion, guidance, and confidentiality. He did what he thought was the right thing to do and I had nothing but respect for his decision. I had just as much admiration for his wife and her willingness to support her husband.

It was a hot summer day when we responded to a multi-vehicle accident on N. Roosevelt Boulevard in New Town. One motorhome had rear-ended another motorhome. There were no serious injuries in the accident, but the front metal rack on the second vehicle was smashed into the back end of the first vehicle. Two LP gas tanks were inextricably trapped amid the wreckage; if the tanks were not removed carefully from the mass of twisted metal, they might explode. I volunteered to crawl underneath the wreckage. I only had enough headroom to lay on my back and creep inch by inch under the wreck, avoiding debris on the hot pavement. I worked slowly, and carefully, aiming to remove one tank at a time. Chief Castro ordered the remaining firemen to retreat from the danger area, remain at the ready in the event of an explosion, and keep the onlookers at a safe distance. The chief, however, remained on the scene to assist me. I won't lie, it was terrifying. I tried to remain calm and attentive to the task.

At one point, I needed an additional tool to continue. I turned my head towards the chief's location and yelled.

"Chief," I yelled, "I need a set of channel locks." He responded quickly, telling me that he was searching through the toolkit. After a minute or two, he called back to me.

"Kevin, we don't have channel locks," he said. "I have a pair of dykes, if you think that would help?" My first thought was that dykes – pliers designed to cut electrical wire – was not going to do the job. I was feeling quite stressed and, before I could think, I yelled a response.

"If the dykes are strong, can you ask them to lift these vehicles and give me some more room to work?" It took a few seconds for him to realize my stupid joke. Out of necessity, I settled on using a set of dykes with ridged, flat ends. I successfully removed one gas tank and carefully brought it over to the edge so the chief could take it away. He asked how I was doing. I was OK, I told him, but the heat of the tarmac was intense; I could feel it through my turnout fire jacket! My back was getting overheated and even a little burned. To add to my distress, there was an awful smell of rotten eggs in the air under the vehicles.

Another 10 minutes or so and the second tank was removed from the mangled metal. My back was still hurting. *It is almost over now, and I can soon get off this hot road.* Once Chief Castro received the gas tank, I quickly withdrew from under the wreckage. As soon as I stood up, I felt a searing pain on my back. My first impulse was to remove my turnout coat. Immediately, both the chief and I could see that it was soaking wet and was the source of that terrible smell I had been experiencing. At the same moment, we realized that it was battery acid! One of the motorhome's batteries was damaged in the accident and had leaked its acid on the road! It was at this moment that the chief ordered me to get in his wife's car so she could take me back to Firehouse 1 and get into a shower. I glanced in the direction he was pointing; there stood the chief's wife. *What the heck was she doing so close to a dangerous scene like this one?!* Heading towards her car, I decided I had to remove my uniform shirt because it, too, was wet with acid. The fire station was only a mile away, and she drove quickly. Unable to control myself, I was continually crying out in pain. "Take off your shirt!" she yelled. I hesitated but removed my undershirt. *Is this real? Am I taking off my clothes in front of the chief's wife!?* In a flash, she screeched into the truck bay of our firehouse, and I flew up the several flights of stairs and into the shower stall. I didn't stop to remove my turnout trousers or uniform pants. I just wanted water gushing down my back as soon as possible. Much to my relief, I had no permanent scarring from the battery acid. I did, however, have a very painful backside for several days.

Later, I asked Chief Castro what his wife was doing at the scene of the accident, and he told me that she feared for his life and wasn't going to abandon her husband at a time like that! It made me think about how Joe would have responded if I had been severely injured or killed in the incident. He knew that I would have volunteered for the dangerous task. I wasn't sure if he would've come close to the dangerous scene, though. We weren't communicating very well these days.

CHAPTER 26: Blaze of Glory

There are times in life when one has an epiphany. One night, we were sent to a residential structure fire on the edge of Old Town. The fire was extinguished with relative speed, but the house had suffered extensive damage. The family was not going to be able to return to it tonight. I noticed them as I finished draining and rolling up the fire hose. There they sat, the couple and their two children – one an infant – on the curb at 2:30 in the morning. Concerned for their disposition, I spoke to Capt. Vega.

"What about this family?" I asked.

"We did our job," he answered, "Someone will take care of them." His tone suggested that he was simply stating a fact and not lacking human compassion. *Who will take care of them?* I pondered that question for a couple of days.

Later that week, I was having breakfast with my friend Terry Rinehart. He was a registered nurse working at the Florida Keys Memorial Hospital. Terry listed patiently as I relayed the story of the family who had lost everything in the fire. *How difficult that must be with two small children!* I explained that I really cared more about people than burning structures; with insurance, you can always rebuild a house. He helped me see myself in a completely different way.

"You're a nurse," Terry said. "Admit it! Go get a license." *A nurse?* I hadn't seriously considered a change of career. I had encountered nurses in hospice that I thought were incredible; their scope of knowledge about illness, medicine, and human behavior was impressive. Nurses were compassionate. Terry reminded me that much of my volunteer work with HELPLINE, hospice, and the American Red Cross AIDS Education program was evidence that I needed to be a nurse. I had to agree that the mounting AIDS epidemic spurred me to learn more about health and disease. The HIV virus, and its effects on the immune system, fascinated me. Admittedly, having numerous friends die of AIDS had fundamentally changed me. I had become more serious and aware of the fragility of life. Death had a finality that made me realize that we cannot waste the time we're given. *What was I going to do to make my life more meaningful?*

Terry was very persuasive. I thought maybe it was time for me to pursue a career that would demand more of my talents and truly inspire me. I wouldn't be *leaving* the Fire Department as much as I would be *moving towards* a career in Nursing. I asked Terry how one becomes a Registered Nurse. Later that afternoon, I walked into the School of Nursing at the Florida Keys Community College and began the process of applying to the program with entry in the Fall semester.

I would be soon quitting my job. I was going to miss some of the guys with whom I was working. Surely, working with men like Capt. "Viti" Vidal had been an honor. I enjoyed working with Frank, Al, Alex, and Alan. Sadly, my hope that we would ever be 'friends' had diminished over time. I was sure that the *black hats* would be thrilled to hear of my decision, but they were not my concern.

After nearly 8 years, Joe and I were breaking up. We had been growing in different directions and were no longer each other's source of joy and energy. We were not communicating with each other as well as we once had and ceased to bring out the best in each other. We realized that this would mean selling the house we had built and moving out. I was the first to leave our Bay Point home. Before quitting my position with the KWFD, I needed to secure a mortgage for the purchase of a small house on Packer Street in Old Town. The tiny, two-bedroom cottage was a 'fixer-upper' that I felt I could afford with profits from selling our house. I had the skills to renovate it to meet my needs. For nearly a month, though, I depended upon the kindness of my friends (Peter Hughes, 'Boomer' Connors, and Dennis Beaver) who provided me with short-term housing until I could close on the new property. By the time my last scheduled shift as a firefighter arrived, I had only a few days left of temporary 'couch surfing' before moving into my new home.

So, in this short period of time, I was ending my long-term relationship with Joe and purchasing a new house of my own. I was also leaving my position in the KWFD and, three days later, beginning a two-year Nursing program at the college. This was a lot to juggle. I hadn't quite figured out how I was going to pay my bills after no longer receiving my regular City paycheck. Joe and I had to sell the house on Bay Point before I would have the necessary proceeds to cover my living expenses. Still, this time of great stress was also a period of endless possibilities for me. I was thankful to have my friends Tom, Joy, and Jan giving me support and encouragement. I was optimistic that all the disparate pieces would fall into place and my future would be full of exciting adventures. I appreciate the adage that "the only constant in life is change" and change didn't frighten me. Still, I could not have foreseen that my final hours in the KWFD would be so unpredictably dangerous.

Well, the day had finally arrived. It was my last shift on the KWFD, and it seemed no different than any other. Capt. Vega was in charge and Alan was my driver. I was the sole rear-end man on the truck. The three of us spoke briefly about it being my last day on the department. The events over recent months had complicated our relationships somewhat. The day passed quickly. Soon enough, we were off to our bunks for the night.

It was still dark when the alarm sounded. There was little more than one hour left for me to serve on the KWFD. We were informed that a guesthouse in Old Town, the El Siboney Inn, was on fire. We all knew the large building on the corner of Truman Avenue and Elizabeth Street. The inn's conch architectural style included the obligatory gingerbread railings, large porches on the first and second floors, and decorative shutters. Unfortunately, those old wooden elements also served as the best fuel for a fast-moving fire.

The El Siboney Inn was a guesthouse. Of course, this immediately conjured up images of rescuing guests. It also meant containing the fire to a single structure in an area of town densely populated with older wooden buildings. One of the great fears for anyone in the KWFD is facing a conflagration in Old Town. It wouldn't take much for several houses in the neighborhood to be set afire by embers sent into the night sky. A mental map of Old Town flashed through my thoughts. Luckily, the school for the Basilica of St. Mary of the Sea, across Truman Avenue, was set back from the main road. However, there were old conch houses on the other three sides of the El Siboney property.

We rushed to dress and slide down the pole to the firetruck. As I was donning my turnout gear, I turned to Capt. Vega and jokingly asked "Oh, come on captain…I don't really have to go to this last fire…do I?"

True to his nature, he muttered something in Spanish, laughed, and winked at me. Though I didn't understand what he had said under his breath, his good-natured response assured me that he took my comment as it was intended. I was attempting to reduce the tension we all felt in this moment. Alan started the truck, and we were off.

It was always an eerie feeling to be on a fire truck in the middle of the night. People were sleeping in their beds while we were wide awake, adrenaline flowing! This is when I most realized the crucial role of firefighters to our island city. We didn't know what we would encounter when we arrived, but it was our job to be prepared for anything. I was trying to anticipate what the captain might order me to do. Alan was an excellent engineer. I knew I could depend upon his guidance.

The truck's siren screamed as we flew down North Roosevelt Boulevard. This main thoroughfare became Truman Avenue. The captain would occasionally blast the air horn as we approached intersections or other potential hazards on the road. In the front cab, Frank and Alan had received additional information via radio as we entered the Old Town area. Blocks away, we could already see a red glow just above the blossoming Poinciana trees lining Truman Avenue. Billowing black smoke was illuminated by what was promising to be an enormous blaze.

"*Coño!*" [damn!] My loud exclamation to myself came out without thinking…and in Spanish! The first glimpse of the enormous structure engulfed in flames took my breath away. I hadn't seen such a sight since the Old Cuban Club fire. Immediately, I began to doubt our ability to contain this fire to a single structure. No time for that, though. It was time to focus.

Alan had turned right onto Elizabeth Street. We were exceedingly close to the fire and the radiated heat was extraordinary. We dropped hose lines and hooked up to the hydrant at the end of the short block. There were trucks on Truman Avenue directing fire streams towards the front of the building.

Capt. Vega and I set ourselves on the west edge of the property in the middle of Elizabeth Street. From this vantage point, we could view the length of the building, the car park area in front of us, and the rear of the property. The property spanned nearly half the length of the block towards Olivia Street. Behind the inn was a large LP gas tank that served the needs of the inn. The gas tank sat on a concrete base, exposed to the elements. Unfortunately, it was also being directly impacted by the heat radiating from the raging structure fire. As the gas tank gets hotter, the gas inside expands; if unchecked, the tank could explode and engulf several other homes in the neighborhood in fire.

The assigned task for me and Capt. Frank Vega was to direct a stream of water onto the gas tank to keep it from exploding. There were, easily, five other houses in the immediate area that might be damaged, destroyed, or engulfed in flames if the tank ruptured. If that happened, it may not be possible to stop the fire from expanding further into the Old Town neighborhood. Frank and I were keenly aware that if there were to be an explosion, our proximity to the detonation would, likely, be lethal. We seemed to be acting in unison, trying to strategically position our hose for maximum water delivery, not allowing fear to overwhelm us. Fear in firefighting can lead to poor judgment, reticence to act, or acting without thinking. Fear can put firefighters in danger and risk the mission.

I took the nozzle and knelt on the asphalt to establish a stable center of gravity. The hose line was bent for maximum control as I knew the kickback would be significant once the nozzle was opened and the water began flowing. Frank was behind me, providing backup with his weight on the hose and guidance as to how best to direct our stream of water. The fire was emanating such heat that I had to occasionally turn my face away to avoid being scorched. Hot embers rained down on us. We were positioned so close to the inferno that we were destined to inhale smoke. "Well," I thought to myself "If you are going to leave the fire department, this is quite a last hour of work!?" Despite the difficulties, Frank and I held our water stream on the gas tank.

ALARM IN THE FIREHOUSE

The first blast took us by surprise. It began with a few moments of loud hissing. The gas in the tank had been rapidly expanding due to the excessive heat. The pressure relief valve on the tank opened to release some of the gas. Upon hitting a superheated atmosphere, the gas ignited. The loud explosion reverberated through my turnout gear. The blast would have knocked me over if I hadn't been locked into the nozzle on my hose. I remember thinking that some windows in the neighborhood were shattered by the impact. The valve was functioning properly. Despite the stream of water we were applying to the tank, though, the pressure was building. It was crucial that we keep the tank cooled.

Large fire scenes are, but their very nature, hectic. My laser-focus was on the task at hand. So, I don't recollect the Navy Fire Department trucks arriving to provide additional firefighting support. As Frank and I were situated in an area of heavy smoke and heat, our field of vision didn't allow us to see the other firefighters or the crowd of onlookers. There were some firefighters rushing back and forth on the sidewalk behind us, but we were largely unaware of them. We had been holding this position for quite a while. We didn't seem to be getting any relief. Why weren't other firefighters on hand to take over for us? After what seemed to be an eternity of heat and smoke, we held our position.

There were several more times when the LP gas tank pressure relief valve opened and released gas. It looked like an enormous flamethrower. The flare would burst out towards the burning structure. Despite the anxiety we felt with each burst, the release of pent-up gas meant a reduction in the tank's internal pressure. It seemed to be a race against time. The El Siboney guesthouse was slowly collapsing into a large pile of burning timbers. I wanted its inevitable destruction to come sooner rather than later. If we cooled the tank and avoided an explosion, the building would be reduced to remains and the fire would no longer pose a serious threat. Apparently, the captain and I were successful, but to be honest, I have no recollection as to how it all ended.

The next thing I remember is waking up in a strange bed. *This is an unfamiliar room.* It took a few minutes to realize that I had moved to this house a few days earlier. It was temporary housing while I waited to close on my new house. But, looking around that morning, I had no memory of how I came to be there. My memory for the previous 24 hours was fuzzy at best. Apparently, Frank and I were eventually relieved of our position on Elizabeth Street. He had suffered some type of cardiac event and was taken to the hospital. I was transported to the hospital after I was found dizzy and confused in the middle of the street. We both had suffered heat exhaustion and smoke inhalation. I don't remember being relieved of our position on the hose line. I don't recall an opportunity for Frank and me to cool down, rehydrate, and recover. It wasn't surprising that both the captain and I were injured. I wondered if their reason for not relieving us was that they were too scared of the potential gas tank explosion. Much later, I learned that Jerry had also been transferred to the hospital from the El Siboney Inn fire.

It seems that I was discharged to a friend's care after several hours in the hospital. It took the nearly three days of recovery before I began to feel somewhat normal. Finally, I got a ride out to Fire Station 1 on Flagler Avenue to retrieve my motorcycle that had been parked in the truck bay since my last day on duty. It was a relief to find it had not been tampered with over the course of several days. I was also pleased that none of the firemen were around as I walked in, started up the engine, and rode home. My time as a professional firefighter had come to an end. Despite there being no send-off party, I could say that I left in a blaze of glory!

Reflections

Looking back on my four years in the KWFD, I realize that I did the best I could in the moment. *In 1981,* I had no way of knowing that I had been the first openly gay professional firefighter in the United States. It was only after several decades had passed – and the availability of the Internet – that the distinction became clear.

In retrospect, I joined the department only a couple of short years after Anita Bryant ran her malevolent, albeit successful, Miami campaign to strip gay men and lesbians of their civil rights. Her national prominence gave undue propriety to a religious crusade based on stereotypes, innuendo, and outright lies about gay men. Unfortunately, her vicious message was internalized by the ignorant. The early 1980s was an era of social, political, and financial change for Conchs in Key West. The uncertain future of their island life made them easy prey for unscrupulous politicians looking to move up the food chain. It was the advent of the HIV/AIDS pandemic. There were many unknowns about the virus. An AIDS diagnosis often revealed secrets that one wanted to keep from family, friends, and coworkers. These events, and others, formed the backdrop for my simple desire to be a professional firefighter.

I don't believe that the *black hats* did the best they could in the moment. These men were professional firefighters and, thereby, should be held to a higher standard. They behaved like adolescent bullies who took twisted pleasure in acting out their personal insecurities. I have more forgiveness for those firemen who stood by, witnessing the assaults, but didn't speak up in my defense. I can now understand how they were caught unprepared to be advocates. More disappointing to me were the ineffectual commanding officers; they were complicit with the assaults, showing no respect for me nor concern for my safety. The willingness to brush off even the most serious offenses by claiming 'boys will be boys' was inexcusable. I could imagine how Black Americans felt when reporting racist assaults; I could imagine how women were treated when trying to bring sexual predators to justice. 'Boys will be boys' is not simply institutional enabling; it is institutional betrayal. It was the officers' duty to discipline the men who assaulted and traumatized me. As firefighters, our safety should never be put in jeopardy because of personal bias.

After I left the KWFD, its reputation continued to be eroded by firemen occasionally being arrested for criminal activity. Yet, they seemed to keep their position in the department. It was unrealistic to think that a city with a long history of corruption and nepotism would be able to turn itself around quickly. I continued to be encouraged by the *white hats*, young firemen who were rising in the ranks and worked to advance professional firefighting. It is my hope that contemporary fire departments would establish a more inclusive environment, leading to a more diverse workforce.

Sadly, it still makes national news when a member of a professional sports team or entertainer comes 'out of the closet.' I am pleased that we have seen tremendous progress in the political arena, with LGBTQ+ candidates running in local, state, and national elections. The progress in America's firehouses, however, has been slow. It is sad to note that four decades after I became a firefighter, it is extraordinarily rare to find open LGBTQ+ persons serving as professional firefighters in the United States.

What did I learn? My experience as a firefighter taught me that I was stronger than I ever thought I could be. I am satisfied that I was able to stand my ground and hold to my principles. I didn't seek revenge on those who terrorized me. My fear and anger morphed into resolve and resilience. The words 'courageous' and 'brave' came to have personal meaning for me. I hope that my restraint and respect for my coworkers had some positive effect on how they perceived gay men.

My experience was mine; I don't expect that every individual will choose to be 'out there' and expose themselves to the slings and arrows I had to face. My life has been fulfilling because I live with the knowledge that I did not compromise my principles. I pursued my dream. If you are to be the 'first' in your field, know why you are committed to the endeavor. Be confident in your principles; know what you will – and will not – compromise on as situations arise. Consider your philosophy in dealing with subtle microaggressions or a more overt assault. How do you stay true to who you are? Where will you find your support? Will you respect the antagonist other and try to understand their perspective?

I offer advice for commanding officers responsible for the 'first' minority firefighter in their workplace. First, and foremost, give the person a safe environment in which to work. Don't expect them to be perfect. Each employee is imperfect in their own way. They are likely to make mistakes and they are just as likely to contribute something unique to the workplace. Acknowledge that hiring the first minority individual will change the workplace; it should be expected and not feared. For those who already have firefighters from minority groups, I implore you to ask them about their experiences. It is unlikely that they feel as comfortable in their position as their colleagues. Hold accountable those who would hurl slurs or sexual innuendos that create a hostile workplace. Find ways to make the firehouse inclusive for all.

We need to rethink masculinity. It is not about being a bully, driving an oversized pick-up truck, or dominating others. What kind of men do we want in our society? How can we instill respect, self-confidence, and compassion in our kids? Women can be excellent firefighters and men can be compassionate nurses. Gay men can command military units and straight men can be warm, loving, and engaged fathers. We need to distinguish masculinity from bravery; they are not synonymous terms. Further, neither is defined by one's sexual orientation. Twenty years after my joining the KWFD, a television reporter was highlighting the lives and families of the passengers on UA flight 93 that courageously fought back against four hijackers, causing their plane to crash near Shanksville, PA on September 11, 2001. When queried why she failed to mention Mark Bingham, an avid rugby player who played a key role in storming the cockpit that morning, the reporter replied: "America is not ready to hear the words 'gay' and 'hero' in the same sentence yet." Such shocking acts of omission result in LGBTQ+ history being diminished or denied; their stories of bravery and selflessness are lost. On that fateful day, September 11th, terrorists murdered LGBTQ+ Americans on the planes and at all three sites. Also, there were LGBTQ+ firefighters, police, first responders, and others who lost their lives in courageous rescue efforts. Bravery is not exclusive to straight, White males.

I only hope that Americans come to recognize how racist and misogynistic stereotypes have been ingrained into our social institutions and remain, largely, unquestioned. Consequently, daily workplace customs and expectations are taken for granted; we don't critically examine how our usual ways of doing things might disenfranchise a newcomer. When a minority group has never been represented in a workplace, the environment may need to adapt to assure equitable opportunities for success. Due to erroneous preconceptions, some of my fellow firemen believed that I didn't even deserve to be in the KWFD. They never stopped trying to get me fired.

Leaving the KWFD, I was not defeated. I wasn't hanging my head in shame. *I* was proud of my years in the department and believe that there were firemen who appreciated what I contributed. So, what about living your truth? I can testify that:

The truth will set you free. First, it will beat you about the head and torso, leaving you bruised and battered. But then, it will set you free!

I have been known to espouse that 'when one door closes, another door opens' and I can attest to it. I entered the Nursing program at the Florida Keys Community College a week after leaving the Fire Department. In the years since, I found my calling, my passion. The profession has allowed me to combine science, communication and compassion in my own unique way to optimize the lives – and deaths – of others in my care. I continued with my education with a baccalaureate degree from the University of Miami and both a master's and PhD in Nursing at the Johns Hopkins University. A more detailed account of my journey can be found online at: https://alarminthefirehouse.com

After the Fire Department

My four years in the KWFD were, in a word, traumatizing. Any number of times since, I would wake up in a cold sweat after dreaming that I was forced to return to the firehouse to work with the *black hats*. In retrospect, I could have done things differently. First, and foremost, I would have made sure that City administrators – the City Manager, Mayor, and Fire Chief – had documentation of the harassment and assaults I endured at the hands of the firemen. It seems that our openly gay mayor was not aware of the barrier I was breaking in the KWFD.

I held out hope that my fellow firefighters would get to know me, appreciate my work ethic, and value my contributions to the KWFD. It was a mistake for me to think that the *black hats* would, eventually, tire of bullying and taunting me and just accept that I was a fellow firefighter. They were not reined in by their commanding officers and I could have ended up being seriously injured. The failure of management to protect me from harassment and harm led me to experience 'institutional betrayal.' It was the duty of the KWFD to assure that no employee suffers from a toxic environment of stigma, discrimination, and assault. They betrayed the trust I had in the system. Of course, there was widespread public acceptance of blatant homophobia, and a lack of legal protections for gay and lesbian persons, in the early 1980s. My colleague, Al Rahming, was right on target when he told me that "they gonna know there's a *faggot* in this firehouse for a very, long time!"

Further, it became clear to me – many years after the fact – that some of the *white hats* did not know the extent to which I had been tormented and endangered by their colleagues. If I had to do it over again, I would have approached the firemen who supported me and spoken more openly about my struggles. They could have learned more about me as a person. Given the chance, I would have invited some of them to bring their families to a social event with me and Joe so that they could see how boring and 'normal' gay men could be. Years after my departure, I learned that the firemen had sons, daughters, and other family members that were gay or lesbian. Hopefully, knowing me encouraged empathy and understanding for their loved ones.

A few months after I had left the KWFD, I received a call from my friend Dan Stahley. He and his partner were the owner/operators of the Curry House gay guesthouse on Fleming Street in Old Town. Dan told me that one of their guests wanted very much to meet me. The young man, Bill Burroughs, was a firefighter from the Tampa area who was visiting Key West for just two days. *Wow! I'd be happy to meet another gay firefighter!* That next afternoon, I met Bill in the beautiful, tropical back garden of the guesthouse. He was a couple of years younger than me, slightly heavier, and quite handsome. Bill had heard about my years as a fireman and wanted to swap stories. He was not open about being gay in his department. He also heard homophobic comments from his fellow firefighters and thought it best to remain closeted. It was clear from his stories that the stress at the firehouse was taking a toll on him. His initial nervousness with me melted away after the first hour and he asked me to join him for dinner. Our conversations eventually drifted from my experience in the KWFD to my pursuit of a career in Nursing. I described how my friends with AIDS had inspired me to do more than just serve as a witness to their struggles; I needed to be actively engaged in helping them fight the disease. Bill heard me decry the stigma and discrimination that so many with HIV were facing.

Once back at the guesthouse, we climbed into the hot tub. The garden was quite dark, except for the well-positioned spotlights lighting up the fronds of the palm trees and creating a dreamlike atmosphere. One crucial element of any Key West guesthouse design was to have a tropical environment so beautiful that the ambience transports the visitor out of everyday reality. The garden at the Curry House provided that fantasy-like setting. *How lucky I am to be here, now, with this charming young man…and he is another gay firefighter!* All too soon, though, the fantasy came to a crashing end.

"I have *Pneumocystis* pneumonia," Bill said.

I was caught off-guard and couldn't think of anything to say.

"That means I have AIDS," he continued.

"Yes," I said with as much compassion as I could muster, "I am quite familiar with PCP." I was looking right into his eyes and reached out to hold his hand on the rim of the hot tub. His eyes swelled quickly, and he started to sob. This was so very cruel, so unfair. *AIDS!? I meet another gay firefighter and he has AIDS?* In 1985, a diagnosis of AIDS was a virtual death sentence. There were no antiretroviral medications yet, and the diagnosis almost always came late in the course of disease. Nearly everyone with an AIDS diagnosis – but not everyone – died within a relatively short period of time. Every bone in my body told me to detach myself from this wonderful young man, to protect myself. I wasn't concerned at all about getting HIV; I was trying to avoid emotional pain. But I wasn't going anywhere. This man had just revealed his terrifying truth to me, and I considered the moment sacred. I leaned over in the hot tub and gave him a big hug.

Bill told me that he had just been discharged from the hospital three days before and caught a flight to Key West. He hoped that the time away on this beautiful island could help him sort out his life. He stumbled upon the Curry House and was lucky that they had a room available. After talking a bit more, he decided it was time he went to bed; he had a flight back to Tampa in the morning. He was notably short of breath when climbing the stairs to the second floor of the guesthouse. To my surprise, he turned to climb the stairs to the third floor.

"Bill, your room is on the top floor?" I asked. I was concerned about the respiratory effort necessary to climb stairs. *Pneumocystis* pneumonia is notorious for leaving patients fatigued and short of breath for weeks after leaving the hospital. I encouraged him to take the stairs very slowly and kept just inches behind him in case I needed to provide physical support. It was increasingly difficult for him to get to the top of the staircase, but he did it. We stood and he caught his breath before going into his room. Bill repeatedly apologized to me for being so slow. Sitting on the edge of the bed, he looked half-dead; the stair climb had been a challenge and he wasn't recovering well at all. He thanked me for dinner and was attempting to say "good-bye."

"I'm not leaving, Bill," I said, "I never have the chance to spend a night in the Curry House. Do you have some medication to take before going to sleep?"

I retrieved some water and his pills. I helped him onto the bed and climbed in alongside him. I sat up against the headboard, took him in my arms, and cradled him until he fell asleep. Once, during the night, he had bout of coughing and I did my best to keep him calm through it. In the morning, his condition had improved considerably, and we had a nice breakfast before we said our good-byes.

A few months later, I was in Tampa for training, and I drove over to Bill's firehouse. Two guys were sitting out in front of the truck bay. I asked if Bill was working that day.

"He's dead. That little faggot had AIDS," said one of the guys. The lack of compassion in his voice communicated his total lack of humanity.

"His name was Bill Burroughs," I responded, "and he was a fellow fireman."

For me, Bill died like so many other gay men in the epidemic. He was alone, frightened, and stigmatized. I had only a brief insight into his shock and despair but could still see his underlying strength and gentle nature. I count myself so lucky to have spent a few hours with such a charming young man. Years later, in memory of Bill Burroughs, I created a panel to be sewn into the AIDS Memorial Quilt, using the t-shirt I received in Orlando at the 1984 Firefighter Olympics.

Odds & Ends

The wooden sign I constructed for Fire Station 1 (described in Chapter 11) is still in place after 39 years. That firehouse is now Station 3, and the number was updated.

In Chapter 12, I described performing CPR on a child. Years later, in 1987, I was working alongside a woman who told me that a firefighter had saved her 8-year-old son's life by initiating CPR after he was injured on a football field. He had suffered a basal skull fracture and recovered with time. I was so pleased to tell her that I was the firefighter that helped her boy that day. It is rare, and wonderful, to hear the outcome of your actions in the field. I was so pleased to receive a mother's heartfelt gratitude.

In Chapter 17, I discussed advocating for changing the exit doors in the *Copa* nightclub that did not meet fire code regulations. The infraction was finally corrected. In 1995, the *Copa* was destroyed in a fire. No lives were lost.

Fire Station 3 at the corner of Virginia and Grinnell Streets is now the Key West Firehouse Museum. It was established to preserve the history of fire fighting in the Florida Keys. For more information, please go to: https://keywestfirehousemuseum.com/Home.php

There are numerous people mentioned in this book that have since died of AIDS. Their names are engraved in stone at the Key West AIDS Memorial at the foot of the White Street Pier on the Atlantic side of the island. To explore the memorial, go to: keywestaidsmemorial.org

ABOUT THE AUTHOR

R. Kevin Mallinson, PhD, RN, FAAN is a retired university professor and Fellow in the American Academy of Nursing. He is a public speaker and researcher who consistently advocates for disenfranchised groups, particularly LGBTQ+ communities and persons with – or at risk for – HIV disease. Dr. Mallinson was the Principal Investigator of *Nurses SOAR!* [Strengthening Our AIDS Response], a 3-year nursing capacity building program in the countries of Lesotho, South Africa, and the Kingdom of Swaziland. Over the academic year 2012-2013, he served as a Fulbright Scholar at the Southern Africa Nazarene University in Swaziland.

Dr. Mallinson and his husband split their time between Washington, DC and Lewes, Delaware. His recreational interests have included gardening, running, scuba diving, skydiving, and bungy jumping.

www.ingramcontent.com/pod-product-compliance
Lightning Source LLC
Chambersburg PA
CBHW051427290426
44109CB00016B/1467